Dolph Schayes and the Rise of Professional Basketball

Sports and Entertainment
Steven A. Riess, *Series Editor*

Other titles in Sports and Entertainment

Beyond Home Plate: Jackie Robinson on Life after Baseball
  Michael G. Long , ed.

Black Baseball Entrepreneurs, 1902–1931:
The Negro National and Eastern Colored Leagues
  Michael E. Lomax

Moonfixer: The Basketball Journey of Earl Lloyd
  Earl Lloyd and Sean Kirst

My Los Angeles in Black and (Almost) White
  Andrew Furman

The 1929 Bunion Derby: Johnny Salo
and the Great Footrace across America
  Charles B. Kastner

The Rise of American High School Sports
and the Search for Control, 1880–1930
  Robert Pruter

Sport and the Shaping of Italian-American Identity
  Gerald R. Gems

The Sport of Kings and the Kings of Crime: Horse Racing,
Politics, and Organized Crime in New York, 1865–1913
  Steven A. Riess

Dolph Grundman

DOLPH SCHAYES

and the Rise of

PROFESSIONAL

BASKETBALL

Syracuse University Press

To the memory of Elkin Isaac,
who touched many lives at Albion College

Dolph Grundman is a professor emeritus of history at Metropolitan State University of Denver. He has published two basketball books, *The Golden Age of Amateur Basketball: The AAU Tournament, 1921–1968* and *Jim Pollard: The Kangaroo Kid.*

Contents

Illustrations

Acknowledgments

In preparing this book I wish to give a special thanks to Sharon Roehling, who typed the manuscript as we worked through several drafts. Without her assistance, I would not have been able to complete this book in a timely manner. I also wish to thank Emilio DeGrazia of Winona State University and Lynette Bousman of Metropolitan State University of Denver for carefully reading the text. Gregory Newsome of Syracuse was extremely helpful in providing photographs of Dolph Schayes from his photographic collection. Katherine Honda of the Auraria Library helped me with my Interlibrary Loan requests. Finally, I received two travel grants from the School of Letters, Arts, and Sciences at Metropolitan State University of Denver that facilitated my research.

In doing my research Dolph Schayes was extremely generous with his time, as we had frequent conversations during the preparation of the manuscript. I was also able to interview a number of Dolph Schayes's former teammates, including Earl Lloyd, Jim Tucker, Bob Hopkins, Bob Harrison, Johnny Macknowsky, Dave Gambee, Togo Palazzi, Al Bianchi, Lee Shaffer, Chet Walker, and Joe Roberts. Naomi and Danny Schayes also shared some of their memories. Vince Boryla provided useful information on the history of the New York Knicks. Norm Drucker gave an official's perspective of the National Basketball Association (NBA). Bob Houbregs shared his memories of the Fort Wayne Pistons. Dennis Gildea shared some of his insights from his work on Clair Bee. Dick Triptow, who played in the National Basketball League (NBL), allowed me to copy a letter from Al Cervi. Gerard Pelisson, the author of *The Castle on the Parkway*, sent clippings and photographs of Dolph Schayes's high school years. Betsy Burton of the Syracuse Public Library sent me copies of game descriptions that I was unable to find. Mary Kay Halbrook shared her scrapbook of Harvey Wade "Swede" Halbrook. Robert C. Johnston, the archivist at LeMoyne College, guided me to the Danny Biasone Collection.

Introduction

My Day with Dolph Schayes

In the 1950s professional basketball was in its infancy. The National Basketball Association played its inaugural season in 1949–50, the result of a merger between the Basketball Association of America and the National Basketball League. The teams in the BAA played in America's big cities such as New York, Boston, Philadelphia, and Chicago. The NBL's teams represented smaller cities such as Syracuse and Rochester in New York, Oshkosh and Sheboygan in Wisconsin, and Fort Wayne and Anderson in Indiana. In 1949–50, there were seventeen teams in the NBA. By 1954 the number of teams had been reduced to eight.

If, like me, you grew up in the fifties and were a fan or an aspiring player, or both, you were oblivious to this rather complicated history. Unless you lived in an NBA city, there was little television exposure to professional basketball. But in 1954–55, the year I entered Bowen High School on Chicago's South Side, Dumont televised an NBA game every weekend, my first exposure to professional basketball. My favorite team was the Minneapolis Lakers, since George Mikan, the team's star center, had helped to put Chicago's DePaul University on the collegiate basketball map in the mid-1940s. Since the Chicago Stags, the Windy City's BAA team, had folded in 1950, Mikan's Chicago roots drew me to the Lakers. Besides, the Lakers were the first NBA power, winning four championships in the league's first five years. The Lakers surrounded Mikan with Slater Martin, Vern Mikkelsen, and Jim Pollard, all of whom would join Mikan in the Hall of Fame. As I watched these professional games, another player intrigued me. His name was Adolph "Dolph" Schayes of the Syracuse Nationals, affectionately called the Nats. We shared the same first name, and in the generation of the 1950s there were not too many Adolphs around. A German dictator made sure of that. More important, Dolph was a star. He stood six foot eight, weighed 220 pounds, and possessed a deadly two-handed set shot. When defenders came out to contest his two-hander, Dolph had the strength and agility to drive to the basket and either score or draw a foul. He was always among the best free-throw shooters in the league. Between 1951 and 1961, Dolph played in every All-Star Game.

In my case the images of this history were tucked away in my memory, as I turned my focus to the study of American history. In the fall of 1977 I moved to Colorado, where I took a position in the Department of History at Metropolitan State College of Denver. In 1978 I was asked to teach a course on the history of sports in America. As I developed this course, I discovered that Denver had been the home of a national basketball tournament sponsored by the Amateur Athletic Union (AAU). After doing a little research, I discovered that some of the great basketball players of the 1940s and 1950s appeared in this tournament. Hank Luisetti, Bob Kurland, Jim Pollard, George Yardley, Jack McCrackan, and Robert "Ace" Gruenig demonstrated their skills on Denver's courts and would eventually earn a place in the Basketball Hall of Fame. This research led to my first book, *The Golden Age of Amateur Basketball.*

When I discovered that Jim Pollard had captivated Denver fans in the 1946 and 1947 AAU tournaments, it brought back memories of the Minneapolis Lakers. I decided to write a biography of Jim Pollard and nail down his life in basketball and refamiliarize myself with the Minneapolis Lakers. As I did my research, I discovered that the Lakers, in two of their four NBA championship seasons, 1950 and 1954, had defeated the Syracuse Nationals. Dolph Schayes led the Nats in scoring, and accounts of those games brought back memories of that two-handed set shot and those powerful drives to the basket. In 2009 the Pollard biography, *Jim Pollard: The Kangaroo Kid,* was completed, and I joined Jim's wife, Arilee, and daughter, Jeanne, for a book signing at the September 2009 Hall of Fame induction ceremonies. Ever since Jim Pollard was inducted into the Hall of Fame in 1978 and even every year after he passed away in 1993, the

Pollards had attended the Hall of Fame ceremonies and knew just about everybody. Among the many former players they introduced me to was Dolph Schayes. He had been inducted into the Hall of Fame in 1972, after fifteen brilliant years in the NBA.

After returning to Denver, I began digging into Dolph's basketball life. In 1948, as a senior, he was an All-America at New York University (NYU) when New York City was the mecca of college basketball. Dolph was the first player to score fifteen thousand points in the NBA and at one point had played in 764 consecutive games, which was briefly a record. Between 1950 and 1961 Schayes was named either to the first or to the second All-NBA teams. During those twelve years, Schayes led the team in scoring every year, in rebounding in ten seasons, and in free-throw percentage ten times. Surprisingly, given these accomplishments, no person had written a biography of Schayes. David Ramsey had written a short chapter on Dolph in his brief history of the Syracuse Nationals, and Charles Salzberg's *From Set Shot to Slam Dunk* also discussed some aspects of Dolph's career.

What makes a biography of Dolph Schayes particularly appealing is that his fifteen years embraced several important transitions in professional basketball history. When Dolph played his first season in the NBA, 1949–50, there were no African American players, there was no shot clock, and games could become long and tedious affairs, as teams stalled or marched to the free-throw line in foul-filled games. By 1960 that phase of professional basketball history had passed, as the shot clock and an influx of African American players changed the nature of the NBA. Dolph excelled in both the old and the new eras. Sometimes old-timers will debate whether player X of the 1940s and 1950s could play in today's NBA. An examination of Dolph Schayes's record answers that question affirmatively. He did it.

With all this history to explore, I flew to Syracuse in August 2010 to meet with Dolph Schayes to discuss the possibility of doing his biography. The highlight of the trip was a guided tour of Syracuse's basketball history. Before we made our first stop, Dolph explained that when he moved to Syracuse in the fall of 1948, its population was about 230,000. Before the Civil War, the Erie Canal passed through Syracuse. Abolitionists also used Syracuse as a skipping-stone to Canada for runaway slaves on the

Underground Railroad. In the mid-twentieth century the Carrier Corporation was the city's largest company, and General Electric had a strong presence. By 2010 Carrier had outsourced most of its manufacturing to Brazil and Central America, and General Electric left the city in the 1960s as a result of a labor dispute. Two of the city's biggest employers today are its many hospitals and Syracuse University. Like many American cities, Syracuse had lost some of its population as people moved to the suburbs.

Our first stop was the State Fair Coliseum. It looked exactly as it did in the fall of 1948, when Dolph played his first home game as a Nat. The Coliseum sat upwards of nine thousand. There was a walkway around the lower level that allowed fans without seats to stand and watch the game. The backboards in 1948 were attached to the balcony by wires, and occasionally the fans tugged on them when a player from the visiting team was shooting a free throw. The place was a real pit and gave the Nats a definite home-court advantage. In 1949–50, Dolph's second year, the Nats compiled a 51-13 record and lost just one game at the Coliseum. After that season the city placed pressure on the Nats' management to move to the newly constructed Onondaga War Memorial in the heart of Syracuse. Dolph thought the move was a mistake. The War Memorial sat two thousand fewer people, and parking was less available.

The War Memorial was our next destination. Around the exterior of the building, carved in stone, were the names of major battles from American wars. Inside there were nicely presented display cases with uniforms, artifacts, and photographs of some of the men and women of Syracuse who served their country. When we entered the arena, Dolph immediately said, "Do you see how much smaller it is?" Today the facility is used for cultural events and is the home of a minor league hockey team. There was one nice connection to the past. Hanging from the ceiling was a banner celebrating the Nats' 1954–55 NBA championship season.

The visit to the Onondaga War Memorial prompted Dolph to tell a story about himself that revealed something about his sense of humor and a little about how he saw himself as a basketball player. During the election of 1976, President Gerald Ford made a campaign swing through Syracuse and held an event at the War Memorial. The sponsors asked Schayes to sit with Ford, since the president had been a star football player at the University of Michigan and would enjoy meeting Dolph. While he was sitting on the stage with the president, Dolph's mind began to wander, and he asked himself what he would do if somebody in the audience had a gun and opened fire on the president. If that happened, Schayes decided, he would shield the president and take the assassin's bullet. As Dolph played this out in his mind, he visualized himself dying on the stage and a guy hovering over him, asking him if he had any last words. Dolph heard himself say, "Tell Naomi [his wife] I love her." Then as an afterthought, Schayes added, "They said I couldn't block shots. Well, I couldn't."

While I filed that story away, it revealed something about Dolph's capacity to laugh at himself and some insight into his athletic ability. At six foot eight and 220 pounds, Dolph was very strong, but I learned he was not blessed with foot speed or leaping ability. As he later admitted, Dolph never dunked the ball. By constantly practicing and playing, Schayes developed a feel for the game, or what we might call basketball sense. When he broke his right wrist in 1952, Dolph became a better shooter with his left hand. He accomplished it the Schayes way. Dolph studied how left handers shot. He used his left hand for all the mundane activities of daily life. As a result, Schayes was ambidextrous on the court, which made him even more difficult to defend. This commitment to basketball excellence, not easily measured by a stopwatch or a tape measure, was what made Dolph Schayes a Hall of Fame basketball player.

We then drove to Syracuse University. Dolph took me to the Carrier Dome, where the Syracuse Orangemen play their home football and basketball games. Dolph's son Danny played there between 1977 and 1981, before enjoying an eighteen-year career in the NBA. While the facility was impressive, our final stop, the Carmelo Anthony Center, was astonishing. Anthony led Syracuse to a National Collegiate Athletic Association (NCAA) championship in 2003, his only year in college. Since then he had made his fortune as a star forward with the Denver Nuggets before he was traded to the New York Knicks in 2011. A gift from Anthony helped to build this facility. The Anthony Center is used exclusively by the men's and women's basketball programs. There was a large basketball floor, but it was what surrounded the floor that caught my eye. On the second floor there were spacious offices for all the coaches, a room with stadium seating to show game film, and a coaches room with computers and television screens to analyze film. On the first floor was a weight room, a training room, a recreation room, and a room to store equipment and uniforms. The training room had small pools with treadmills on the bottom to help athletes recovering from injuries. An outer corridor was home to the Syracuse University Basketball Hall of Fame.

The State Fair Coliseum, the Onondaga War Memorial, and the Carmelo Anthony Center were only miles apart, but they were light-years apart as a measure of how the game has changed. When I asked Schayes if the Nats had a scout, he laughed and said, "The team could not afford one." What about game film of the opponent? This question brought another chuckle from Schayes. He explained that his first coach, Al Cervi, thought that if you knew your stuff, you should be able to figure out what the other team was trying to do in the first five minutes of the game. When Schayes played at New York University, he remembered that the team met at a restaurant for a meal before the game. At Syracuse the players have a daily catered meal. Before games the Orangemen stay at a nearby hotel, where they can be closely monitored.

This game is no longer an amateur sport. The expectation is that college men's football and basketball will generate enough revenue to fund other university athletic teams such as tennis, golf, and track, sports that make no money. In the 2009 fiscal year, the largest athletic program reportedly generated $138.5 million, while the median value of schools eligible to play football in the Bowl Championship Series (BCS) was $45 million. Yet only fourteen BCS schools made a profit. These figures highlight the gap between contemporary sports culture and the sports world Dolph Schayes entered at NYU in 1945. Academic institutions have had to wrestle with how the reality of collegiate sports meshed with the academic values of higher education. Some have concluded that the dilemmas posed by professionalized college sport were impossible to resolve. One of those schools was New York University, Dolph's alma mater, which dropped basketball and Division I sports in 1971.

The changes in college basketball are mirrored by professional basketball. In 1948 Dolph Schayes signed his first contract with the Syracuse Nationals for $7,500. In August 2010, Carmelo Anthony rejected an offer from the Denver Nuggets reportedly valued at $65 million for three years, which forced Denver to trade him to the New York Knicks. From 1948 through 1971, Dolph Schayes was a player, a coach, and a director of NBA officials. As a college player, Schayes played in every major college event. Through his eyes and his career, it is possible to gain insight into the life of a basketball player during the decades of basketball's emergence as a major American sport.

In the course of doing my research, I was able either to interview or to find information on a significant number of Dolph's teammates. I have written a number of biographical vignettes covering their careers as a means of revealing the variety of basketball experiences of those men who played with Dolph between 1948 and 1963.

Dolph Schayes and the Rise of Professional Basketball

1

New York's Golden Age of Basketball

In the decades between 1890 and 1910, waves of immigrants from southern and eastern Europe poured into the United States speaking languages other than English and bringing cultural traditions that were foreign to their Protestant hosts. Despite what it says on the Statue of Liberty, these immigrants were not particularly welcome. Organizations emerged during these decades that sought to restrict immigration to the United States. They believed that these new immigrants would resist assimilation and threaten American democracy.

During this period of rapid industrial growth in the United States, immigrants sought a better life. In some cases they were fleeing conscription or, in the case of European Jews, pogroms or other forms of anti-Semitism. After being processed at Ellis Island, immigrants headed for cities and neighborhoods that shared their language and culture. Dolph Schayes's parents, Carl Schayes and Tina Michel Schayes, were part of this immigrant experience. They emigrated separately from Romania in 1920, shortly after World War I, and just before the 1924 National Origins Act, which placed severe limits on immigration from eastern Europe. Carl Schayes was nineteen when he left Dorohoi, a small town in northeastern Romania, for the United States. Two brothers and a sister had preceded him. Carl's plan was to go to Youngstown, Ohio, where a job was waiting for him at a steel mill. He did not like the work, though, so he quit and headed back to New York City, where his family lived. He found work with Consolidated Laundries, which supplied restaurants, hospitals, barbershops, and salons with clean linens and towels. Carl had a route in midtown Manhattan. On the side he drove a taxi. Likable and hardworking, after World War II he became a supervisor.

1

Tina Michel came from Jassy, about fifty miles south of Donohoi. Members of her family had also preceded her. Carl Schayes met Tina Michel at an English-language school in Manhattan, and they were married after a short courtship. While Carl and Tina were part of the Jewish Diaspora, they were not religious and did not attend a synagogue. They moved to a three-room flat in a five-floor walk-up at 2275 Davidson Avenue and 183rd Street in the Bronx. They had three boys, Fred, the oldest; Adolph, born on May 19, 1928; and Herman, the youngest. Even in the worst days of the Depression, Carl made sure the Schayes family never wanted for food or clothing. Tina was a stay-at-home mother who kept a close eye on her children.

Because Dolph's father put in a long day, Dolph did not spend a lot of time with him. The time they did spend together, Dolph remembered, was meaningful, especially the hours spent watching the Yankees play at the stadium. Roughly twelve times a season, they would take the Jerome Avenue elevated to Yankee Stadium to watch a Sunday or holiday doubleheader. For fifty cents you could buy a seat in the bleachers. Dolph and his father would usually get to the stadium at eleven so they could watch batting and infield practice. By six or seven in the evening, they returned home rather blurry eyed. But it was worth it, since on any given day they might see the great Jewish slugger Hank Greenberg, or Jimmy Foxx, or Bob Feller, as well as the great Yankee teams. Carl Schayes was not a Yankee addict; he just enjoyed a day at the ballpark with his son.

As Dolph reminisced about his childhood, he said that his father hit him only once. Carl, like many in the neighborhood, liked to play the numbers. It was like playing the lottery today. Dolph's responsibility was to drop his father's wager off at the neighborhood barbershop on his way to school. One morning, for whatever reason, Dolph failed to make his drop. When he stopped at the barbershop after school, Dolph learned that it was too late; the numbers had already been picked up. The next day when the winning numbers were published, Carl was delighted to see that he had won, or so he thought. When Dolph revealed his story, Carl reacted angrily and gave him a smack that he remembers vividly today.

As a child and teenager, Dolph was extremely shy and a little naive. A story that Dolph likes to tell about himself is that one day, he happened to find ninety dollars, which seemed like a fortune in the Depression. Wondering what he should do, an older boy advised him to take the money to the local police station. Dolph followed this advice, and the police assured him they would find the rightful owner of the money. Dolph would later realize that the boy and the police had taken advantage of Dolph's ignorance of the ways of the world.

Another one of Dolph's stories captured his relationship with his mother. When he was a boy, Dolph and Herman slept in the living room on a pullout bed. When he was around nine or ten, Dolph recalled, he was afraid of the dark. Because the apartment buildings in the Bronx were so close together, at night it was especially dark. One restless night, Dolph looked up and saw a small orange light at the end of the room. It was his mother smoking, staying up until her son fell asleep. For Dolph, this story epitomized his mother's devotion to her children.

Once a month, Schayes remembered, his family would visit relatives in Brooklyn. The adults would play cards and the kids whatever games captured their fancy. Today Schayes maintains this tradition with his grandchildren. He invites all of them to his house, provides each with a stake, and they play a variety of poker games. Schayes also remembered that as a boy, for five or six years, he and his mother and brothers would spend the summer on a farm outside the city. His father would join them on the weekends. Although Carl and Tina were not affluent, they were resourceful enough to provide their children with a stable and loving family life.

Although Dolph received no formal religious training, he had no difficulty developing a Jewish identity. He was surrounded by Jews in his neighborhood, so that as a kid, Dolph "thought everyone was Jewish." As a result, Schayes rarely encountered any anti-Semitism. Except for the summer trips to the farm and family visits to Brooklyn, Dolph's childhood days were spent in two or three blocks around his apartment. Outside of his family, the institutions that had the biggest impact on his life were neighborhood social clubs. The first club that Dolph joined was called the Trylons, named after one of the symbols of the 1939 World's Fair, located in Queens. When Schayes got a little older, he and a group of friends formed the Amerks, short for Americans, and they focused their energy on playing all sports, especially basketball.

1. The Schayes family enjoying a summer's day in the Catskills. *From left:* Fred, Herman, Tina, and Dolph. Family photograph.

Basketball is the perfect city game. All you need is a hoop, a ball, and a space large enough to play a game. You can practice by yourself as you learn to dribble and shoot with both hands. In every neighborhood, in every major city, there is a gym or outdoor court where some kind of game, one-on-one, three-on-three, or five-on-five, is being played. For Dolph Schayes, the blacktop court adjacent to Public School (PS) 91 at 181st Street and Aqueduct Avenue was that place. Winter did not discourage him or his friends, as they climbed the fence surrounding the court and continued playing. This court is where Schayes began to develop his skills. When the Amerks were old enough and through their high school years, they played in organized leagues and tournaments throughout the Bronx. Dolph recalled that they played in Italian and Irish neighborhoods. While the fans rooted vociferously for their teams, there were no fights, and anti-Semitic remarks were very rare and considered out of line. The Amerks were a tight-knit group, and Schayes remembered their camaraderie as the highlight of his childhood and teenage years.

After elementary school Dolph attended Creston Junior High, where his basketball coach was Lou Rossini, later the basketball coach at Columbia and NYU. When Dolph was ready for high school, he chose to attend Townsend-Harris, a prep school on the campus of the City College of New York (CCNY). The school was for bright students who had to pass a test before gaining admission. Although the academic program was outstanding, the subway ride and the school's weak basketball program left Dolph disenchanted. Whether he would remain at the school became a moot question when, after six months, the school closed its doors for financial reasons. As a result, Dolph enrolled at DeWitt Clinton High School, located at 100 West Mosholu Parkway on 205th Street, near Bedford Park in the Bronx.[1]

Until 1983 DeWitt Clinton was an all-boys school. Its extraordinary history is told in *The Castle on the Parkway*. In the 1930s approximately twelve thousand boys attended DeWitt Clinton. By the time Dolph entered in 1941, construction of new public high schools reduced the size of the school to about four thousand boys. Because it was an open-admission school in a predominantly Jewish neighborhood, the school was 80 percent Jewish. Its list of alumni includes prominent writers, actors, composers, lawyers, and judges. Richard Rodgers, Burt Lancaster, James Baldwin, Irving Howe, William Kunstler, Neil Simon, and Lionel Trilling were a few of Clinton's graduates. Johnny Most, the legendary voice of the Boston Celtics, graduated from Clinton. Schayes was a good student and remembered his teachers as especially gifted and dedicated. Unlike the student body, the faculty was less Jewish, perhaps approaching 40 percent.[2]

Because of the Depression and World War II, DeWitt Clinton dropped baseball and football. While Schayes attended the high school, the competition to make the basketball team, coached by Nat April, was fierce. Schayes and Joel Kaufman soon emerged as the stars of the team. In their junior years, the spring of 1944, Schayes, now six foot five, and Kaufman led Clinton to the semifinals of the Public School Athletic League City basketball tournament. Schayes was the center on the All-City high school basketball team. As Dolph's team gained a reputation, college coaches began to recruit members of the team. Schayes remembered Purdue University offered the starting five scholarships to play for the Boilermakers.

Nat Holman, the celebrated coach at CCNY, offered the five an opportunity to work at his summer camp in the Hudson Valley, Camp Scatico. If Holman was using the offer of a summer job as a recruiting device, his brother Frank turned the team off, when the players learned they would have to sleep in tents. Ironically, that summer Schayes worked at another summer camp and slept in a tent.[3]

DeWitt Clinton won the city basketball championship in March 1945, but because Schayes graduated from high school in January 1945, he was not part of that championship team. The Schayes family was very proud of their son's success. New York City had a host of newspapers, and Mrs. Schayes joyfully cut out articles from the sports section detailing Adolph's successes.

On January 12, 1945, Len Heideman, who covered sports for the *Heights Daily News*, NYU's student newspaper, revealed that a couple of students had scouted Schayes in a game against Evander High School. Heideman reported that "Schayes was almost a head taller than any of the men on either team." While Schayes's "pivot shot was excellent," he also showed "a very fine set shot." For a big man, Schayes was also "quick on his feet." If Schayes decided to attend NYU, Heideman concluded, he would be the answer to "one of Coach Cann's pet prayers," a player "who could score from the keyhole."[4] In January Schayes answered those prayers by enrolling at NYU.

Although Schayes had opportunities to go to St. John's University, Columbia, CCNY, and even West Point, there were several reasons for selecting NYU. At that time NYU's main campus, which dated back to the 1830s, was in Greenwich Village. But it also had an uptown Bronx campus called University Heights, founded in 1894, that focused on the arts and sciences. The gym and the aeronautical engineering program, the two focal points of Dolph's college years, were located at the Heights, within walking distance of the family's apartment. Walking to school rather than spending hours on public transportation made sense to Dolph, who lived at home during his three and a half years at NYU.

The Violets also appealed to Schayes because they played almost all their home games at Madison Square Garden. By 1945 the Garden was the "mecca" of college basketball. Beginning in 1934 Edward "Ned" Irish,

2. DeWitt Clinton High School—Bronx champs, 1943–44. Dolph holding the ball, Coach Nat April behind him, and Joel Kaufman to the right. *DeWitt Clinton Yearbook, 1944.*

sportswriter turned promoter, sold the Garden's management on the idea that college basketball doubleheaders could be a profitable venture. In March 1938 the Metropolitan Basketball Writers Association sponsored the first National Invitational Tournament (NIT), an event that only added to the Garden's luster. By 1945 the Garden doubleheaders regularly drew eighteen thousand fans. Finally, NYU's academic prestige played a role in Dolph's decision. For the son of immigrants, Dolph's decision to attend NYU, with its academic reputation, was a source of individual and family pride. Dolph had been an excellent student in high school, and his scholarship was for academic rather than athletic excellence.[5]

The opportunity for Dolph Schayes to play immediately as a freshman in 1945 was the result of World War II. After Pearl Harbor a host of collegiate basketball players were among the men who either enlisted or were drafted into military service. Between 1942 and 1945 many of the best basketball players in the United States were playing in the armed forces. Hank Luisetti, Bob Davies, Jim Pollard, Jack Coleman, Kenny Sailors, and Dick McGuire were just a few of the great players of the era who played for service teams. College and university athletic programs responded to this talent drain in several ways. Some conferences simply suspended competition. Others were able to add players stationed nearby their campuses. Dick McGuire, a star at St. John's University, played for Dartmouth College in the 1944 NCAA Tournament. Still another response was to make freshmen eligible for varsity competition. In 1944 the University of Utah, led by Arnie Ferrin, won the NCAA Tournament with five freshmen and a sophomore. So Dolph Schayes was just one of many freshmen playing at the varsity level.[6]

When Schayes reported for his first practice, Howard Cann was in his twenty-first year as the NYU coach. Cann had been a basketball, football, and track star at NYU. In 1920 he led NYU to the Amateur Athletic Union National Championship, held in Atlanta, and the Helms Athletic Foundation named him the basketball player of the year. In the same year Cann finished eighth in the shot put in the Olympics, held in Antwerp, Belgium. Cann had great success at NYU. When he retired in 1958, his record was 429-235. In 1968 he was inducted into the Basketball Hall of Fame.[7]

Yet Dolph quickly discovered that Howard Cann did not have set plays and was not terribly interested in the X's and O's of basketball. As a coach he had a simple philosophy, which was to embrace the New York style played by high school kids throughout the metropolitan area. Schayes called it "pure basketball." You kept the floor balanced, and the players spread out. There was constant movement, with the players using the give-and-go and pick-and-roll, passing, and cutting. On defense NYU always played man-to-man. Cann also believed in conditioning. His practices emphasized a variety of running drills designed to promote a fast-breaking offense. In this style of play Schayes was not a traditional center limited to the high or low post. Later he recognized that Cann's offense was the best possible preparation for his career. Because Schayes was only sixteen when he joined the team, it helped that Cann had a nice sense of humor and a knack for getting along with his players. On the bench Cann was not a screamer, but remained cool, almost stoic. Schayes clearly flourished in Cann's approach to the game.[8]

Snapshot

New York City College Basketball

Although there was no New York City collegiate league, New York University, St. Francis, St. John's University, the City College of New York, Long Island University (LIU), Manhattan College, Brooklyn College, Columbia University, and Fordham University competed for media and fan attention. The Metropolitan Basketball Writers Association published the records of each team so that there could be a mythical city champion. This notion was flawed, because no school played all of the other teams. Each season NYU played five or six of the other city schools, with the balance of the schedule filled by schools such as Notre Dame, Temple, and North Carolina (UNC). Its biggest city rivalries were with St. John's University and CCNY. During Dolph Schayes's career at NYU, the Violets never played Long Island University, a perennial basketball powerhouse. Schayes thought NYU shunned LIU because of the athletic program's perceived low academic standards. Norm Drucker, who played for CCNY in the early 1940s, also remembered that CCNY never scheduled LIU.[9]

Beginning in 1936 the Metropolitan Basketball Writers Association gave an award to the Metropolitan collegiate player of the year. In 1943 the award was named after Frank Haggerty, who played baseball and basketball at St. John's. (Trained as a naval pilot, Haggerty died in a plane crash on September 23, 1942, near Morris Field in Charlotte, North Carolina, the first St. John's alumnus to die in World War II.)[10] The first fifteen winners of the award came from LIU, NYU, CCNY, and St. John's, which is one measure of their preeminence in New York City basketball. They were the big four of New York City basketball.

Another aspect of the city's basketball culture was the prominence of Jewish players on all of the college teams. Dolph Schayes's Jewish background, then, was no novelty. CCNY, with its large Jewish enrollment, almost 90 percent between the wars, had the largest percentage of Jewish players. If a student had a specified student grade point average, attending City College was tuition free. For the bright children of immigrants, City College was a natural choice. Jewish basketball players played prominent roles at NYU, LIU, St. John's University, and other New York City schools.[11]

By the time Schayes suited up for NYU, there was an aspect of New York college basketball that led to scandal. In January 1945 five Brooklyn College players were removed from their team for accepting a bribe to throw a game against the University of Akron. Although this event set off alarm bells, Al Figone, a historian of the scandal, argues that basketball was becoming so profitable that some colleges ignored the warning signs of a possible crisis. As Figone explains, bookies by the early 1940s had developed a point spread to encourage gambling. Before the point spread, bookies engaged in straight gambling, which meant that when they made one team a 9–6 favorite, for example, the gambler would put up nine dollars to win six if the gambler bet on the favorite. If gamblers could get the players to throw or lose the game, they would make more money by betting on the underdog. Bookies developed the point spread to allow gamblers to bet on the underdog with points or on the favorite to beat the point spread. The point spread made it easier for gamblers to approach players and offer them money to shave points or control the score so that the underdog could win with points offered by the bookie. The players accepting the money could rationalize the deal by arguing that they were not throwing the game but merely winning by a certain number of points. Just as Madison Square Garden had earned the reputation as college basketball's mecca, all the elements were in place to destroy that image.[12]

Snapshot

The Coaches

Despite Howard Cann's success, Dolph Schayes believed that the basketball writers and fans ranked Cann behind Nat Holman of CCNY, Joe Lapchick of St. John's University, and Clair Bee of LIU. Nat Holman, born on October 19, 1896, grew up on the Lower East Side of Manhattan. Like many Jewish boys, he gravitated to the settlement centers, where he honed his athletic skills. At Commerce High School he led its basketball team to one city championship, but also excelled in soccer and baseball. He was also president of the student council. Holman graduated from the Savage School of Physical Education and in 1919 took a position at CCNY as an instructor in the Hygiene Department, varsity soccer coach, and freshman basketball coach. In 1920 CCNY named him the varsity basketball coach, yet Holman continued to play basketball, somehow juggling his coaching and playing responsibilities. As the floor leader of the Original Celtics, Holman reportedly made as much as $12,500 a year. When the Celtics disbanded in 1928, Holman played with the Chicago Bruins and Syracuse All-Americans, until he retired as a player in 1933. In 1921 the enterprising Holman and his brother Jacob purchased 250 acres in Elizaville, New York, where they built the Camp Scatico summer camp. Between 1930 and 1939 Holman was also director of physical education at the 92nd Street Young Man's Hebrew Association. Impeccably dressed, well groomed, and extremely articulate, Holman was an impressive figure.[13]

Because all the students at CCNY attended tuition free, there were no athletic scholarships. According to the rules, athletes had to have the required high school average or, like other students who fell short, pass a rigorous entrance exam.

Norm Drucker, who played for Holman in the early 1940s and enjoyed a long career as an NBA and American Basketball Association (ABA) official, remembered Holman as one of the best teaching coaches of his generation but not a good bench coach. Holman had the ability, according to Drucker, to accomplish a great deal with average players. Because Holman discouraged dribbling, his team would sometimes practice their offense without a ball. While some in the media considered Holman aloof, even arrogant, Drucker remembered that Holman regularly wrote to him while he was stationed in Europe during the war. Other players found his screaming and harsh criticism insufferable.[14]

By the time Dolph Schayes entered NYU, Holman had compiled an outstanding record, but had won no major championship. This changed in 1950, when CCNY became the only team to win the NIT and NCAA championships in the same year. Unfortunately, in February 1951 the press reported that New York City district attorney Frank Hogan had announced the arrests of four CCNY players for accepting bribes to shave points. The New York City Board of Higher Education suspended Holman without pay for neglect of duty. An investigation also revealed that several players were admitted without the required high school average or test scores. After a hearing he was dismissed on April 2, 1954, but successfully appealed the dismissal before the State Education Commission. With his back pay restored, Holman returned to coaching basketball at CCNY, now de-emphasized, which he would do until 1960.[15] After retiring from coaching, one of Holman's passions was promoting basketball in Israel. In 1932 he helped organize an American basketball team for the first Maccabiah Games, or Jewish Olympics, in Palestine. In 1949, under the sponsorship of the State Department, he established clinics to promote basketball throughout Israel. Between 1973 and 1981 Holman was the president of the United States Committee Sports for Israel, which sponsors the US teams that compete in the Maccabiah Games. Holman died in 1995.[16]

When Joe Lapchick signed a contract for twenty-five hundred dollars with St. John's University to coach baseball and basketball in 1936, he was already a basketball legend. The son of immigrants from Czechoslovakia, Lapchick was born in 1900 in Yonkers. After the eighth grade, Lapchick had to leave public school to help support his family. Eventually reaching six foot five, Lapchick played semipro basketball until he joined Nat Holman and the Original Celtics in 1922. After the Celtics disbanded, Lapchick continued to play professionally until he signed with St. John's. Lapchick was bright and worked diligently to overcome the limits of his eighth grade education. He had an engaging personality, and the basketball writers loved to join him after games as he dissected the night's play. Lapchick recruited some of the city's best players, such as Harry Boykoff, Hi Gotkin, Andrew "Fuzzy" Levane, Ivy Summer, Dick McGuire, and Bill Kotsoris. In 1943 and 1944 St. John's won back-to-back NIT championships. Because of Lapchick's collegiate success and professional experience, Ned Irish named him the coach of the New York Knicks in the newly formed Basketball Association of America. In 1947 Lapchick moved over to Madison Square Garden, where he would coach until 1956 and then return to St. John's until 1965. Five years later Lapchick suffered a fatal heart attack.[17]

Clair Bee was born on March 2, 1896, in Grafton, West Virginia, where he graduated from high school and played football and basketball and wrestled. In 1920 Bee earned his associate's degree in business from Mansfield College in Ohio. Five years later he graduated from Waynesburg College in Pennsylvania. When he went to Rider College in Trenton, New Jersey, to teach business courses, the administration persuaded him to coach football and basketball. At Ryder College Bee's basketball teams were 53-7 between 1928 and 1930. In 1931 he moved to Long Island University to teach accounting; serve as the athletic director, head of physical education, and special assistant to the president; and coach basketball and football until the latter sport was dropped in 1940. For wearing all these hats, Bee earned twenty thousand dollars a year, an impressive salary during the Depression. In 1931 Long Island University was only three years old and had fifteen hundred students. The first classes were held in a renovated factory near the Brooklyn Bridge. The university's mission was to serve the immigrant population.

It was in basketball that Bee made his name. He had ten basketball scholarships, which were particularly attractive to Depression-era athletes. In the 1930s and 1940s Bee conducted tryouts for these scholarships. In

1936 and 1939 his teams were undefeated. In 1939 and 1941 the Blackbirds won NIT championships. Ossie Schectman, Irv Torgoff, Art Hillhouse, and Danny Kaplowitz were some of his star players. After World War II Bee also authored the Chip Hilton series, which was popular with children. Between 1944 and 1963 twenty-three books were published. The books taught that those individuals who competed the right way would succeed in the end. Given the message of these books, it was a bitter irony that in 1951, three of Bee's players were arrested in the point-shaving scandal that shocked basketball fans. Bee resigned from LIU in 1951, and LIU dropped college basketball for six years. Bee ended his coaching career in 1954 after two unsuccessful years at the helm of the NBA's Baltimore Bullets. Afterward, Bee served as the athletic director for the New York Military Academy, near Cornwall, New York, and the director of Kutsher's Sports Academy. Clair Bee died on May 20, 1983.[18]

Schayes thought he played at the zenith of New York college basketball, and he might be right. The basketball scandals of 1951 ended New York City's preeminence in college basketball. Through 1950 the NIT's prestige matched, if not exceeded, the NCAA's tournament, which got its start in 1939. As a result of the scandals, the NCAA increased its field to sixteen teams and prohibited college teams from playing in both tournaments. As the NCAA continued to enlarge its field, the NIT became the tournament for teams not selected to play in the NCAA Tournament. The Madison Square Garden doubleheaders also ceased to be a part of New York City basketball. Besides CCNY and LIU, Toledo University, Bradley University, and the University of Kentucky were implicated in the scandals.

In 1951, when the scandals were exposed, Dolph Schayes was in his third year with the Syracuse Nationals, and the news shocked him, as it did most basketball fans. While at NYU, Schayes was focused on balancing basketball and academics. He was never approached by gamblers and was unaware of any efforts to manipulate games. Like all basketball fans, Schayes saw the scandals as one of the great tragedies of modern American sport.

Adolph Schayes

1945–48

On February 10, 1945, Adolph Schayes was the starting center in his first varsity basketball game. At six foot five, he was the tallest NYU player in five years and three months away from his seventeenth birthday. NYU's opponent was Notre Dame, the second-ranked team in the Midwest. The Violets and the Irish had inaugurated the Madison Square Garden doubleheaders in 1934, and the Irish had won nine of the previous eleven meetings between the two teams. Larry Dobrow of the *Heights Daily News* thought the matchup that could determine the outcome of the game was Adolph Schayes's ability to contain Vince Boryla, Notre Dame's leading scorer.[19] (Ironically, five years later they would be battling each other in the NBA.)[20] The oddsmakers considered the Violets the underdog, but NYU was a solid 10-3 going into the game. Their leader on the floor was Sid Tanenbaum, a six-foot sophomore who was an All-City guard at Thomas Jefferson High School. Al Grenert, a senior, was a high school star at Boys High, in Brooklyn's Bedford-Stuyvesant neighborhood, a former marine, and a husky six-footer. He was the team's leading scorer, just ahead of Tanenbaum. Another sophomore, Frank Mangiapane, from George Washington High School, was a strong rebounder, despite measuring just five foot eleven. A freshman from Boys High School, Don Forman was beginning to clock more playing time. As a high school senior, he was the city's leading scorer, hit for forty-nine points in one game, and made the All-City first team. Forman had a good two-handed set shot and liked to drive to the basket. Forman would be a key player for four years and play a year with the Minneapolis Lakers before practicing law.

A crowd of 18,210 screaming fans watched Notre Dame beat the Violets, 66–60. Before the game one of Schayes's teammates said that Dolph was "scared stiff."[21] After the opening tip-off, Schayes shook off the butterflies and finished with sixteen points, high man for the Violets. Louis Effrat, who covered the game for the *New York Times*, wrote that Schayes "was all over the court, capturing rebounds, feeding his mates and turning in a herculean all-around job, offensively as well as defensively." On the basis of one game, Effrat thought Schayes "gave evidence of future greatness."[22] What Schayes remembered about the game was that at one point, he was so exhausted that he had to sit on the floor during a timeout. While Schayes had to adjust to the faster pace of college basketball, he also had to adjust to the Madison Square environment. Not only were there more than 18,000 fans jammed into the Garden, but so many were smoking that Dolph remembers that by the second half, he could not see the balcony seats.[23]

NYU ended the season 14-7, but had two big wins over Temple and CCNY and accepted a bid to play in the NCAA Tournament. After defeating Tufts by fifteen in the opening round, NYU rallied to win the Eastern Regional by beating Ohio State University (OSU), 70–65, in overtime. Trailing by ten points with 2:00 left, the Violets tied the game at 62 at the end of regulation play. Louis Effrat thought the outcome turned on a "mental lapse" on the part of the Buckeyes. In 1945 the rules gave the team with the ball the option of shooting a free throw or taking the ball out of bounds after a foul was committed. With 1:14 left, the Buckeyes were fouled three times, and rather than keeping possession they chose to shoot the free throws. They proceeded to miss all three. After the last two misses, Schayes and Forman made clutch shots to tie the score. The Buckeyes entered the overtime without their star center, Arnie Risen, who had scored twenty-six points. "Brimming with confidence," according to Effrat, NYU outscored OSU 8–3 in the overtime to capture the win.[24]

On March 24 NYU met Oklahoma A&M, the winner of the Western Regional, for the NCAA championship. Coached by Henry Iba, who was on his way to a Hall of Fame career, the Aggies were led by Bob Kurland, their seven-foot center. Iba's teams played tough defense and ran a methodical offense. The Aggies prevailed, 49–45, before 18,000 fans. Kurland scored twenty-two points to lead all scorers and earned most valuable player (MVP) honors for the tournament.[25] Schayes guarded Kurland, and fifty-five years later recalled that he simply could not contain him. If the Aggies had fed Kurland, Schayes thought, he would have scored considerably more points.

By mid-August 1945 World War II was over, and the United States emerged as the world's undisputed military and economic power. Rationing came to an end, and Americans looked forward to spending some of the savings accumulated during the war. Richard Rodgers and Oscar Hammerstein's *Oklahoma* was a smash Broadway hit, and "Oh, What a Beautiful Morning," its opening song, captured the optimism of the moment. The end of the war also meant the return of college athletes from the service.

Because Al Grenert was NYU's only graduate, Howard Cann had high expectations for his team in the fall of 1945. The Violets did not disappoint their fans, as they won their first five games, including a one-point victory over Arkansas before a record-breaking Madison Square Garden crowd of 18,398. After losing to North Carolina by two points, the Violets won their next thirteen games. During this run NYU's biggest victories were against Notre Dame, St. John's, and Temple. On the evening of the Notre Dame game, Louis Effrat claimed that "many thousands" were turned away from the Garden's gates. In summing up NYU's 62–58 victory, Effrat said, "The faster, more imaginative and better team won." Schayes held Vince Boryla to thirteen points, while scoring eleven of his own. Don Forman led all scorers with eighteen.[26]

Against the St. John's Redmen, NYU trailed by fourteen points with seven minutes left in the game. After the Redmen slowed the pace of the game, the Violets managed to tie it at 48. Louis Effrat wrote that in the overtime, St. John's "did not have the stamina to keep pace with the beautifully-conditioned Violets." NYU's Frank Mangiapane's twenty-one points just edged Harry Boykoff, St. John's six-foot-nine center, by one point for scoring honors. The victory was particularly sweet for the Violets because they had lost the previous five meetings against St. John's.[27] NYU won another nail-biter, 59–57, over the Temple Owls at Philadelphia's Convention Hall. The game ended in a brawl when, according to NYU sportswriters Howard Rosenblum and Leonard Heideman, Dolph Schayes retaliated after being "roughed under the backboards time after time." They wrote, "The usually meek Violet center connected with a hard right to giant Max Wharton's jaw in retaliation for a hard shove and a slap across the face."[28]

CCNY broke the Violets' winning streak in the last game of the season, 49–44. Before the game the Inter-Fraternity Council held a "'Beat City' rally and dance" at the Heights gymnasium. For one dollar a couple could dance to a "twelve-piece orchestra and a vocalist." After the loss Daniel J. Robins in the *Heights Daily News* lambasted some of the NYU fans. He was offended by comments made after the game that NYU had thrown the game. His point was that in sports, an inspired underdog can win.[29] The column reflected a widespread concern about the extent to which gambling permeated Madison Square Garden; Larry Dobrow, another NYU journalist, wrote that one just had to walk through the "Garden lobby" to hear bets being made.[30]

By finishing 18-2 NYU earned its second straight NCAA bid and faced North Carolina in the first round. Once again the Tar Heels, led by John Dillon, defeated the Violets.[31] NYU defeated Harvard in the consolation to finish the year with a 19-3 record. The New York Basketball Writers Association placed Tanenbaum, Mangiapane, and Forman on the All-Metropolitan college basketball team. For the second straight year, Dolph Schayes made the second team.[32]

In 1946 Dolph Schayes spent the first of several summers playing basketball and working in the Catskill Mountains, nicknamed the "Borscht Belt." The hotels and resorts were a popular retreat for Jewish New Yorkers. Schayes worked and played at the Nevele, owned by a graduate of NYU. The country clubs saw basketball as part of their entertainment package and recruited the nation's best players. The players worked in the athletic department, waited tables, or served as bellhops. Technically, they were not paid to play basketball, so they maintained their amateur standing. The teams played two games a week, one at home and one away. All the games were played outdoors under the lights. There were big-time referees and lively crowds. Bob Cousy, the future star of the Boston Celtics, played at the Tamarack Lodge with some of his Holy Cross teammates, and George Mikan of DePaul and then the Minneapolis Lakers played for Klein's Hillside.

There was a dark side to these pleasant summers. Gamblers frequented the games, and spectators bet on the total score of the games. Historians of the college basketball scandals agree that it was in the Catskills that gamblers developed relationships with players who were subsequently persuaded to shave points during the regular season. In the summer of 1946, Schayes saw none of it in the games he played.[33]

When Howard Cann called his team together for its first practice in the fall of 1946, expectations for the new season were extremely high. Al Sauer, writing in the *Heights Daily News,* declared that some fans were predicting an undefeated season. Although Frank Mangiapane had graduated, Ray Lumpp, a six-foot-one guard with great skills, returned from the service after playing at NYU in 1942–43. The Violets started the season by crushing Connecticut. Schayes's play caught the eye of Louis Effrat, who thought "the 18-year-old junior appeared to be the most improved player of the young season." Effrat wrote that Schayes, now six foot seven, was "bigger and stronger than before" and "has added aggressiveness to his other assets and will be tougher than ever on rebounds."[34]

The Violets won ten of their next twelve games. Their only losses came against Oregon and North Carolina. Then NYU registered wins against Arkansas, Duke, and the University of California at Los Angeles (UCLA). Just when it looked as if the Violets were headed for another tournament bid, the season turned sour. NYU finished by losing seven of its last eight games. In the loss against Canisius, Schayes, who was not particularly physical, was tossed out early in the game when he retaliated after being punched by an opponent. St. John's nipped NYU, 57–56, in what Louis Effrat called "the standout performance of the season."[35] The season ended on a dismal note when CCNY crushed NYU, 91–60. The one bright spot in the game, according to the student newspaper, "was the stellar play of Dolph Schayes."[36]

After the season the Metropolitan Basketball Writers Association gave the Frank C. Haggerty Award to Sid Tanenbaum, who was the only Violet named to the All-Metropolitan first team. Tanenbaum finished his career with 1,074 points, the first Violet to pass the 1,000-point mark. He also won All-America honors. The honors won by Tanenbaum were small consolation for a season that Jonas Kiken of the *Heights Daily News* called "a nightmare of memories."[37] Another writer wondered how a team with enormous potential could be reduced "to such utter futility." This thoughtful writer believed the Violets lacked that "innate, compelling

3. Dolph playing for New York University in the 1946–47 season. Family photograph.

force that is intrinsic in champions. As individuals they were superb, as a team they were flops."[38]

In 1946–47 Dolph Schayes scored 195 points in twenty-one games, 46 more than the previous season. He had 20 points in a loss against Temple and 23 in a game won by Fordham. In an interesting story in the *Heights Daily News*, Dave Glinert observed that during the losing streak, Schayes "was generally heartbroken, he could not eat or sleep but just sulked all day and kept aloof of his friends." Schayes impressed Glinert as a person "who is concerned only in his team's record and not in his personal glories." Unfortunately, rebounding statistics were not kept or at least published in the 1940s, but Glinert reported that Schayes "did yeoman work off the backboards with practically no help from his teammates." While Howard Cann repeatedly mentioned how indispensable he was to the squad, Schayes failed "to do himself even the slightest justice."[39] In short, Dolph Schayes exhibited a trait that he would carry with him throughout his career—he was a worrier. Perhaps it was this part of his personality that drove him to seek excellence on the basketball court. While he would continue to improve and to gain more confidence, would the Violets recapture that team chemistry they had possessed in Schayes's first two seasons?

In the fall of 1947, Howard Cann looked forward to his twenty-fifth season as the coach of NYU's basketball team. The most experienced players, Don Forman, Ray Lumpp, and Dolph Schayes, were expected to provide leadership and to carry the scoring load. Other starters were Joe Dohlon, a two-year letterman from Yonkers who played one guard position, and Tom Kelly, from Regis High School in the Bronx, who started at one of the forward spots. Kelly, who flew twenty-nine combat missions with the Eighth Air Force, also had two years of varsity experience. Joel Kaufman, who played at DeWitt Clinton with Schayes, was the sixth man.

The team chemistry that was missing the prior season returned in Schayes's senior year. The Violets won their first nineteen games, as Forman, Lumpp, and Schayes took turns winning the scoring honors. On March 1 Notre Dame was NYU's twentieth opponent, and the *Heights Daily News* declared "studies and classes are secondary today." The editorial page described Notre Dame "as the very epitome of basketball" and "the mecca of all that is exemplary of an athletic spirit." The school newspaper declared that eleven thousand of the more than eighteen thousand seats would be filled by NYU students and alumni.[40] The pregame euphoria ended in disappointment, as the Irish edged the Violets, 64–59. But the game generated more controversy after a Notre Dame player called Don Forman a "no good Jew." The *Heights Daily News* thought the Notre Dame player had "no right to appear in intercollegiate ball again." Notre Dame, the editorial concluded, "won the game, but lost prestige."[41] In another column in the *Heights Daily News*, Norman Jackman reported that before the game, Jinx O'Connor, the freshman coach, said, "Don't forget fellows, they're the 'Fighting Irish' and will be tough to beat." Joe Dohlon replied, "That's all right, we're a mixture . . . that's even better." Although Jackman readily acknowledged that Notre Dame outplayed NYU, he thought it was the "cooperation between men of different faiths as exemplified by the names of Kelly, DeBonis, Benanti, Derderian, Kaufman and the rest, that make us still one of the top teams in the nation."[42] Although NYU had been defeated by Notre Dame, the *Heights Daily News* turned the game into a celebration of tolerance over intolerance, the melting pot over the salad bowl.

The Violets finished the season by defeating Fordham and losing to CCNY. By defeating Fordham, NYU clinched the mythical metropolitan championship. Before the Fordham game, NYU, in honor of his twenty-five years of service, presented Cann with an automobile and a certificate guaranteeing enough gasoline to drive twenty-five thousand miles. Although NYU lost to CCNY, 60–57, Dolph Schayes finished with 19 points, which gave him 315 for the season, establishing a new regular-season record for the Violets.[43]

At the end of the regular season, the Metropolitan Basketball Writers Association showered the Violets with awards. The writers named Howard Cann coach of the year and voted Dolph Schayes the city's most valuable player and recipient of the coveted Haggerty Memorial Award. Don Forman and Ray Lumpp joined Schayes on the All-Metropolitan first team, while Joe Dohlon, Tom Kelly, and Joel Kaufman earned honorable mentions.[44]

For the students who followed NYU basketball closely, the Violets' success was a mystery. The disastrous ending to the 1946–47 season haunted NYU's basketball junkies. The loss of Sid Tanenbaum and the lack of team chemistry did not auger well for the 1947–48 season. For whatever reason, NYU found that mysterious glue that characterizes winning teams in Schayes's senior year. Joe Hirsch of the *Heights* sports desk wrote that the Violets were like "a phoenix rising from the ashes of a disastrous 1946–47 season."[45]

While Cann and his players accepted their awards, they also prepared for postseason play. NYU elected to accept a bid to play in the National Invitational Tournament at Madison Square Garden. Because 1948 was an Olympic year, the winner of the NIT earned a spot in the Olympic tournament to decide who would represent the United States in London. Basketball was added to the Olympic program in 1936. In the first round NYU played the Texas Longhorns, led by Slater Martin, who would go on to enjoy a Hall of Fame career with the Minneapolis Lakers and St. Louis Hawks. With just a little more than a minute left in a hotly contested game, Schayes scored to cut Texas's lead to two points, 43–41. Lumpp then stole a pass and hit Fred Benanti, who tied the score with a pretty hook shot. With ten seconds left, Schayes grabbed a missed shot and hit Dick Kor with an outlet pass, and he won the game when he sank a one-hander. Benanti and Kor were unlikely heroes, because they had rarely played during the season and between them had scored a mere twenty-two points. Although Schayes was often double-teamed, he led all players with fourteen points.[46] In the semifinal game Ray Lumpp poured in twenty-nine points to lead the Violets past DePaul, 72–59. The St. Louis Billikens dominated NYU, 65–52, in the championship game, as "Easy" Ed Macauley led all scorers with twenty-four and was named the outstanding player of the tournament.[47] Despite the loss, NYU's season was not over. St. Louis's athletic board decided that its basketball players had missed enough class and voted against sending the Billikens back to New York to play in the Olympic tournament. As the second-place team, NYU took their spot.

The eight-team tournament included three AAU teams: the Denver Nuggets, the Oakland Bittners, and the Phillips 66ers. There were four college teams: New York University, the University of Kentucky (NCAA champions), Baylor University (NCAA runners-up), and the University of Louisville (National Association of Intercollegiate Basketball champions). The Brooklyn Young Men's Christian Association was the eighth team in the tournament. Including a YMCA team was a method of rewarding the Y for its role in spreading basketball to other parts of the world in the early decades of the twentieth century. The two teams that reached the finals of the tournament would select five players each to represent the United

States. The American Olympic Basketball Committee would add four at-large players from the competition.

In the opening round the Baylor Bears nipped NYU, 59–57. Louis Effrat reported that the game was "a torrid struggle that produced fifteen ties and seventeen lead changes." NYU's Joe Dohlon's free throw tied the score at 57 apiece with less than a minute to play, but Jimmy Owens's one-hander with forty-five seconds left was enough to give Baylor the victory. Unfortunately for the Violets, a back problem prohibited Don Forman from playing. Ray Lumpp led the Violets with fourteen, and Dolph Schayes followed with eleven.[48]

In the championship game Bob Kurland limited Alex Groza, Kentucky's All-America center, to four points and scored twenty of his own to give the Phillips Oilers a 53–49 victory. Ralph Beard, Kentucky's All-America guard, kept the Wildcats in the contest with a game-high twenty-three points. By virtue of the victory, Omar "Bud" Browning, the Phillips coach, earned the right to coach the Olympic team. Adolph Rupp, Kentucky's coach, would be his assistant. Jesse "Cab" Renick, Gordon "Shorty" Carpenter, R. C. Pitts, and Lew Beck joined Bob Kurland as the Phillips five on the Olympic squad. Along with Groza and Beard, Ken Rollins, Cliff Barker, and Wallace "Wah Wah" Jones were selected to represent Kentucky's contribution to the Olympic team. Ray Lumpp of NYU was added to the Olympic squad as an at-large selection, along with Vince Boryla from the Denver Nuggets, Jackie Robinson from Baylor, and Don Barksdale from the Oakland Bittners. Barksdale was the first African American to play on an Olympic basketball team. Dolph Schayes was named an alternate, but did not go to London to watch the competition. The 1948 Olympic basketball team went on to win the gold medal in London.[49]

The loss to Baylor in the Olympic tournament was Dolph Schayes's last college basketball game. He was still two months shy of his twentieth birthday. By his senior year Schayes had clearly made great progress as a basketball player. A student sportswriter marveled at the "Houdini-like deception he imparts to his passing." The writer continued, Schayes "lost his propensity for fouling recklessly and his inordinate fear of shooting from the outside."[50] Schayes managed to develop his basketball skills while completing a major in aeronautical engineering in three and a half years.

Professor Frederick K. Teichman, assistant dean of the College of Engineering, described Schayes as "a good student, despite the fact that both basketball and the aeronautical engineering program he was following were very time consuming. It is unusual for a star athlete to be a good student in such a tough course."[51]

After Dolph's three and a half years at NYU, now twenty years old, he was still the shy young man who had entered college in January 1945. Academically, he finished with a B average. Dolph never missed class and managed to complete his homework. There was an adjustment to doing college work. In the spring of 1945, Dolph was on the baseball team and not playing much. He was struggling in Analytic Geometry and had failed a test miserably with a 20. The baseball coach approached Dolph and recommended that he drop baseball and take care of his schoolwork. Dolph agreed and managed to pass the course with a D, his only poor grade at NYU. Although good in mathematics, Dolph thought of himself as a "grinder" and made no pretense of being brilliant.[52]

Because he lived at home, he did not mix much with his teammates, most of whom took their classes at the Washington Square campus, so socially Dolph was somewhat isolated. There was also an age gap between Dolph and his teammates that could be intimidating. A few of the players were also returning from the service and were older than the average student.

As for romance, Dolph did not date much, if at all. DeWitt Clinton was an all-boys school, and the University Heights campus was 95 percent male. Besides, Dolph was very quiet and did not have much money to spend on social activities. Later when he was running his basketball camp, he would always get a laugh from the kids when he would say, "I didn't date much; girls were secondary to basketball." Except when he played basketball at Madison Square Garden, he did not explore the cultural life of Manhattan. Dolph's life was pretty much circumscribed by the Bronx. Basketball was his outlet, the court a place where he was most comfortable. Howard Cann remembered that Dolph was the first at practice and the last to leave.[53]

In the summer of 1948, Schayes was not particularly interested in pursuing a career in aeronautical engineering and had no pathway to a business career. Because he wanted to continue playing basketball, Schayes had the option of playing for a corporation that sponsored basketball teams under the umbrella of the Amateur Athletic Union or playing professionally. From a player's perspective, the advantage of playing for a corporation offered the prospect of lifetime employment with the company after the completion of one's playing career. Teams and players were also eligible to compete for a spot on the US Olympic basketball team. Dolph Schayes received letters from the Boeing Corporation in Seattle and Allen-Bradley in Milwaukee but did not pursue them. By 1948 Schayes had an opportunity to watch the New York Knicks play, a charter member of the BAA. He was impressed with what he saw and was determined to play professionally.[54] In deciding to play professional basketball, Dolph did not know where this road would take him. As it turned out, he would become one of the pioneers of professional basketball who helped build the foundation of what would become a global enterprise.

2

The Syracuse Nationals

The Al Cervi Years

When Dolph Schayes completed his college basketball career, almost sixty years had passed since James Naismith formulated the first rules for basketball as a student at the Young Men's Christian Association in 1891 in Springfield, Massachusetts. By 1948 professional basketball had yet to win a place as a national sport in the hearts of the American sports fan. Although there were professional teams as early as the 1890s, basketball, whether collegiate or professional, was a dull affair. Games were low scoring and boring except for periodic fights. Professional leagues, concentrated in New York, New Jersey, Pennsylvania, and the Midwest, were fly-by-night operations. In the 1920s the best-known teams were barnstorming outfits such as New York's Original Celtics or African American teams such as New York's Renaissance Big Five and Chicago's Harlem Globetrotters.[1]

On collegiate campuses, basketball became more interesting in the late 1930s for two reasons. The first involved rules changes such as the adoption in 1932 of a line at half-court that the offensive team had to cross in ten seconds or give up the ball. No longer could a team use the entire court to hold the ball or stall. By 1935 no player could park in the foul lane for more than three seconds, and the game speeded up dramatically in 1937 when the rule makers eliminated the center jump after every basket.[2]

Another development involved what some coaches considered a radical shift in the style of play that was generated by the imaginations of players rather than coaches. Between 1936 and 1939 Angelo "Hank" Luisetti, the great Stanford star, dazzled basketball fans with his deadly one-handed shot. Upon watching Luisetti at Madison Square Garden, Nat Holman said, "That's not basketball. If my boys ever shot one-handed, I'd quit coaching." In the 1940s Wyoming's Kenny Sailors and others astounded old-timers by introducing the jump shot. By the end of the 1930s, basketball, after football, was America's most popular college sport. A built-in fan base, natural rivalries, and a more interesting game accounted for this popularity. After the war, the big question for sports entrepreneurs was whether they could build on this popularity and make the professional game profitable.[3]

In the spring of 1948 when Dolph Schayes contemplated his future in professional basketball, there were two leagues struggling to capture the attention of basketball fans. The older league, the National Basketball League, dated back to 1935, when it was called the Midwest Basketball Conference. The heart of the league, which became the NBL in 1937, was in the Midwest, and its most stable franchises were the Oshkosh All-Stars and the Sheboygan Redskins, both of Wisconsin, and the Fort Wayne Zollner Pistons of Indiana. The first two teams were financed by businessmen in the community. The Pistons were the best-financed team in the league, as Fred Zollner put his corporation's money behind the team. Except for these three teams, other teams bounced in and out of the league. Until after the war, the league schedule never exceeded thirty games. To make any money, these teams scheduled a great number of exhibition games. The NBL acquired an eastern presence when the Rochester Royals in 1945 and Syracuse Nationals in 1946 purchased franchises. The Royals were the brainchild of Les Harrison and the Nationals the passion of Danny Biasone. Both men were small businessmen who ran their teams on a shoestring.[4]

The other league was the Basketball Association of America, organized in 1946. The sports entrepreneurs who invested in this new league were men who operated sports arenas from the Midwest to the Atlantic Coast. Ned Irish of Madison Square Garden, Walter Brown of the Boston Garden, and Arthur Wirtz of the Chicago Stadium were prominent players. Given the popularity of college basketball, they reasoned that basketball fans would follow the fortunes of college stars as they competed as professionals. Located in big markets, they were confident that they could ultimately put the NBL out of business.[5]

In its first year a BAA franchise cost one thousand dollars, and a salary cap for a twelve-player roster was set at fifty-five thousand. The Board of Governors named Maurice Podoloff commissioner of the league. Born in 1890 near Kiev, Russia, Podoloff and his family immigrated to the United States to pursue the American dream when he was three months old. Valuing education, Podoloff's father eventually moved the family to New Haven, Connecticut, so that Maurice could attend Yale. He entered Yale Academy in 1909 and left in 1915 with bachelor's and bachelor of law degrees. Afterward, Podoloff practiced law briefly and then went into the real estate business. When he purchased the ice arena in New Haven, he also got a hockey franchise in the Canadian American League. In 1935 Podoloff became president of the American Hockey League. When the BAA's Board of Governors sought a president, one of its members, Al Sutphin, owner of the Cleveland Arena and the AHL's Cleveland Barons, recommended Podoloff for the position at a salary of between eight and nine thousand dollars a year. Podoloff admitted that he knew nothing about basketball, but he did know something about running a professional sports league. Only time would tell if the arena managers had found another vehicle to keep their doors open.[6]

By 1948 the status of professional basketball was extremely fragile. After the first season, four franchises folded, leaving seven teams in the BAA until Baltimore entered the league to make eight. After the BAA's second season, Podoloff delivered a severe blow to the NBL when he enticed Fort Wayne, Indianapolis, Minneapolis, and Rochester to jump to the BAA. The big prize was Minneapolis with George Mikan, who was the first dominant center in professional basketball and always a popular draw wherever he played. This move was a significant step toward crushing the NBL and ending the bidding war between the two leagues for star players.[7] In 1947 Jim Pollard, the former Stanford and AAU star, was able to take advantage of the bidding war to sign with Minneapolis for twelve thousand dollars and a signing bonus of one thousand. Most first-year players were signing for five thousand dollars.[8]

Although the NBL was on life support, its existence favored Dolph Schayes. In the summer of 1948, he was drafted by the NBL's Tri-Cities Blackhawks, who played in Moline and Rock Island, Illinois, as well as Davenport, Iowa, and by the BAA's New York Knicks. With the defection of Rochester, the NBL's only presence in the East was in Syracuse. The NBL thought that the best way to strengthen the Syracuse franchise was to transfer the draft rights to Schayes from Tri-Cities to Syracuse. Thus, the bidding war began between Syracuse and New York. As a New Yorker, Schayes seemed like a natural fit for the Knicks. When the Knicks offered Schayes five thousand dollars, Syracuse countered with seventy-five hundred. Ned Irish refused to raise his offer.[9] In 1948 twenty-five hundred dollars was a lot of money, and Schayes, with his father looking on, signed a contract to play with Syracuse. To be sure, there were many, including his coach Howard Cann, who were skeptical about Schayes's chances of succeeding in professional basketball. There were some who simply thought he was not tough enough to survive in the professional game; he was just too nice. When Schayes became a star, the New York press never failed to remind Ned Irish of what he had lost for a few thousand dollars.[10]

As noted, the majority owner of the Nats was Danny Biasone, whose Italian family landed at Ellis Island on Christmas Day 1919, when Danny was eleven years old. His father took him to Syracuse in 1920. Growing up in Syracuse in the 1920s was not easy for Biasone. He spoke little English and struggled in school. There were many days when he came home with a torn shirt following a fight. Biasone recalled, "They acted like I didn't belong in this country."

But Biasone was determined to prove that he did belong. Later in life, Danny remembered that his father advised him, "You play sports and you won't land in jail." So Biasone immersed himself in sports. He umpired softball games and officiated basketball games, and when he got older he formed the Syracuse Bisons semipro football team.

As the result of a rather amusing story, in 1946 Danny Biasone purchased a basketball franchise in the National Basketball League. In 1945 Biasone had put together a semipro basketball team. During the season Biasone attempted to schedule a game with Les Harrison's Rochester Royals, who won the NBL title in the 1945–46 season. After Harrison

4. Danny Biasone, owner of the Syracuse Nationals. Courtesy of Gregory Newsome.

canceled twice, Biasone said to himself, "What league is this team in? I want to play this guy Lester Harrison at basketball." Upon learning that the Royals played in the NBL, Biasone took a train to Chicago, where he met with Leo Fischer, the league president. When Biasone asked Fischer what it would take to join the league, the latter replied, "Just give us a down payment." Biasone responded by handing over a certified check for one thousand dollars. After this point, the financial side of the story becomes murky. The going rate for an NBL franchise was twenty-five hundred dollars, but Biasone later claimed that he paid five or six thousand dollars. Biasone said he named the team the Nationals because he hoped "that someday the team would be national champions." By 1948, in addition to owning a basketball team, Biasone had established himself as a successful businessman and was the owner of the Eastwood Sports Center, a combination bar and bowling alley, where people could get a sandwich and a drink and talk sports.[11]

Danny Biasone helped to make playing basketball in Syracuse a good experience. He sat on the bench at every game, usually with a cigarette in his mouth. When the NBA passed a rule prohibiting owners from sitting on the bench, Biasone made himself an assistant coach. Although Biasone did not interfere with coaching decisions, he did get on officials. In a game at Anderson, Indiana, at the end of the 1948–49 season, Biasone drew four technical fouls. After practice or home games the team congregated at the Eastwood Sports Center for beer and sandwiches and to rehash the night's game. When Carl Schayes came up to watch his son play, he had a seat on the bench.[12]

One constant in the history of the Nationals was that the players respected and liked Danny Biasone, but found him a tough negotiator. Al Bianchi, who joined the team in 1956, never made more than fifty-two hundred dollars as a Nat. Once when he asked Biasone for a five-hundred-dollar raise, Biasone countered by replying that Bianchi would get at least that much from the playoffs. Bianchi remembered that he did not push too hard, because he feared that Biasone just might cut him. After the 1961 season Larry Costello, who had been with the Nats since 1957, thought his average of 14.5 points per game was worthy of a five-hundred-dollar raise. Biasone replied, "Have no money. Can't do it." When Costello persisted, Biasone caved in and gave him the raise. Thirty-four years later Costello recalled that Biasone had made him feel "guilty getting that $500. I still feel guilty."[13]

Beyond Danny Biasone, the front office of the Nationals was streamlined. There were no frills. The general manager was Leo Ferris, a native of Elmira, New York. Ferris's experience in professional basketball began in Buffalo, where he helped Ben Kerner establish a franchise in the NBL.

For a brief time in 1948, Ferris served as president of the NBL. Lawrence J. Skiddy, the sports editor of the *Syracuse Herald-Journal,* recalled that in 1948, "Leo Ferris bobbed up in Syracuse, waving the magic wand, and put on the campaign which produced 25 new directors at $1,000 each." Dolph Schayes remembered Ferris as professional basketball's version of baseball's Bill Veeck. Ferris believed that the way to sell professional basketball was to make it part of an entertainment package. When you attended a Syracuse game, there would be halftime entertainment and occasionally a dance afterward with a big band. Art Deutsch assisted Leo Ferris. He would handle publicity and assist with promotions. There was no staff, but Deutsch was energetic and effective.[14]

In the fall of 1948 Dolph Schayes boarded a train at Grand Central Station for Syracuse. Except for summers in the Catskills, he had never been far from home for an extended period of time. Dolph was unfamiliar with Syracuse, but he knew it was cold. Before he left Tina made sure that her son would be properly clothed for the Syracuse winters.

Without fanfare Schayes found the offices of the Nationals and then looked for a place to live. In his first year with the Nats, Dolph boarded with five of his teammates at the home of Mr. and Mrs. Woody Williams and their two daughters at 312 Highland Avenue. Woody Williams had been a former professional baseball player, so the family was familiar with the world of professional athletes. The modest accommodations had the look and feel of a small fraternity house.[15]

In its first two years, Syracuse posted losing seasons. This outcome changed in the 1948–49 season. In part, it was because of the defection of Minneapolis and Rochester, the two best teams in the NBL the previous year, to the BAA.[16] As important, the Nationals emerged as a stronger team. Biasone began to alter the face of the team when he hired Al Cervi to serve as both player and coach. An all-sports star at East High School in Buffalo, New York, Cervi had elected to play semipro basketball and work after graduating in 1936. In 1938 he hooked up with Les Harrison, who ran a number of basketball teams in Rochester, New York. Except for the war years, Cervi played for Harrison and the Rochester Royals until they split over a contract dispute in 1948. Cervi was five foot eleven, 170 pounds, and powerfully built. His relentlessness on defense earned him the nickname "Digger." On offense Cervi was confident in his ability to come through at crunch time. Between 1946 and 1949 Cervi earned all-league first- or second-team honors. At a time of low-scoring games, Cervi averaged in the low teens.

To the youthful Schayes, Cervi at thirty-one was a grizzled veteran who had been through the basketball wars. Schayes remembered Cervi as an "overpowering personality with a great will to win." In trying to understand Cervi's hypercompetitiveness, Schayes, in 1958, speculated that Cervi might have been overcompensating for his decision not to attend college. Was he trying to prove to the college guys that he was tougher, smarter, better? If Cervi's intensity rubbed some of his players the wrong way, Schayes acknowledged that his coach's competitiveness was infectious and that he and his teammates "always played very hard for Al." Like most of the professional coaches of this period, Cervi was not an X's and O's guy. Alex Hannum, who played for Syracuse between 1949 and 1951, said, "Maybe the toughest guy I ever saw in the game was Al Cervi." According to Hannum, Cervi always exhorted his players to use their hands and "hit the bangboards." Hannum remembered that "Cervi's hands were in a constant state of motion." He told his players "to use your hands at all times on the court. You got to be hitting someone." Why Cervi called the backboards the "bangboards" was a mystery to Hannum, but the message was clear to all but a few.[17]

Along with Cervi, an infusion of new talent also made the Nats more competitive. Joining Schayes as rookies were "Bullet" Billy Gabor, Johnny "Whitey" Macknowsky, Hank O'Keeffe, and Ed Peterson. Gabor, a five-foot-eleven guard, starred at Syracuse University and was a hometown favorite. He was a tough guy with a good outside shot. Blessed with a quick first step, Gabor was strong enough to force contact and finish the play when driving to the basket. Macknowsky was a six-foot guard from Seton Hall with a deadly two-handed set shot. After playing on the freshman team in 1941–42, Macknowsky served in the US Navy for three years. When he returned to Seton Hall for the 1946–47 season, one of his teammates was Bobby Wanzer, who went on to star for Rochester. Their coach was Rochester's great star Bobby Davies, who commuted to his alma mater while playing for the Royals.[18] O'Keeffe was a six-foot-three guard from

Canisius, and Ed Peterson was a six-nine center from Cornell who gave the Nats much-needed size.

Although he had not played much the previous year, Paul Seymour would blossom into an outstanding player in 1948–49. Seymour grew up in Toledo and starred at Woodward High School. After playing a little at the University of Toledo, Seymour left college to play briefly for the Toledo Jeeps in the NBL. In the fall of 1947 Seymour then signed with New Orleans of the Pro Basketball League of America. When the PBLA folded, Seymour moved on to Baltimore in the BAA, before winding up with Syracuse in the spring of 1948.[19] As a competitor Seymour had many of the qualities of Al Cervi. The holdovers from the previous season were John Chaney, who starred at Louisiana State University and was in his third year as a Nat; Jim Homer, a forward from the University of Alabama; and Jerry Rizzo, a fiery guard from Fordham.

The new coach and his team had a new home court for the 1948–49 season. The Nationals traded the Jefferson Street Armory for the more spacious State Fair Coliseum. They would play in the Eastern Division of the NBL, which included the Anderson Packers, the Dayton Rens, and the Hammond Buccaneers. The Western Division included the Oshkosh All-Stars, the Tri-Cities Blackhawks, the Sheboygan Redskins, the Waterloo Hawks, and the Denver Nuggets.

By the end of the season the Syracuse Nationals had the second-best record in the NBL but were eight games behind Anderson in the Eastern Division. The keys to the dramatic improvement were Dolph Schayes and Al Cervi. Schayes got stronger during the season, and at one point in March scored 144 points in eight games. His 12.8 scoring average was the fifth best in the league, as Schayes scored 809 points in sixty-three games. The NBL rewarded Schayes by naming him the rookie of the year and placing him on the all-rookie first team. Al Cervi finished the season as coach of the year and earned a place on the All-NBL's first team.[20]

In the playoffs the Nats eliminated the Hammond Buccaneers in the first round. The Anderson Packers knocked out Syracuse in the Eastern Division finals by capturing the best-of-five series, 3–1. The Packers defeated the Oshkosh All-Stars to win what would prove to be the last championship in the NBL's short history.[21] In early March Bill Reddy, the sports editor of the *Syracuse Post-Standard*, reported that he expected the Nationals to jump to the BAA. Because of its location in upstate New York, the travel requirements of the NBL made no sense for Syracuse. With Boston, Rochester, New York, and Philadelphia in the BAA, the Nats would have a number of natural rivalries. On August 3, 1949, the BAA and NBL merged to form a seventeen-team league now called the National Basketball Association. Bill Reddy thought the merger was a "good gamble" for the Nationals because they would be playing in larger cities and travel would be more manageable.[22]

In orchestrating the merger of the NBL and BAA, Maurice Podoloff was able to end the bidding war between the two leagues that drove up player salaries. However, the new league was extremely unwieldy. There were three divisions: Eastern, Central, and Western. Syracuse was in the Eastern Division with New York, Washington, Philadelphia, Baltimore, and Boston. The Central Division included Minneapolis, Rochester, Fort Wayne, Chicago, and St. Louis. Placing Rochester in the Central Division was an anomaly, as it made no sense geographically. The teams that played in the Western Division were Indianapolis, Anderson, Tri-Cities, Sheboygan, Waterloo, and Denver. Although Syracuse was in the Eastern Division, it played a Western Division schedule. Therefore, it played Denver five times but New York just twice.[23]

In one of the most interesting franchise moves, the Indianapolis Jets became the Indianapolis Olympians. Desperate to generate interest in the pro game, the NBA awarded a franchise to the stars of the two-time NCAA champions, the Kentucky Wildcats. Five of the Olympians—Alex Groza, Ralph Beard, Wallace "Wah Wah" Jones, Cliff Barker, and Ken Rollins—had played on the 1948 gold-medal Olympic team. Groza and Beard were immediate stars.[24]

After the 1948–49 season Dolph Schayes returned to New York City. Rather than taking the train home, Dolph showed up in a brand-new sporty Dodge convertible, purchased for eight hundred dollars.

For Carl and Tina Schayes, the hardships of the Depression and war years were over, and they were about to share some of the prosperity of postwar America. Rather than working multiple jobs, Carl became a supervisor for Consolidated Laundries. With a part of his salary Dolph

5. After his first season Dolph shows off his brand-new Dodge. Family photograph.

helped his parents put a down payment on a house on Long Island valued at ten thousand dollars. For the first time in his life, Carl Schayes had some leisure time and more opportunities to see his son play basketball. Dolph recalled that his father was "happy as hell."[25]

When Dolph returned to Syracuse, he and Johnny Macknowsky rented rooms with Mrs. Catherine Quick on Tipperary Hill. In the uncertain world of professional basketball three of their roommates from the previous season, John Chaney, Jim Homer, and Jerry Rizzo, were gone, as was Hank O'Keeffe. As the Nats geared up for the 1949–50 season, they continued to strengthen their lineup. From the defunct Oshkosh All-Stars, Syracuse picked up Alex Hannum. As he would be the first to admit, Hannum was not a great offensive player. In his eight years in professional basketball, he averaged just six points a game. At six foot seven and 220 pounds, however, Hannum was strong, smart, and incapable of being intimidated. Hannum had played for Sam Barry at the University of Southern California and during the war served as a medical reconditioning officer in the army, a stint that earned him the nickname "Sarge." Because Hannum had a successful construction business, he did not need basketball for financial reasons. But he told me, "Once you get the basketball bug, you get it for life."[26] After his playing career was over, Hannum enjoyed a successful coaching career, winning NBA championships with the St. Louis Hawks and Philadelphia 76ers, an ABA championship with the Oakland Oaks, and an AAU championship with the Wichita Vickers.

With the addition of six-foot-six, 220-pound George Ratkovicz, the Nats added more bulk to their front line. Ratkovicz played high school ball at Lindbloom, in Chicago's public league, but he did not play college ball. By 1949 he was a veteran who started playing professionally with the Chicago Bruins in 1940 and made stops with the Chicago Gears, Tri-Cities Blackhawks, and Rochester Royals. Cervi and Ratkovicz had been teammates in Rochester. In the 1948–49 season, Ratkovicz was sitting on the bench at Tri-Cities. According to Cervi, "I asked Ben Kerner, owner of Tri-Cities, if he'd trade for him—jokingly he said hell—you can have him." When Ratkovicz played for Syracuse, Kerner asked Cervi what accounted for his increased productivity. Cervi explained that Ratkovicz "had to start—he couldn't play well coming off the bench—funny but it's true." Cervi thought Ratkovicz was "the main reason for my success" in Syracuse's first year in the NBA.[27]

Still another veteran pickup was Andy "Fuzzy" Levane, who starred at St. John's under Joe Lapchick. Cervi said Levane "played very well—he was a heady player—not like today—hell—I think we could win games with just the turnovers they commit today."[28] Levane played four years with the Royals before joining the Nats. Leroy Chollet from Canisius

College and Ray Corley from Georgetown University were rookies and played little during the season.

In 1949–50 the Nationals compiled the best regular-season record, 51-13, in the franchise's entire history. Al Cervi called the season "the most pleasant in my life." He praised Biasone for making it possible for the Nats to travel "first class" and "stay at the best hotels."[29] Obviously, there were some extra incentives when former NBL teams played teams from the BAA. Many of the NBL players believed that they were as talented as the players in the BAA. Against BAA teams the Nats were 16-4. Their record against Eastern Division teams was an almost perfect 9-1. One of those victories was on March 12, when the Nats crushed the Boston Celtics, 95–72. The game was special for Schayes because he became the first Syracuse player to score one thousand points in a season. While Carl Schayes made the trip up to Syracuse frequently, this game was Tina Schayes's first time watching her son play at the State Fair Coliseum.[30] Of all the happy spectators, Carl and Tina were the most pleased.

By virtue of winning the Eastern Division, the Nats picked up an extra $2,500. If the Nats won the NBA championship, they would pick up another $13,000, or roughly $1,636 per player. In the first round of the playoffs the Nationals eliminated the Philadelphia Warriors in two games. This win set up a best-two-of-three series with the New York Knicks, the winner advancing to the NBA championship series.

The Knicks had the second-best record in the Eastern Division and were coached by Joe Lapchick, a New York favorite. After coaching St. John's to two NIT championships, Lapchick was in his third year with the Knicks. In assembling the Knicks, Ned Irish tried to build the team around a core of New York collegians. Dick McGuire, who played for Lapchick at St. John's, triggered the offense. McGuire was a two-time Haggerty Award winner who was best known for his uncanny passing ability. Carl Braun, New York's leading scorer, was a star at Garden City High School on Long Island who as a freshman set a single-season scoring record at Colgate University. Ernie Vandeweghe from Oceanside, New York, held Colgate's career scoring record. While attending medical school, Vandeweghe was a reliable sixth man. Vince Boryla and Harry Gallatin, from Kirksville State College in Missouri, started at the forward positions. Boryla told me that the Knicks were like minestrone soup. There was no star but a "little of this and a little of that."[31]

Before the Nats-Knicks series, Al Cervi reminded Syracuse fans that beating the New Yorkers assured the team another $8,000.[32] Besides the money, there were other themes that Cervi could play on to motivate the fans and his team. The Nats had beaten the Knicks during their two meetings, so they were not in awe of their big-city rivals. In New York Ned Irish gave each Knick a $1,000 bonus for their second-place finish.[33] The message was that the Knicks were the real champions of the Eastern Division because the Nats played a Western Division schedule. There was also the issue of the arrogance of Ned Irish, who did not hide his displeasure with the small-market teams.

The first game of the series in Syracuse drew 9,674 fans and lived up to all the pregame expectations. Bud Vander Veer, who covered basketball for the *Syracuse Herald-Journal*, compared the game to "all the storybook finishes by the Merriwells and other poor little boys who became stars." The Knicks were leading the game by five points with forty-three seconds left to play, 76–71. The Nats hit four free throws and took the lead, 77–76, when John Macknowsky scored on a drive to the basket. When Carl Braun was fouled in the act of shooting, he converted just one of his two free throws to take the game into overtime. Schayes had kept Syracuse in the game in the second half by scoring seventeen of his game-high twenty-six points and dominating the boards. By overtime Schayes had fouled out, along with Gabor, Cervi, and Hannum. In overtime the Nats outscored the Knicks, 14–6, as Ed Peterson, John Macknowsky, and Leroy Chollet hit key baskets. When the game ended the Nats were left with five eligible players; the Knicks had lost five to personal fouls. The officials, constantly badgered by Cervi and Lapchick, called forty-eight fouls on the Knicks and forty on the Nats.[34] Naturally, the Knicks thought they had been robbed, but Carl Braun had had a chance to win the game in regulation.

During the game the State Fair Coliseum was a madhouse. This scene led to an unusual exchange in Bill Reddy's column, "Keeping Posted." A fan wrote Reddy, "The conduct of Al Cervi in particular and the Syracuse fans in general, contradicted all the principles of fair sportsmanship that we Americans are supposed to be famous for. When the Nats fell behind,

Cervi went into his Durocher-like act in which he rants and raves at the officials at the least opportunity." The result, the unhappy fan concluded, was that the fans "behaved like bloodthirsty Romans at a lion fight." Reddy did not try to defend the fans and agreed that "Syracuse is as bad as any other city." He defended Cervi by arguing that the Syracuse coach "couldn't out do Lapchick in the color and tone of his remarks."[35]

Before the second game the *New York Times* reported, "There is a bitter feeling between the rivals."[36] Before 10,000 fans at the Garden, the Knicks tied up the series, 80–76. Boryla led the Knicks with twenty-one points. Ratkovicz led the Nats with seventeen, followed by Schayes with fourteen.[37]

A record 10,270 fans saw the Nationals take the rubber game, 91–80, in Syracuse. Louis Effrat wrote that there were no excuses: "Joe Lapchick's lads simply did not have it—Syracuse did." Schayes led all scorers with twenty-four points, and Ratkovicz, Gabor, and Macknowsky were in double figures.[38] The victory meant that the Nats would face off against the Minneapolis Lakers for the NBA championship.

The Lakers were built around George Mikan, the league's leading scorer, first dominant center, and major drawing card. Mikan's supporting cast included three future Hall of Famers. Jim Pollard could run, shoot, jump, and handle the ball. Nicknamed the "Kangaroo Kid," Pollard was the prototype of the small forward. Vern Mikkelsen was a sturdy six-foot-eight power forward who was a rookie but already showed signs of stardom. Slater Martin started the offense from his guard position and played tough defense. The Lakers had won the NBL title in 1948 and the BAA title in 1949.

Because it had the best record in the NBA, the Nationals had the home-court advantage in the seven-game series. On April 9 a spring snow limited the crowd to 7,552. Late in the game the Nats held a 61–54 lead, but the Lakers scored the next 7 to knot up the game at 61. The Nats scored next, but Bud Grant, who would have a successful career as the coach of the Minnesota Vikings, tied the game again at 66 with a set shot, his only points in the contest. Cervi called time and elected to freeze the ball for the last shot. The question was, who was to take the last shot? As Johnny Macknowsky remembered it, Cervi asked the players, "What are we gonna do?" Some thought the Lakers would expect Schayes to take the last shot. Because Macknowsky had shot well, some thought that it might catch the Lakers off guard if they set him up for the last shot. Finally, as Dolph Schayes recalled, Cervi said he would drive for the basket and try to draw a foul.

With fifteen seconds left, Cervi drove to the basket and his shot was blocked, but no foul was called. The outlet pass went to the Lakers' Bobby Harrison, who dribbled a few strides across the half-court line and took a forty-foot shot that hit nothing but the bottom of the net for a Laker victory. Harrison took just three shots during the entire game and made all of them. (Ironically, his running mate and best friend at Woodward High School in Toledo, Ohio, was Paul Seymour.)

According to Johnny Macknowsky, an angry Cervi, who thought he was fouled on the play, grabbed his clothes, stormed out of the locker room without taking a shower, and drove home in his uniform. Mikan's 37 set a Coliseum scoring record, and Pollard added 14, so the two accounted for 51 of their team's 68 points. Schayes's 19 and Ratkovicz's 13 led the Nats. The loss was only the second for Syracuse on its home floor during the 1949–50 season.[39]

When the fans filed in the next night for the second game, many were lighting up cigars. After the Lakers' win, Mikan mentioned that the smoke in the Coliseum bothered him. If the smoke bothered him, the Syracuse fans were intent on making him even more uncomfortable. The Nats bounced back and topped the Lakers, 91–85. Ratkovicz with 17 and Schayes with 13 led a balanced scoring attack. Mikan had another great night with 32.[40]

The next day Cervi unwisely gave the Lakers some bulletin-board material in his guest column for the *Syracuse Herald-Journal*. He began by making the reasonable statement that the difference between the two teams was Mikan. Then Cervi wrote, "Even with him in the game we're just as good." With a few breaks, Cervi predicted, "we will win the overall championship."[41]

Because the Minneapolis Auditorium was in use, the third game was played at the St. Paul Auditorium. Cervi declared that his plan was to run the Lakers into exhaustion. Instead, the Lakers won rather easily, 91–77, before 10,288 fans.[42] Mikan, Mikkelsen, and Pollard scored 28, 27, and 13, respectively. Macknowsky led Syracuse with 25, while Schayes with 12 and Hannum with 10 were the only other Nats in double figures. The Lakers stretched their lead to 3–1 when they beat the Nats again, 76–69. The Lakers' big three led the way, as Mikan had 28, followed by Pollard's 17 and Mikkelsen's 14. Schayes and Hannum each had 18 for the Nats.[43]

When the series returned to Syracuse, 9,024 fans turned out to watch their team win, 83–76. Five Nats hit in double figures, with Schayes leading the pack with 19. Jack Andrews of the *Post-Standard* wrote that the "highlight of the staunch defense thrown up by the Nats was Paul Seymour's tight as skin guarding against the great Jim Pollard. Pollard was able to collect only two field goals and two fouls." After the game Seymour told the press, "I hugged him and he had no place to go with Mikan clogging the middle."[44]

Game six in Minneapolis got physical. Early in the contest Pollard and Seymour squared off, a carryover from game five. Then Macknowsky fouled Pollard in the act of shooting, and the Laker threw a punch at him, drawing a technical. In the third period Cervi drew his first technical foul after he threw a towel after Johnny Nucatola failed to call a foul when Slater Martin and Billy Gabor charged into each other. Later in the period, following a scrum for the ball involving Cervi, Nucatola called a jump ball rather than a foul, and the Syracuse coach cursed the referee. Nucatola immediately assessed a second technical, which banished Cervi from the game. In the meantime, the Lakers were on fire. Mikan had 40, Pollard 16, but all the Lakers were making a contribution. Schayes, with 23, had his best game, but the Lakers won handily, 110–95. The Lakers' victory was worth $2,027 for each Laker, while each Nat picked up an extra $1,409.[45]

The team's success also yielded individual honors for the Nationals: Al Cervi earned a spot on the All-NBA's first team. Schayes, who led the team in scoring during the season with a 16.8 average, found a spot on the second team. During the playoffs Schayes also led the Nationals with a 17.1 average.

By the end of his second year, Dolph Schayes was clearly the star of the Syracuse Nationals, and he loved it and the city that embraced him. In 2010 Schayes told Bud Poliquin, sportswriter for the *Syracuse Post-Standard*, that in 1950 when he would walk down to Salina Street, Syracuse's Fifth Avenue, "on Saturdays after games on Thursdays or Fridays, everyone would wave or pat me on the back or stop to talk. It was 'Hey, Dolph, how ya doing?' And 'Hey, Dolph, great game last night.'"[46] Dolph Schayes was literally and metaphorically a big fish in a small supportive pond. Syracuse was his town.

Obviously, playing professional basketball had its psychic and economic rewards, but it was hardly a glamorous life at the beginning of Schayes's career. Each player received two uniforms: one for home games, the other for away games. On the road you were responsible for washing your uniform in your hotel room. The team gave each player $5.00 for meal money. If the team left in the afternoon, meal money was reduced to $2.50. Trainers did not travel with their teams, so players taped their own ankles or, if lucky, relied on the home team's trainer. Travel could be tedious. Teams often traveled by train, bus, or even automobile. When the Nats flew, it was on a DC-3. Most players dealt with the tedium of travel by playing card games, usually poker. After games beer was the drink of choice. Dolph was a reader, not a card player. Although he might have had a couple of beers with his teammates, that was Dolph's limit. Finally, while the schedule could be grueling, as teams often played three or four games in a row, Schayes found that he was often more relaxed on the road. There was less time to dwell on losses or mistakes so that Schayes thought he often played best on the third or fourth game of a road trip.

In 1948 there had been basketball experts, including his college coach, Howard Cann, who were skeptical about Dolph's ability to succeed in the pro game. When reminded of his skepticism, Cann simply laughed and said, "I was wrong."[47] Why were the skeptics wrong? Part of the answer was that at twenty Schayes had not matured physically. By twenty-two he had filled out and was much stronger. Second, for a big man, he could play facing the basket and as a college player had been accustomed to moving without the ball. When I asked Bob Houbregs, who played with the Fort Wayne Pistons, to comment on Dolph's game, he said that Schayes "never stopped moving." While everybody remembers Dolph's set shot, they have forgotten that he often faked that shot to set up a running one-hander, which he could hit with either hand, or take the ball to the basket.[48] Schayes also had a great feel for the game. He was not fast and did not jump well, but he always led the Nats in rebounding. When a shot went up, Schayes had a knack for sensing how the ball was going to bounce off the rim and beating his opponent to it. Finally, Schayes was tireless. He took physical conditioning seriously and took good care of his body. Another one of Dolph's trademarks was that after making a shot, he would raise his right fist to express his satisfaction. Although no player had done that before and some might have thought it was showboating, for Schayes it began as a spontaneous reaction to making a basket.

Syracuse was a great place for Dolph Schayes to launch his career. From the beginning, he was a starter and played a lot of minutes. When the Nationals practiced, most of the time was spent scrimmaging and no time was given to offensive or defensive schemes. Dolph said to me more than once, "We just played." In these scrimmages Al Cervi's aggressiveness rubbed off on Schayes. The scrimmages were also opportunities to work on different aspects of his game. While the personalities of Cervi and Schayes were polar opposites, they shared a passion for winning and excellence. In this sense, they were both relentless.

As the Nats improved on the floor, the team's bond with the fans became tighter. Schayes thought of Syracuse as the Green Bay of professional basketball. Visiting teams hated to play in Syracuse. The weather was cold, and the Syracuse fans were obnoxious. Referees hated to call a game in Syracuse. The fans dared officials to call a foul on their team. If they did, Cervi was in their face or turning to the crowd as if to plead his case. Syracuse was a blue-collar town, and its basketball fans came to games prepared to vent all their emotions in support of their team.

The 1950–51 season was significant for professional basketball. As expected, a number of franchises dropped out of the NBA for financial reasons. The league shrank to eleven when Anderson, Chicago, Denver, St. Louis, Sheboygan, and Waterloo folded. The Philadelphia Warriors, Boston Celtics, Syracuse Nationals, New York Knicks, Baltimore Bullets, and Washington Capitols completed the Eastern Division. The Washington Capitols dropped out after thirty-five games, leaving the Eastern

Division with five teams. The five Western Division teams were the Indianapolis Olympians, the Fort Wayne Pistons, the Minneapolis Lakers, the Rochester Royals, and the Tri-Cities Blackhawks.[49]

The biggest news of the professional season was the decision to open up the NBA to African American players. The Boston Celtics drafted Chuck Cooper from Duquesne, and the Washington Capitols selected Earl Lloyd from West Virginia State College. Ned Irish, eager to bring a championship to the Knicks, purchased the contract of Nathaniel "Sweetwater" Clifton from the Harlem Globetrotters.[50]

Finally, on March 2, 1951, before 10,094 fans, the NBA played its first All-Star Game. The game was the idea of Haskell Cohen, who had just become publicity director for the NBA in 1951. Along with Maurice Podoloff and Walter Brown, owner of the Boston Celtics, Cohen was trying to figure out how to attract more attention to the NBA. Baseball had its All-Star Game every July, and, in the 1950s, the National Football League's champions played the College All-Stars. Each player, selected by sportswriters who could not vote for players in their city, received a television set. In the NBA's first All-Star Game, the Eastern All-Stars beat the Western All-Stars, 111–94.[51] Dolph Schayes scored 15 points and grabbed 14 rebounds. The players, as Schayes recalled, took the game seriously. Schayes and his teammates were eager to prove the superiority of the Eastern style of play.[52]

In the 1950–51 season Syracuse finished fourth in the Eastern Division with a disappointing 32-34 record. Dolph Schayes had a great season. He led the team in scoring with 17 points a game, in rebounding with 16.4 a game, and even assists with 3.8 a game. This season was the first time that the NBA kept rebounding statistics. Schayes won the rebounding title with 1,080 boards, 108 more than George Mikan.[53]

In the playoffs the Nats faced off against the Philadelphia Warriors, who had the best record in the Eastern Division at 40-26. The Warriors had two high-scoring players in the front court: "Jumping Joe" Fulks and Paul Arizin. Fulks, who signed with the Warriors in 1946, was one of the pioneers of the jump shot. Arizin, who was a rookie in the 1950–51 season, also had a deadly jump shot. Directing the Warrior offense was Andy Phillip, who led the league in assists.

During the season the Nats strengthened their roster by picking up Freddie Scolari from the disbanded Washington Capitols. A native of San Francisco, Scolari, who left the University of San Francisco after his sophomore year, perfected his game and a soft one-hander by playing AAU ball until the Capitols drafted him in 1946. In the first playoff game at Philadelphia, Scolari earned whatever Syracuse paid him. With forty-five seconds left in the game, Scolari hit a shot to tie the score at 89 and send the game into overtime. The Warriors won the tip to begin the extra session, but Joe Fulks, who scored 30, missed a jumper and the Nats secured the rebound. Cervi elected to stall for the next four and a half minutes. With ten seconds left, Scolari hit another shot to give the Nats a 91–89 victory. Scolari led the Nats with 23 points, and Schayes followed with 18. Jack Andrews thought the win "was the sweetest victory of the campaign for the Nats and they richly deserved it."[54] The Nats eliminated the Warriors when the teams played the second game in Syracuse. Schayes led the way with 24 points, as the Nats cruised to a 90–78 victory.[55]

For the second consecutive year, the Nats met the Knicks to determine who would represent the Eastern Division in the NBA championship series. In 1951 the Knicks were a different team. Their center was the former Globetrotter Nathaniel "Sweetwater" Clifton. At six foot six and 230 pounds, Clifton was extremely strong. In his first season Clifton snagged 491 rebounds, which made him the second-leading rebounder on the team behind Harry Gallatin. After the Chicago Stags folded, the Knicks picked up Max Zaslofsky, a six-foot-two guard who had been Chicago's leading scorer. Zaslofsky had played his high school ball at Thomas Jefferson in Brooklyn and collegiately at St. John's. Because Zaslofsky was Jewish, Ned Irish also thought he would help at the gate. Irish did not get Zaslofsky without a fight from Eddie Gottlieb, the owner of the Warriors, and Walter Brown, the owner of the Celtics. When Maurice Podoloff could not resolve the conflict between the three owners, he put Zaslofsky's name in a hat, along with the name of another Stag, Andy Phillip, and that of Bob Cousy, who had just graduated from Holy Cross. Irish drew Zaslofsky, Gottlieb picked Phillips, and Brown drew Cousy. On that day nobody knew that Brown was the big winner.[56] While the Knicks added Clifton and Zaslofsky, they lost Carl Braun to the service.

The five-game series opened at Madison Square Garden, where a mere six thousand fans watched the Knicks hold off the Nats, 103–92. Louis Effrat described the game as "one of the roughest court battles of the campaign." He thought the turning point in the game came with 9:30 left in the fourth quarter when Schayes fouled out and Syracuse was behind, 90–87. Vince Boryla led the Knicks with 30, but Effrat had special praise for Connie Simmons, who "played his best game of the season" as he tallied 20 points. Ratkovicz with 22 and Schayes with 15 led the Nats.[57]

When the series returned to Syracuse's State Fair Coliseum, the fans were wild. Louis Effrat wrote, "Their heroes can do no wrong, and when fouls are called against the home club, the hoots directed against the officials are sharp." Charley Eckman, one of the officials, demanded police protection after being cursed by some fans. By the end of the third quarter the Nats were up by 17 and finished with a 102–80 thumping of the Knicks. Schayes with 21 and Ratkovicz with 20 led a balanced scoring attack.[58]

In the third game at the Garden, Vince Boryla hit a shot with fifty-three seconds left in regulation to tie the score at 70 apiece, and both teams failed to score again as time ran out. In the overtime Harry Gallatin scored with two seconds left to give the Knicks a 77–75 victory. Schayes was high man for Syracuse with 17.[59]

Back in Syracuse the home-court advantage held, and Syracuse evened the series with a 90–83 victory before 7,767 spectators. Syracuse made 42 of 49 free throws, which was the difference in the game, since the Knicks had four more field goals. Schayes led all scorers with 34 points. Louis Effrat of the *New York Times* wrote that "Schayes was the most versatile player on the floor." He scored on "sets, hooks, one-handed jumps, lay-ups—every conceivable way." From the free-throw line Schayes was a perfect 12 of 12. Zaslofsky and Boryla led the Knicks with 20 and 19, respectively.[60]

In the deciding game, played at the 69th Regiment Armory before 5,300 fans, the Knicks rallied from a 12-point deficit in the fourth quarter to win 83–81. Once again Boryla with 23 and Zaslofsky with 17 were high for the Knicks. One key to the victory was that the Knicks limited Schayes to 14, high for the Nats.[61] The victory meant that for the first time in its five-year history, the Knicks would play for the NBA championship. In a hard-fought seven-game series, the Rochester Royals emerged as the NBA champions.

In the off-season Syracuse added three important players. In a trade with the Baltimore Bullets, the Nats picked up Ephraim "Red" Rocha for Alex Hannum and Fred Scolari. Rocha was born and raised in Hilo, Hawaii. He played briefly at the University of Hawaii before transferring to Oregon State University (OSU), where he played for "Slats" Gill. At six foot nine and 215 pounds, Rocha was agile and possessed a good one-handed shot. A three-time All–Pacific Coast Conference selection, in 1946–67 Rocha was one of OSU's "thrill kids" who won the Pacific Coast Conference title and an invitation to the NCAA Tournament, where they lost to Oklahoma in their first game. Rocha represented the Baltimore Bullets in the first NBA All-Star Game and had four years of professional experience before coming to Syracuse. Vince Boryla told me that playing against Rocha was like coping with an "overgrown spider."[62] One measure of Rocha's defensive talents was that he always guarded Bill Sharman, Boston's great shooter, when the Nats and Celtics tangled.

George King, a six-foot, 175-pound guard, had been a two-time national small-college scoring leader at Morris Harvey in Charleston, West Virginia. Before coming to Syracuse, King played a year with the AAU's Phillips 66ers. Dolph Schayes described King as a "revelation." King's ball-handling skills reminded Schayes of an early version of Pete Maravich. Earl Lloyd, who joined the team in 1952, likened King to Marques Haynes, the dribbling wizard of the Harlem Globetrotters. A heady player with a good jump shot, King possessed the handsome features of a Hollywood leading man. He was extremely popular with the Syracuse fans.[63] Another first-year player was Wally Osterkorn, a six-foot-five, 215-pound forward from the University of Illinois. Nicknamed "Ox," his aggressive, tough-guy style of play made him another fan favorite.

In October 1951 the college basketball scandals reached into the NBA when it was revealed that Alex Groza and Ralph Beard had taken money from gamblers while playing for the University of Kentucky. The duo seemed headed to the Hall of Fame until this transgression led the NBA to ban them for life. The Indianapolis Olympians finished the season and played one more year before folding.[64]

The new additions paid off, as Syracuse, playing its home games at the Onondaga War Memorial, won the Eastern Division in 1952 with a 40-26 mark that was worth twenty-five hundred dollars for the team. Rocha was the team's second-leading scorer, and King was third. Schayes led the team in scoring with a 13.8 average, but his numbers were down due to a broken right wrist. He played a portion of the season with a cast, but used that injury to perfect his left-handed shot. In the first round of the Eastern Division playoffs, the Nats met the Philadelphia Warriors for the third straight time. In his second year with Philadelphia, Paul Arizin had emerged as a major star, as he led the NBA in just about every offensive category.

In the playoffs Syracuse and Philadelphia split the first two games, each winning on their home floor. The Nats took the deciding game on their home floor, 84–73. With five minutes left in the game, only a few points separated the teams, but at that moment Paul Arizin fouled out. Arizin left the game with 26 points and 15 rebounds, and the Nats took advantage, outscoring the Warriors 12–4 in the final three and a half minutes. Red Rocha led the Nats with 20 points, and Schayes and Seymour followed, with 17 and 16, respectively. The victory added twenty-five hundred dollars to the twenty-five hundred earned for coming in first during the regular season. It also meant that the Nationals would play the New York Knicks for the third straight time to determine who would play in the NBA finals.[65]

By 1952 the Nats-Knicks rivalry was quite heated. Before the series Bill Reddy wrote that "there's nothing much in the NBA to equal the Syracuse–New York hostility. Uncle 'Nedso' Irish had much to do with stirring up the feud, and nothing would give Syracusans greater pleasure than to knock off the hired hands of 'Nedso.'" One of those "hired hands," Vince Boryla, was out of the series with a knee injury.[66]

In a rivalry where the home-court advantage had been crucial, the Nats managed to lose a 16-point lead and drop the opener in Syracuse, 87–85. Louis Effrat wrote, "Seldom have the Knicks been as sloppy as they were throughout the first twenty-four minutes." Connie Simmons hit 23 of his 24 points in the first half to keep the Knicks in the game. In the second half Max Zaslofsky got hot and finished with a game-high 26 points.

Schayes, with 25 points, led the Nats, but Rocha and Osterkorn were the only other teammates to hit in double figures.[67]

The following night the Nats evened the series with a 102–92 victory. Five Nats scored in double figures, with Paul Seymour and Red Rocha hitting 21 and 20, respectively. Close until midway in the fourth quarter, the game was rough, and on at least three occasions Louis Effrat reported that players were ready to exchange blows. He said, "The crowd of 7,064 was in an ugly mood and it would not have required much to light a fire." A riot almost occurred when Dick McGuire, the Knicks' playmaker, appeared ready to tangle with an out-of-control fan.[68] While the Nats won, they had lost their home-court advantage and had to play the next two games at New York's 69th Regiment Armory.

The bad blood from the second game spilled over to the third game before a capacity crowd of fifty-two hundred. Louis Effrat wrote, "The feuding quintets, hated enemies for years, finally made good on their hints to do something about their mutual loathing." The Knicks controlled the first half, but at the end of the third period the Nats were only down by three, 67 to 64. With less than a minute left and the Nats up 92–90, Effrat wrote, "Suddenly, Schayes pushed Harry Gallatin, and the officials, ruling it a deliberate foul, awarded two shots to Harry. Then Schayes was seen to charge after Gallatin with unmistakable gestures." The officials then hit Schayes with another foul, his sixth, which meant he was out of the game. As Schayes walked back to his bench, he and the Knicks' George Kaftan, who had spent much of the game on the bench, had words and then exchanged blows. Then, according to Effrat, "the free-for-all got under way. Kaftan, Schayes, Al McGuire (Dick's brother) and innumerable spectators all were swinging and some were going down." One of those spectators was Carl Schayes, who was more than willing to defend his son. After the dust cleared, the Knicks managed to win, 99–92. Effrat summarized the game this way: "Both sides, it appeared early were concentrating more on mayhem than on basketball. When they forgot about their emotions, however, they exhibited wonderful basketball." Effrat singled out Schayes, who had 20 points; Rocha, with 22; and George King's floor play as standouts for Syracuse. Zaslofsky, high for the Knicks with 20, Vandeweghe, Clifton, and Dick McGuire sparkled for the Knicks. Effrat thought that

Clifton's play, in particular, "won the hearts of the fans." He scored 17 points, rebounded, passed, and played defense. Effrat concluded, "Clifton had promised to play his 'heart out' and he did."[69]

Three days later the Knicks eliminated the Nats, 100–93, before another standing-room crowd of fifty-two hundred at the 69th Regiment Armory. While security was in force, Louis Effrat reported that, "aside from the normal tugging, pushing and hacking . . . nothing out of the way happened. And because of that it was one of the better-played games in the series." For the first time in eight weeks, Schayes played "without his special protective foam rubber wrist wrapper" and led all players with 22 points.[70] Bud Vander Veer, writing for the *Syracuse Herald-Journal*, thought that one of the keys to the game was Dick McGuire's ability to limit Paul Seymour to two points.[71] For finishing first and playing in the playoffs, the Syracuse players split seventy-five hundred dollars. The Knicks lost to the Minneapolis Lakers in the NBA finals.

In the winter of 1951–52 at a Syracuse University basketball game, a mutual friend introduced Dolph to Naomi Gross, a dark-haired beauty who grew up in a small town near Plattsburgh, in upstate New York. In elementary school Naomi's parents, Bill and Ruth, discovered that she was gifted musically and sent her to McGill University for voice lessons. By her late teens Naomi sang the lead role in several Gilbert and Sullivan operettas performed at Lake Champlain Air Force Base. Naomi followed one of her sisters who had moved earlier to Syracuse. Sixty years after they met, Dolph and Naomi recounted that when they were introduced, sparks flew, generated by static electricity from the false-fur coats they were wearing. In their family history this episode was a sign that their match was love at first sight. After the Syracuse basketball game, they went to a club, where they dined and danced. Naomi quickly discovered that dancing was not one of Dolph's talents. She also remembered that while they were dancing, Dolph suddenly stopped to engage her in conversation, which she found amusing.

After dating for several months, Dolph and Naomi eloped and found a justice of the peace to marry them. Afterward, they repeated their marriage vows at Temple Beth El in Plattsburgh in a small wedding before family and friends. Dolph fitted comfortably into the Gross family. Naomi's father worked for US Customs and enjoyed telling stories of life on the Canadian American border, and Dolph was a willing listener.

Between 1952 and 1960 Dolph and Naomi had four children—Debbie, Carrie, David, and Danny. Raising a family dominated Naomi's life, but she and the wives of other players became a very close-knit group. Beyond attending games, the wives would host dinners featuring steak and lobster tail. Although Naomi was too busy with her family to perform musically, she remembered that playing the piano helped her deal with Dolph's absences on road trips. She also quickly discovered the degree to which Dolph was focused and self-critical of his own performance. "No matter what he did," Naomi remembered, "it was never good enough."[72]

Snapshot

Earl Lloyd

In 1952–53 Earl Lloyd played his first season with the Syracuse Nationals. He had already become the first African American to play in an NBA basketball game. Drafted by the Washington Capitols in the ninth round in 1950, Lloyd played his first NBA game on October 31, 1950. A few days later Chuck Cooper and Sweetwater Clifton joined Lloyd in the first class of black NBA players.

Lloyd grew up in segregated Alexandria, Virginia, where he was born on April 3, 1928. After excelling in basketball, baseball, and football at Parker-Gray High School, Lloyd attended West Virginia State College, a black college in Institute, West Virginia, just outside Charleston. West Virginia State was a power in the Colored Intercollegiate Athletic Association, winning conference and tournament championships in 1948 and 1949. Named to the all-conference team three times, Lloyd would later be named the CIAA "Player of the Decade, 1946–56." Until Lloyd reported to the Capitols, he had had no significant contact with white people. In his first major exposure Lloyd thought he was fortunate to have Horace "Bones" McKinney as his coach. Surviving that training camp was one of the first of many defining moments for Earl Lloyd. In 1950 Lloyd played just seven games for the Capitols when he received his draft notice from the US Army. In the middle of the season the Washington Capitols folded, and Syracuse selected Lloyd in a dispersal draft of all of Washington's players. Lloyd had actually caught a lucky break. In that draft the Nats had picked up Fred Scolari, who encouraged Danny Biasone to pick up the six-foot-six, 200-pound forward. Lloyd's role would be to guard the highest-scoring forward on the opposing team and to rebound. Lloyd was comfortable with his role and executed it well.[73]

When Lloyd joined the Nats the United States was on the cusp of a civil rights revolution. In 1954 the Supreme Court issued its momentous decision in *Brown v. Board of Education*, which declared state laws requiring or permitting public school segregation unconstitutional. The following year Martin Luther King Jr. gained national recognition as the spokesman for the Montgomery bus boycott. The integration of collegiate and professional sports was a part of the struggle for equality. Lloyd understood that he was under a microscope. During the season Lloyd lived in the Fifteenth Ward, Syracuse's black residential area. While the opportunities to find an apartment outside the Fifteenth Ward were limited and racism hurt a lot, Lloyd was a hero in the black community. Life in the ward also gave Lloyd the opportunity to frequent the Embassy jazz club, where he could relax and indulge his taste for jazz. He knew all the hot spots in every NBA city.

Lloyd also liked his teammates and Danny Biasone. Ironically, one of his best friends on the team was George King, who played collegiately at Morris Harvey in Charleston, West Virginia, just ten miles from West Virginia State. But because of segregation they never played against each other or saw each other play in college. Their years together with the Nats made up for that lost history. Following King's death in 2006, his wife called Earl and said, "I want you to know that my husband truly loved you."[74]

While Lloyd told me he had "six fantastic years" in Syracuse, racism was unavoidable. In cities such as Fort Wayne, Indianapolis, and St. Louis, the fans could be brutal. Only once did the Nats let him down. In 1954, when the team scheduled an exhibition game in Greenville, South Carolina, Lloyd was told he could not travel with the team. When his teammates failed to tell Lloyd that they believed it was wrong, he was disappointed. Nonetheless, for Lloyd, the bottom line was that Syracuse "professionally was the right place for me." He stressed that his teammates were unselfish and meshed well together. In describing Dolph Schayes, Lloyd used phrases such as "good guy," "dependable," and "ultimate athlete." Schayes, Lloyd observed, "was always ready to play, never whined, and wanted to take the last shot." Lloyd described himself as a person "driven to succeed," and his teammates thought of him as a "tough guy" who would not back down from anybody.[75]

Following the 1958 season, Syracuse traded Lloyd to the Detroit Pistons. In 1960 Dick McGuire, the Pistons' head coach, made Lloyd his assistant coach, the first African American to hold this position in the NBA. Lloyd left the Pistons in 1968 to work for the Chrysler Corporation. He returned to the Pistons in the 1971–72 season as their head coach when Butch van Breda Kolff left the team after ten games. Before Lloyd, Bill Russell was the only African American to coach an NBA team. Lloyd finished the season with a 20-50 record. The following season the Pistons released him after the Pistons lost five of their first seven games.[76]

After his NBA career Lloyd worked for Chrysler, the Detroit Board of Education, and the Bing Group. On September 5, 2003, Earl Lloyd was inducted into the Naismith Memorial Basketball Hall of Fame as a contributor. Lloyd was a basketball pioneer in the truest sense of the word. He was the consummate team player who conducted himself as a professional. By overcoming racial barriers, Earl Lloyd paved the way for a host of gifted black basketball players.[77]

The 1952–53 Season

In 1952–53 the Nats finished in second place in the Eastern Division with a 47-24 record. Only a few games separated the first-place Knicks from the third-place Boston Celtics. But the real news was the report that Danny Biasone was considering an offer from Ike Duffy, former owner of the Anderson Packers, to sell the team for $150,000 and move it to Chicago. According to Bill Reddy, only New York drew better than Syracuse, but Biasone and Leo Ferris thought the rental at the War Memorial was too steep. The War Memorial assessed Biasone 15 percent of the gate, with a ceiling of $1,000 a game.[78]

While Biasone mulled over Ike Duffy's offer, his team took on the Boston Celtics in the first round of the Eastern Division playoffs. It was the first time the Nats had met the Celtics in the playoffs, but a heated rivalry with the Bostonians had developed over the previous three years. Arnold "Red" Auerbach coached the Celtics, and his team featured Bob Cousy, a perennial all-star at guard; Bill Sharman, a deadly outside shooter; and "Easy" Ed Macauley at center. They upset the Nats, 87–81, in the series opener at the War Memorial. The game also underscored a problem that the NBA had not yet resolved. The officials called 96 fouls that produced 107 free throws.[79] In Boston the Celtics ended Syracuse's season by topping the Nats, 111–105, in four overtimes. Bob Cousy was the star of the game with 50 points, 30 from the free-throw line on 32 attempts. One of the keys to Boston's victory was that the officials banished Dolph Schayes from the game early in the second quarter for fighting with Bob Brannum, Auerbach's enforcer. There was some speculation after the game that Brannum's role was to provoke a fight with Schayes so that the Syracuse star would be ejected from the contest. The officials called 107 fouls, 55 against the Nats.[80]

When the team's plane arrived at the Syracuse airport, almost seven hundred fans were there to greet them. This expression of fan loyalty helped to persuade Danny Biasone to keep the team in Syracuse. The players also told Biasone that they would "rather play for him than for anyone else in basketball." At the end of the season Al Cervi announced his retirement as a player. He would remain as the team's coach.[81]

By the end of his fifth season, Schayes had established himself as a star in the NBA. For five straight years he led the Nats in scoring and rebounding. Schayes played in every All-Star Game. Bill Reddy wrote that Schayes was the "bellwether of the Nats." Reddy believed that "over the past four seasons it has been fair to remark that 'as Schayes goes, so go the Nats.'" Despite his star status, Schayes never rested on his laurels. Art Deutsch, who briefly served as general manager, told Frank Woolever that "Adolph frets, fumes, and broods over his shooting, passing, rebounding, defensive technique, fouling, ball-handling, as well as his own physical condition and that of every member of his team."[82]

In the 1953–54 season the Nats finished in a second-place tie with Boston at 42-30, just two games behind the New York Knicks. The Nats played without Red Rocha, who took the year off to work for the McCormick Spice Company in Baltimore and tried retirement. The Nats hoped that two rookies, Jim Neal and Billy Kenville, could compensate for Rocha's loss. Neal was a six-foot-eleven, 235-pound center from Wofford College, and Billy Kenville was a six-foot-two, 187-pound guard from St. Bonaventure. Six weeks into the season the Nats traded for Bob Lavoy, another center, who started the year with the Milwaukee Hawks after playing three years with the Indianapolis Olympians. In 1954 the NBA replaced the traditional playoff system with a round-robin format. In the Eastern Division the Knicks, the Celtics, and the Nats would battle each other to determine which team would represent the division in the NBA finals. The teams would play each other two times, and the two teams with the best records would play for the Eastern Division championship. Bill Reddy of the *Post-Standard* was extremely critical of this complicated format and wrote, "When sillier playoffs are devised the National Basketball Association will think them up."[83]

The Nats broke out of the gate with an exciting 96–95 overtime victory at Boston. Schayes scored nine of his twenty points in overtime to lead all Syracuse scorers.[84] The Nats returned to Syracuse, where they topped the Knicks, 75–68. Schayes once again led all scorers with twenty-three, while Paul Seymour tallied thirteen and George King collected sixteen.[85] Syracuse won its third straight game in Madison Square Garden by edging the Knicks, 103–99. Schayes scored thirty-six, a career high for him, at the Garden. Jack Andrews wrote that "Schayes was fantastic with his long shots and his drive-ins from the start and he set a club record for a regulation game with 10 field goals on 20 shots and 16 free throws on 18 chances as well as 21 rebounds."[86] Because this one was New York's fourth consecutive loss, the Knicks were eliminated from postseason play. The one sour note for the Nats was that Earl Lloyd broke a bone in his right hand fighting for a rebound. The Nats beat the Celtics for their fourth in a row, 98–85, in Syracuse.[87] The victory meant that the Nats would have the home-court advantage in the best-of-three series with Boston for the Eastern Division title.

In the opener of the series at Syracuse, the Nats hit on 59 percent of their shots in dominating the Celtics, 109–94. Schayes remained hot with twenty-seven, and five teammates reached double figures. Bob Cousy uncharacteristically made only one shot out of eighteen attempts.[88] In the second game at the Boston Garden, the Nats eliminated the Celtics, 83–76, in a game marred by a near riot. The fisticuffs of the so-called Boston Massacre broke out at the three-minute mark of the third quarter when Bob Harris decked Dolph Schayes as he drove toward the basket. Jack Andrews wrote, "Dolph flew up in the air and came down with a thud, his hands clapped to his right eye." Wally Osterkorn charged Harris, and "they exchanged punches and soon there were a flock of contestants." Just when tempers cooled, Osterkorn went after Ed Macauley, who cracked, "I guess we are supposed to bow down to you guys and cry olay [sic] as you go by." The second brawl took fifteen policemen along with Garden ushers to put the fire out. The game was delayed for twenty-five minutes while Schayes got three stitches to close the cut around his eye. Schayes missed the two free throws awarded him and sat out the rest of the game, nursing a broken left wrist. Besides Schayes, Paul Seymour was another casualty of the fight, as he sat out with a bandaged right thumb. Ironically, when the melee interrupted the game, the Nats were down, 53–47. They won the game without Schayes, Seymour, and Lloyd. Osterkorn, Bob Lavoy, and George King led the Nats to the victory. After the game Al Cervi called the game the "greatest thing I've ever seen in my life." Danny Biasone chimed in: "I'll never forget this. We turned the Celtics into chokers. We've got more moxie than all the other clubs put together."[89] The victory meant that the battered Nationals would face the Minneapolis Lakers in the NBA finals.

The Lakers were gunning for their third straight NBA title and fourth in the NBA's five-year history. George Mikan, Vern Mikkelsen, Jim Pollard, and Slater Martin still composed the team's foundation. To that core the Lakers added Clyde Lovellette, a six-foot-ten center who led the University of Kansas to the 1952 NCAA championship. Whitey Skoog, an All-America guard from the University of Minnesota, gave the Lakers another good shooter from the outside.

In the series opener in Minneapolis, Dolph Schayes and Earl Lloyd played just six minutes and ten minutes, respectively. Fortunately for the Nats, Paul Seymour had not broken any bones in the fight against the Celtics. Despite being shorthanded, the Nats were down by only four points, 60–56, with six minutes left to play. At that point the Lakers went on a 14–4 spurt and wound up winning, 79–68. Despite losing, Al Cervi remained confident. By slowing the game down, Cervi thought, "We played it just about right." The difference for the Lakers was Lovellette, who led all scorers with sixteen. Cervi said, "Lovellette killed us. He was hitting and getting those rebounds." Johnny Kundla, the Lakers' coach, agreed and thought Lovellette played "one of his best games." The Nats had reasons for optimism. Mikan scored only fifteen, and Jack Andrews wrote that he "looked anything but the Player of the Half Century." Paul Seymour, who had given Pollard fits in the 1950 finals, limited the Laker star to four points. After the game Pollard thought Seymour "just played good position on me, and didn't let me get off any shots. He's a tough one anytime."[90]

In the second game the Nats stuck with their ball-control strategy and evened the series with a 62–60 victory. The Laker loss was its first in the Minneapolis Auditorium in its playoff history. At the end of the third quarter, the Nats were up by ten points, 48–38, but then, according to Jack Andrews, the "Nats went into an orgy of misses on easy shots." With eighteen seconds left in the game, Mikan tied the score at 60. The game ended in dramatic fashion when Paul Seymour hit a shot from near midcourt with seven seconds left. Jack Andrews reported that "the entire Nats contingent carried Seymour off the court on their shoulders." Wally Osterkorn led all scorers with twenty points, and King and Seymour hit for double figures. By winning the Nats had eliminated the Lakers' home-court advantage. According to Jack Andrews, they "said they needed to set up a sweep of the next three games in Syracuse." Another reason for optimism was also that Schayes and Lloyd logged more minutes in the second game than in the first game. The only sour note was that George King broke his left wrist near the end of the game.[91]

Before 8,719, the largest crowd ever to see a game at the Onondaga War Memorial, the Lakers trounced the Nats, 81–67. With thirty points and fifteen rebounds, Mikan had his best game of the series. Osterkorn, Lavoy, and Seymour scored in double figures for the Nats. Schayes had one point in thirteen minutes of play.[92] In the fourth game, Syracuse evened the series with an 80–69 win. Paul Seymour, with twenty-five points, was Syracuse's hero in its second win. Schayes played twenty-five minutes and scored ten points, while Kenville and Lavoy joined him in double figures. The Nats limited Mikan to twelve, as Whitey Skoog led the Lakers with sixteen. Unfortunately, the injury bug hit the Nats again, as Billy Gabor had to leave the game with a knee injury.[93] Two nights later the Lakers took a 3–2 advantage in the series by winning 84–73. The key to the victory was a 65–37 rebounding edge. Vern Mikkelsen led the Lakers with twenty-one, and four other Lakers scored in double figures. Schayes had his best game of the series with a team-high seventeen points.[94]

While the Nats were down, their fans and the media marveled at their competitiveness as they played through injuries. Nicknamed the "Bandage Brigade," the Nats traveled to Minneapolis with a nothing-to-lose attitude. Going into the sixth game as decided underdogs, the Nats led most of the game until Jim Pollard hit two free throws to tie the game at 63 with thirty-six seconds left to play. Cervi called time-out to plot Syracuse's strategy. Schayes was the natural player to take the last shot, but he had fouled out with fifteen points. As Cervi considered his options, Cervi put in six-foot-eleven Jim Neal, who had scored just one point in the game. Cervi figured that there was a good chance that Neal would get a good look at the basket in the waning seconds. When the Nats returned to the floor, they held the ball for twenty-seven seconds and then hit Neal, who sank a twenty-foot one-hander to extend the series to game seven. Jack Andrews, in a bit of journalistic hyperbole, anointed Neal "one of the all-time heroes of professional basketball." The Lakers, he thought, expected the Nats to "roll over" against the Lakers' "expensive talent." Maurice Podoloff, the NBA commissioner, was almost speechless when he said, "I don't believe it, but I saw it." Danny Biasone's comment on the stunning conclusion was "How do you like that for a believe it or not."[95]

The Cinderella season came to an end the following night, as the Lakers prevailed, 87–80. Dolph Schayes led the Nats with eighteen, while Jim Pollard topped all Lakers with twenty-one. Paul Seymour had contained

Pollard but graciously said, "I knew Pollard would get mad at me one of these days and kill me." Jack Andrews concluded that Syracuse's performance was "one of the most inspiring bids in the history of professional basketball."[96] The next day the mayor of Syracuse and a host of basketball fans met the Nats at the airport. Years later Al Cervi wrote Dick Triptow, a former NBL player, that taking the Lakers to seven games "has to be my most precious memory—more so than winning the NBA title the next year 1954–55—and as much as being inducted into the Hall of Fame."[97]

As in the previous season, there were rumors that Biasone might sell the team. During the regular season the Nats drew a mere 106,000 and lost $35,000. In April 1954 the club had sold $118,000 shares of stock toward a goal of $200,000. When asked about selling the team after eliminating the Celtics, Biasone responded, "Forget it." After the fifth game of the Lakers series, Maurice Podoloff declared, "I'm gratified the team will stay here." He urged the public to get behind the drive to sell $200,000 worth of stock. The result was that the Nats remained in Syracuse.[98]

The 1953–54 season also introduced the splendid voice of Jim McKechnie to the basketball fans of Syracuse. Sports broadcasting was still in its infancy, and McKechnie would reproduce away games from ticker tape that was sent to WNDR. According to Dick Clarke, who wrote for the *Syracuse Herald-Journal*, McKechnie had a nickname for every Nat. Schayes was "Rudy," and Lloyd was the "the Cat." When Al Bianchi joined the team, he was "Blinky," and Johnny Kerr was "Big Red." When Schayes hit one of his set shots, McKechnie announced that it traveled "through the rafters." An impressive shot was "good—good all around like Schaefer beer." Betsy Burton, today a Syracuse librarian, recalled that her father regularly listened to games and that McKechnie could drive him "into a frenzy." McKechnie died in 1996 and entered the Broadcasting Hall of Fame posthumously in 2004.[99]

The 1954–55 season was a year of transitions for the NBA. In April Danny Biasone renewed his campaign to persuade the owners to adopt a shot clock. Biasone's contention was that the practice of holding the ball or stalling was hurting the game. The fans, he contended, wanted action. While Biasone's argument made sense, it was rather ironic, since Cervi had just used the slowdown strategy so effectively against the Lakers.

Biasone, with the help of Leo Ferris, estimated that in a normal game that lasted 48 minutes, or 2,880 seconds, the two teams took 120 shots. By dividing the number of seconds by the number of shots, Biasone and Ferris arrived at 24 seconds as the time a team would have to shoot the ball. On August 10, 1954, a shot-clock demonstration was held at Blodgett Vocational High School in Syracuse. Schayes played in that game and felt rushed by the time limit. If Schayes was initially cool to the idea, he came to see it as an innovation that saved the pro game. The owners who watched the exhibition liked what they saw and voted to implement the use of a 24-second clock for the 1954–55 season. In addition to stalling, the pro game was marred by excessive fouls. Games often degenerated into free-throw-shooting contests. To correct this issue the NBA passed a rule that gave a team a bonus free throw when the opposing team committed its seventh foul.[100]

In September 1954 George Mikan announced his retirement. In his seven years with the Lakers, Mikan had been the game's greatest draw. The following year Pollard retired, and then the Lakers traded Slater Martin and Clyde Lovellette. The Lakers never won another championship in Minneapolis. In 1960 the Lakers moved to Los Angeles and returned to prominence on the shoulders of Elgin Baylor and Jerry West. In another development, the Baltimore Bullets dropped out of the NBA thirteen games into the season, leaving four teams in the Eastern Division and four in the Western Division.

Snapshot

Johnny Kerr

In the 1954 NBA draft the Nats were able to select six-foot-nine Johnny "Red" Kerr from the University of Illinois. Kerr grew up near the Chicago Stockyards and graduated from Tilden Tech High School. Nicknamed "Red" for obvious reasons, Kerr's first sport was soccer, but he grew eight inches in his senior year and led the Blue Devils to the Chicago Public League City Championship in 1950. As Kerr recalled, young men from his working-class neighborhood did not go to college, but went to work after graduating from high school. Basketball was Kerr's ticket out of the stockyards. After sorting through basketball scholarship offers, Kerr chose to play his college basketball for Harry Combes at the University of Illinois. In 1952, as a sophomore, Kerr was the leading scorer for an Illini team that won the Big Ten Championship and made it to the NCAA's Final Four. Kerr was the Illini's leading scorer as a junior (17.5) and as a senior (25.3), when he earned All-America honors.

Danny Biasone saw Kerr play in the East-West College All-Star Game in Madison Square Garden and made up his mind to draft Kerr. He was the sixth selection in the first round and gave the Nationals the center they needed to win a championship in 1955.[101]

All of the Nats thought of Kerr as a great teammate. Blessed with a great sense of humor and a fondness for pizza and beer, Kerr helped to keep the team loose. One teammate told me you might find Kerr's false teeth on your plate at a team meal. He fitted in beautifully with the Syracuse offensive scheme and in a typical self-deprecating way said his autobiography would be titled "Ten Years in the Pivot without the Ball." Johnny Kerr never missed a game with the Nats and later the 76ers and jokingly said that before every game, he had to "tell some lies to my legs."[102] The 1965–66 season with the Baltimore Bullets was Kerr's last in the NBA. His streak of consecutive games played in the NBA ended at 917 (844 regular season). Ironically, when his streak came to an end, his coach was Paul Seymour. Inexplicably, his former teammate decided to keep Kerr on the bench for one game.[103] There never was a good explanation for Seymour's decision. Cincinnati's Jack Twyman thought because of Russell and Chamberlain, Kerr "never received the recognition he deserved. He's a great one."[104] Al Bianchi, his teammate, thought Kerr was one of the top-five passers from the center position in NBA history.[105]

Between 1966 and 1968 Kerr coached the Chicago Bulls, followed by a season and a half with the Phoenix Suns. In 1975 Kerr became the color commentator for the Chicago Bulls, a position he held through the 2007–8 season. On February 26, 2009, Johnny "Red" Kerr died of prostate cancer. On February 10, 2009, before he died, the Bulls unveiled a sculpture of Kerr that remains at the United Center. At this halftime ceremony, Kerr also received the Basketball Hall of Fame's Lifetime Achievement

Award. Dolph Schayes was there to honor his old friend and teammate. Chicago columnist Bob Greene captured Kerr best when he wrote, "A big, amiable man, Red Kerr was about as beloved a figure in Chicago as a person can possibly be."[106]

In the 1954 draft the Nats also picked up Dick Farley, a guard from Indiana, and Jim Tucker, a forward from Duquesne. Tucker was the second African American to play for the Nats. Tucker played sparingly in his first year, but Farley saw significant action. After a year out of the game, Red Rocha could not shake the basketball itch and returned to Syracuse.

Snapshot

Jim Tucker

Jim Tucker's professional basketball career was short, but his story is worth telling. Born on December 12, 1932, Tucker grew up in Paris, Kentucky, a town of sixty-seven hundred, northeast of Lexington. Neither his stepfather, Ed "Snow" Fields, nor his mother, Willie Mae Fields, graduated from high school. Snow Fields earned his nickname, Tucker chuckled, because he was so black. He worked at Claiborne Farms, popularized in the 2010 movie about Secretariat. Growing up, Tucker recalled, "We were poorer than poor."

By the time Tucker was a senior in high school, he was the team's star. Like all southern states, Kentucky's public schools were segregated, so black schools had their own state basketball tournament. In the finals of the 1950 tournament, Tucker's team lost by one point. After the game, one of those events that can change a person's life occurred. In the locker room, a white man approached Tucker and told him that he liked his game. Because of segregation, however, he could not offer him a scholarship to the University of Kentucky. The white man was Adolph Rupp, the University of Kentucky's legendary basketball coach. Rupp explained to Tucker that he would use his contacts with coaches in the Northeast to get him a scholarship. The result was that Long Island University's Clair Bee invited Tucker to New York City for a tryout. It was the beginning of an adventure, since Tucker had never ventured so far from home. While at LIU Tucker received a telegram from Duquesne University, offering him a scholarship and asking him to visit the campus. So Tucker returned home and three days later boarded a plane, his first flying experience, for Pittsburgh, Pennsylvania. When Tucker arrived at the Pittsburgh airport, he was the last person to leave the plane. Duquesne's basketball coach was Donald "Dudey" Moore, and obviously neither Moore nor Tucker had seen each other before. When Tucker approached Moore, the coach said to him, "Is there anyone else on the plane?" The slender Tucker was six foot seven and 175 pounds and not exactly what Moore expected. Nonetheless, the recruit reassured him and said, "I'm Tucker."

The first stop on the recruiting trip was dinner at the Crawford Grille, a landmark in Pittsburgh's black community. In the 1930s Gus Greenlee operated his numbers operation out of the Crawford Grille and used some of the profits to build the Pittsburgh Crawfords, which for a half-dozen years was a powerhouse in the Negro National League. Tucker did not know that piece of baseball history, but he did enjoy his first steak and remembered taking half of it back to his room. The next day Coach Moore watched Tucker work out. While Tucker was shooting, Moore interrupted him and asked, "Can you dunk?" Tucker proceeded to dunk the ball. Then Moore said, "Can you dunk from a standing position?" Tucker obliged. Finally, Moore wondered if Tucker could dunk with two hands with his back to the basket, and Tucker passed the third test. After watching that exhibition, Moore told Tucker, "I think we can find a spot for you," and offered him a scholarship.

When Jim Tucker enrolled for classes in the fall of 1950, Duquesne was a basketball power. Black athletes were not a novelty at Duquesne. In the spring of 1950, the Boston Celtics drafted Duquesne's Chuck Cooper, the first black player selected in an NBA draft. During Tucker's three varsity years at Duquesne, the Dukes flourished under the direction of Dudey Moore. In 1952 Duquesne lost to La Salle in the NIT semifinals and to Illinois in the NCAA regional finals. In the Illinois game Tucker scored twenty-nine, which helped him win All-America recognition. In 1953 Duquesne lost to St. John's in the NIT semifinals. The following year Duquesne finished 24-2 and lost to Holy Cross in the NIT finals. Holy Cross was led by two future NBA players, Togo Palazzi and Tommy

Heinsohn, a Hall of Fame player with the Boston Celtics. In 1954 two of Tucker's teammates, Dick Ricketts and Sihugo Green, would also be among the first wave of black NBA players.

In 1954 Syracuse drafted Jim Tucker in the third round. In his rookie season he commuted from Pittsburgh to Syracuse so that he could complete the courses he needed to graduate from Duquesne. Tucker was just the sixth black player to play in the NBA. As a player he said that he was never the target of racism from the players he competed with or against. Once the game began, he said, "you're just another player." In making the transition from the college to pro game, he found Earl Lloyd an excellent mentor. He described Lloyd as "one of the nicest guys I have ever known." The highlight of Tucker's career at Syracuse was winning the 1955 NBA championship. He and Earl Lloyd were the first black players to play on an NBA championship team. In 1955–56 Tucker played a full season. Syracuse released Tucker in the fall of 1956, and he played the season with the Harlem Globetrotters. After that year Tucker moved to Minneapolis, where he worked nineteen years for Pillsbury. He retired after working sixteen years for Northwest Airlines.[107]

The Championship Season

In early October 1954 the *Syracuse Herald-Journal* reported that Schayes had not signed a contract and was practicing on his own at the YMCA. Leo Ferris, the general manager, said that Schayes's demands were unreasonable, and the Nats star agreed that there was "quite a difference in our salary viewpoints."[108] For six years Schayes had led Syracuse in points scored and total rebounds. The *New York Times* reported that Schayes had played for $12,500 and sought a new contract for $15,000.[109] By the end of the month, Schayes signed a contract and was practicing with the team.

On March 4, 1955, the Nats clinched the Eastern Division title, which was worth $4,000. The Nats won seventeen of their last twenty-one games, which included an eight-game winning streak at the end of the season. Syracuse and the Fort Wayne Pistons, champions of the Western Division, had identical 43-29 records. Schayes had his most productive year as a Nat. He scored 1,333 points (17.8 average), which exceeded his old record of 1,262. His 887 total rebounds also led the team.[110] To get to the finals the Nats were going to have to beat the Celtics in a best-of-five series. In the opener at Syracuse Johnny Kerr sparkled with 27 points and 14 rebounds, King had 21, and Schayes and Lloyd hit double figures in points and rebounds as the Nats won, 110–100.[111] Two nights later, before 8,186 fans, Syracuse edged Boston, 116–110. Ahead by 14 points in the third period, the Nats fell behind 96–93 when the Celtics outscored Syracuse 18–1. Then the Nats went on a scoring run to secure the 6-point victory. Schayes led all Nats with 22, but Jack Andrews thought his 18 rebounds were one of the keys to the game's outcome. Five other Nats hit for double figures, with Red Rocha's 21 leading this group. Bill Sharmen led all Celtics with 32, followed by Macauley's 21.[112]

Boston stayed alive in the series by winning the third game in overtime before 13,091 fans at the Boston Garden. Tied at 89 in regulation, the Celtics outscored the Nats 11–8 in overtime. Kerr led all Nats with 20, while Cousy took game honors with 23. The ill will that existed between the two teams resurfaced in this game. In the second period Bob Brannum, Boston's hatchet man, clobbered Paul Seymour on the forehead with both fists when the Syracuse guard tried to score on a drive. At halftime Seymour followed Brannum to the Boston dressing room and had to be restrained by the police. Seymour had scored 18 points in the first half and did not score in the second half. One Boston writer thought Brannum's blow threw Seymour off his game. While Brannum claimed the hit was an accident, he also said, "I haven't got any friends out there. I don't care who they are."[113]

The next day the Nats dominated the Celtics, 110–94, to win the Eastern Division playoff at the Boston Arena. The win was the first for Syracuse on a Boston court that season. The Nats picked up $3,500 for winning the Eastern Division playoffs. Jack Andrews thought that Dolph Schayes played "a gutty, poised game" and "was the team's hottest shooter, sinking 28 points, 14 in each half." Schayes made all of his 14 free-throw attempts and hit on 7 of 16 from the field. He also had 11 rebounds. Earl Lloyd also had a great game, snatching 18 rebounds and tallying 22 points. Four other Nats were in double figures. For the Celtics, Bill Sharmen kept them in the game with 29. Red Auerbach, the Celtics' coach, was famous for lighting up a cigar on the bench when Boston had iced a game. In a bit of gamesmanship, Jack Andrews reported that Cervi "sat on the bench happily smoking two cigars as the Nats slammed in 13 points against 4 for Boston in the closing moments." If the Nats were the "Bandage Brigade" in 1954, Jack Andrews dubbed them the "men of destiny" in 1955.[114]

To win the NBA title, the Nats had to beat the Fort Wayne Zollner Pistons, another throwback to the early history of professional basketball dominated by small cities. Unlike the Nats, the Pistons were probably the richest team in the NBA. Theodore Zollner had founded the Zollner Machine Works and passed it on to his son Fred. Like many large corporations, the Zollner Machine Works developed an athletic program to provide recreation and entertainment for its employees. In 1939 Fred Zollner hired Carl Bennett to direct the athletic program. Bennett had been an outstanding softball player, but also had basketball experience. In 1941 the Pistons entered the National Basketball League and jumped to the BAA in 1948.

In the previous two seasons the Lakers had eliminated the Pistons in the playoffs. In 1955 the Pistons got their revenge and beat the Lakers to set up the championship series with the Nats. Fort Wayne's rookie coach was Charley Eckman, who had been an NBA official and had no coaching experience. When Zollner hired the thirty-three-year-old Eckman, he raised a lot of eyebrows around the league. Eckman had a reputation of being a likable free spirit with a bagful of jokes. Although an unusual move, Zollner knew that his players did not like their previous coach, Paul Birch, a hard-nosed authoritarian who liked to intimidate his players. Perhaps Zollner recognized that a lighter touch would produce better results. Besides, at this point in the NBA's history, most coaches were not great technicians.[115]

The Pistons were a talented team with a blend of springy youngsters and seasoned veterans. Their leading scorer was George Yardley, who had starred at Stanford University and was drafted by Fort Wayne in 1950. Instead of signing a contract with the Pistons, Yardley chose to play AAU ball and led San Francisco's Stewart Chevrolets to the 1951 AAU championship. One of Yardley's dreams was to represent the United States in the 1952 Olympics as a member of its basketball team. In 1951 he enlisted in the navy and played for Los Alamitos Air Station. Just before the 1952 AAU tournament, Yardley broke his wrist, and his Olympic dreams were dashed. In 1953 Yardley led Los Alamitos to the finals of the AAU tourney and made the AAU All-America team for the second time. After the tournament the Pistons and Yardley agreed upon a contract for ninety-five hundred dollars, plus a fifteen-hundred-dollar signing bonus.[116]

Yardley's rookie year started slowly, as he and Birch did not get along, which meant limited playing time. Another Piston rookie who had worked himself into the starting lineup was Jack Molinas, a six-foot-six forward who had starred at Columbia University. Growing up in the Bronx, Molinas developed a passion for basketball and an addiction to gambling. On March 24, 1954, Maurice Podoloff announced that Molinas was permanently banished from the NBA for betting on Piston games. Podoloff said that gambling "was a flagrant violation of a written contract." Given what had happened in college basketball a few years earlier, the NBA had to enforce a zero-tolerance policy on gambling.[117] With Molinas gone, Yardley played more and excelled in the 1954 playoffs. Although the 1953–54 season was a rough one, in 1954–55 the combination of Charley Eckman's relaxed style and the shot clock was a tonic for Yardley, who led his team in scoring with 17.2 points per game.

At the other forward the Pistons started Mel Hutchins, who had starred at Brigham Young University. Hutchins could run, jump, and play good defense. At the guard positions the Pistons featured three veterans: Andy Phillip, a playmaker; Max Zaslofsky, a shooting guard; and Frank Brian, another scoring threat. The starting center was six-foot-nine veteran Larry Foust, who alternated with Bob Houbregs from the University of Washington.[118]

On paper the two teams were evenly matched. The psychological edge favored the Nats. The Pistons had never won a game on a Syracuse floor, and the Nats had the home-court advantage because they had won the season series with the Pistons. Before the season the managers of Fort Wayne's Allen County War Memorial Coliseum thought there was no way the Pistons would play for the NBA championship, so they scheduled the American Bowling Congress's tournament during the finals. Therefore, Fort Wayne's home games, to Fred Zollner's consternation, were played in Indianapolis. While Cervi worried about overconfidence, Charley Eckman said, "Don't let those seasonal figures fool you. This club is going all the way."[119]

In a nip-and-tuck affair, the Nats hung on to win, 86–82, in the first game. Red Rocha led the Nats with 19 and held Yardley to 13. Seymour followed with 17, and Schayes fouled out with 10. With seven minutes left in the contest, Syracuse was down 75–71 when Dick Farley entered the game and hit a basket and free throw before hitting Rocha with a pretty pass to give Syracuse the lead, 77–76. With thirty seconds left, Earl Lloyd's basket gave the Nats an 84–82 lead, and Seymour added two free throws with three seconds left. After the game Jack Andrews reported that Syracuse's "dressing room resembled a funeral home." Earl Lloyd broke the ice by hollering, "Never mind fellows, we got by with a win on a bad night."[120] By contrast Fort Wayne's locker room was bubbling with enthusiasm. Ben Tenny, who covered basketball for the *Fort Wayne News-Sentinel*, quoted Charley Eckman as saying, "We shook 'em up last night and have them thinking." Larry Foust, who led the Pistons with 26, said, "Well, we can beat them now. Luck can't stay with them forever." When Fred Zollner walked into the locker room, he pulled an expensive watch out of his pocket and said to the team, "I'll give each of you one of these if you win."[121]

Before the second game in Al Cervi's pregame talk, he said, "This is the big one men. We've got to have this one." According to Jack Andrews, Red Rocha piped up and said, "This makes the 78th big one in a row. When do we get a little one?" With thirty-four seconds left in the game, the Nats were up by one slender point. With the clock running out and the "big one" on the line before 5,845 fans, Red Rocha banked a thirty-footer off the backboard to ice the game and give the Nats an 87–84 victory. Afterward, Rocha said, "Chalk that one up to luck." Schayes bounced back from the first game to lead all scorers with 24. Kerr's 17, Seymour's 15, and Rocha's 11 supported Schayes. Yardley and Frank Brian were high for the Pistons, with 21 and 20, respectively. The Nats' Charley Eckman could only hope that "the worm will turn."[122]

Before a mere 3,200 in Indianapolis, Mel Hutchins scored 24 points to lead the Pistons to their first win in the championship series, 98–89.

Schayes and Rocha each had 21 to lead the Nats. Although the crowd was small, it was rowdy, with about half from Fort Wayne. In the third period one fan threw a chair at referee Mendy Rudolph and almost sparked a riot. Ben Tenny wrote, "The Ft. Wayne fandom v. Rudolph feud has become so heated that it does appear that the NBA should take Mendy off the series." Charley Eckman was upbeat and predicted, "We'll win Tuesday, pull even and then kill those Nats with the pressure on."[123]

Eckman proved himself a prophet when the Pistons beat the Nats, 109–102, to even the series at two apiece. Frank Brian had 19 points, and six other Pistons hit in double figures. Brian was a speedy guard who was first-team All-NBL in 1948–49 and held in high regard by teammates and opponents. Schayes, with 28, was high for the Nats. As usual the ebullient Eckman said, "We'll knock 'em in the creek again here on Thursday night and then somehow manage to win one at Syracuse for the title in Fort Wayne."[124]

The fifth game had a wild ending. Down 60–45 at the end of the third quarter, the Nats fought back to close the gap to a point, 72–71. The Nats had two opportunities to take the lead but failed on both and lost, 74–71. On the second possession Dick Farley drove for the basket and was whacked on the arm by Andy Phillip, who said, "I fouled him and got away with it." After the game Jack Andrews reported that a fan attacked Al Cervi, who "responded by tearing the shirt off his assailant while a host of Piston partisans crowded around him." Ben Tenny added that "quite a melee ensued before calmer heads and police could get it stopped." The loss marked the first time the Nats had lost three consecutive games all season. Jack Andrews observed that "the Nats haven't been the stylish, fast-moving club since they added the Eastern Division playoff title."[125]

On Friday night the Pistons boarded the company plane that had "Zollner Pistons" blazoned on its side. Almost 2,000 well-wishers were at the airport to see them off. Although the Pistons had regained the momentum, they also knew that they had lost their last nineteen games in Syracuse, where the championship would be decided.[126]

On Saturday afternoon 4,997 spectators watched the Nats bounce back to even the series by beating the Pistons, 109–104. Late in the fourth quarter, the game was tied at 103. A basket by Kerr and a steal by Farley, who then tipped in a shot by Schayes, sealed the victory for the Nats. Seymour hit two free throws at the end of regulation time. Schayes led the Nats with 28, and Kerr followed with 20. Yardley's 31 topped all scorers, and Brian followed with 24. Bud Vander Veer of the *Herald-Journal* reported, "There were two near riots and a delegation of motor policemen were needed to quell the uprisings." A fight for a loose ball between Bob Houbergs and Wally Osterkorn evolved into a fight that prompted both benches to empty and led some fans to swarm the floor. At halftime a fan hit referee Sid Borgia in the head with his program. Vander Veer wrote that the Pistons checked out of their hotel before the game, expecting to fly home on Saturday evening. Instead, the two teams met the next afternoon to determine who would take home the NBA crown. If the Nats won, Alex Hannum, the former Nat, promised the players an all-expense-paid trip to California.[127]

Before the title game on Easter morning, Al Cervi went to church and prayed, "Lord give us a break let us win one." On Sunday afternoon 6,697 rabid fans watched the Nats capture the NBA crown by the narrowest of margins, 92–91. The Pistons jumped out to a 17-point lead in the second quarter, but the Nats were down only 6 by halftime. They had been helped by Biasone's twenty-four-second clock. With eighty-three seconds left in the game, Dolph Schayes hit two clutch free throws that gave the Nats a 91–90 lead. George Yardley's free throw tied the game at 91 with a minute left to play. After Earl Lloyd missed a shot, Yardley was called for palming the ball with eighteen seconds left to play. On the next possession Brian fouled George King, who had been struggling with his free-throw shot. King calmly sank his free-throw opportunity, but the Pistons had time for one last shot and the title. As Andy Phillip brought the ball into the front court, Seymour directed him into the corner, and then King left his man and from behind stole the ball. The Nats produced a balanced scoring attack, as seven players reached double figures. King and Billy Kenville were high with 15 apiece. The Pistons' Larry Foust captured scoring honors with 24. Although Dolph Schayes played the championship series with a bruised thigh and jammed thumb, he led all scorers with 133 points (19 average) and all rebounders with 83.[128]

6. The 1955 NBA champion Syracuse Nationals. *Front (L–R)*: Dick Farley, Billy Kenville; *center*: Earl Lloyd, Paul Seymour, Al Cervi, George King, Jim Tucker; *back*: Daniel Biasone, Wally Osterkorn, Bob Sexton, Dolph Schayes, John Kerr, Billy Gabor, Red Rocha, Art Van Auken. Courtesy of Gregory Newsome.

The celebration that began with the presentation of the championship trophy by Maurice Podoloff continued in the dressing room and then into the night, as the players joined Danny Biasone at his Eastwood Sports Center. Reflecting on the game, Al Cervi said, "I don't think I could stand another game like that. I've waited a long time for this, it's wonderful."[129] The next afternoon the Optimist Club hosted a luncheon for the team at the Hotel Syracuse. When asked to say a few words about the championship season, Dolph Schayes praised the contribution of the rookies and said he thought, "The spirit of the entire squad was the greatest I've ever experienced." In the evening a dinner was held at the Bellevue Country Club. Amid all the joy was the unhappy reality that during the regular season, low attendance produced a deficit of fifty thousand dollars. The receipts from the 39,290 who saw the playoffs and the finals helped to reduce that deficit, but the bottom line was that the team's investors had to be motivated by civic pride as much as by profits. For winning the championship, the players split fifteen thousand dollars.[130]

In the fall of 1955, the Nats returned with essentially the same lineup that had won the NBA championship in the spring. The only addition to the team was Ed Conlin, a six-foot-five, 200-pound All-America from Fordham. The Nats also lost two popular players—Billy Gabor and Wally Osterkorn. In the championship season, Gabor had been sidelined by hepatitis and played only three games. In the spring of 1955, the Nats and their fans showered the popular Gabor with gifts in a celebration of his career with Syracuse. Osterkorn was limited to nineteen games after having a calcium deposit removed from his thigh.

The only change in the eight-team NBA was that Ben Kerner moved his Hawks from Milwaukee to St. Louis. The most significant coaching change came on February 10, 1956, when Joe Lapchick coached his last game for the New York Knicks. While always popular with the press, tension had developed between Lapchick and Ned Irish. To replace Lapchick, Irish turned to Vince Boryla, one of his favorite players. Boryla's playing career came to end in 1954 following an injury to his right wrist. In 1954–55 Boryla coached the Denver Central Bank in the AAU's National Industrial Basketball League. When Boryla took the coaching position, he told Irish, "I will give you one hundred percent and straight answers." In return he asked that he not hear of complaints through the press.[131]

As the college game became more popular, the collegiate talent pool became richer. In 1955 Philadelphia added Tom Gola, who had led La Salle to an NCAA championship in 1954 and a second-place finish in 1955. Rochester drafted Maurice Stokes, a powerfully built six-foot-seven center and the most talented rookie. With only eight teams and an ever-improving crop of collegians, the NBA was becoming more competitive and interesting.[132]

After having won the championship in 1955, the Nats finished in 1956 with a disappointing 38-42 mark, which left them tied with the Knicks for third place. Nonetheless, the Nats reached the playoffs by defeating the Knicks, 82–77, in a single elimination game. The Nats turned their attention to the Boston Celtics and a best-of-three series for the right to play the Philadelphia Warriors for the Eastern Division title. During the regular season, the Celtics had beaten the Nats in eight of twelve meetings. In the series opener in Boston a terrible snowstorm limited attendance to 5,446, as Bob Cousy hit for twenty-nine points to lead the Celtics to an easy 110–93 victory.[133] Despite Cousy's twenty-eight points, the Nats evened the series in game two by edging the Celtics, 101–98, in Syracuse. Kerr's twenty-three, King's eighteen, and Schayes's fifteen led the Nats.[134] Although Schayes had scored a total of only six baskets in the first two games, he broke out of his shooting slump in the deciding game in Boston to hit ten baskets and four free throws for twenty-four points to lead Syracuse to a 102–97 victory to end Boston's season.[135] The playoff victory meant that the Nats would meet Philadelphia for the Eastern Division championship.

The Philadelphia Warriors were the brainchild of Eddie Gottlieb, who ran the team out of his briefcase. Born in Kiev, Russia, in 1898, Gottlieb and his parents immigrated to South Philadelphia. A few years after graduating from high school, Gottlieb formed an all-Jewish team called the Philadelphia SPHAs (South Philadelphia Hebrew Association). While the SPHAs barnstormed across the United States, they won championships in the Eastern League and American League. In addition to managing, coaching, and promoting basketball, Gottlieb also promoted Negro baseball teams and wrestling. In 1946 Gottlieb, as owner and coach of the Philadelphia Warriors, was one of the driving forces behind the creation of the Basketball Association of America. In 1947 Gottlieb's Warriors won the BAA title and lost in the finals to Baltimore in 1948. In the summer of 1949 Gottlieb played an important role in the merger of the NBL and BAA to form the NBA. Nicknamed "the Mogul," Gottlieb was probably the most knowledgeable basketball man among the early owners and a shrewd operator. Dolph Schayes knew Gottlieb well and said, "You could never win an argument with Gotty. He would just wear you down."

Always working the angles and thinking ahead, Gottlieb made one of his boldest moves in 1955 when he drafted Wilt Chamberlain, who had just completed his senior year at Overbrook High School. At the time the NBA still had a territorial draft, and Gottlieb feared that somehow he would lose the seven-foot phenom. The owners caved into Gottlieb's request, provided that he agree not to sign Chamberlain until 1959 when his class would graduate from college. In 1955 Gottlieb turned over the coaching duties to George Senesky, a former player. The Warriors had won the Eastern Division by six games and were led by three future Hall of Famers—Neil Johnston, who had a deadly sweeping hook shot; Paul Arizin, who had one of the best jump shots in the game; and Tom Gola, who was skilled in all facets of the game. Joe Graboski and Walt Davis gave the Warriors size in the front court, and Jack George and Ernie Beck were strong back-court players.[136]

In the fourth quarter of the opener at Philadelphia's Convention Hall, the Warriors broke the game open to post a 109–87 victory. Arizin had twenty-nine points to lead the Warriors, and Schayes topped the Nats with nineteen.[137] The Nats evened the series in Syracuse, 122–118. Schayes led the Nats with thirty-three, while five other Nats reached double figures. Johnston's forty-three and Arizin's thirty-seven led the Warriors.[138] Before a record crowd of 11,292 at Philadelphia's Convention Hall, Joe Graboski scored twenty points, and five other Warriors hit for double figures, as the Warriors trounced the Nats, 119–96, to take the third game. Ed Conlin had nineteen and Schayes had sixteen for the Nats.[139] The Nats bounced back in game four and edged the Warriors, 108–104, before a capacity crowd at the War Memorial. George King played all forty-eight minutes of the game and tossed in twenty-five points to lead the Nats. Schayes and Conlin were right behind, with twenty-one and nineteen, respectively. Johnston with thirty-five and Arizin with thirty-two continued to pace the Warriors.[140] In the deciding game the Nats played their best game in Philadelphia but lost, 109–104. Schayes led the Nats with twenty-eight, but Arizin countered with thirty-five.[141]

For the Nats the season was bittersweet. Their postseason play compensated for the disappointing regular-season record. The playoffs drew well, and Syracuse made twenty thousand dollars, which helped to cut into the estimated deficit of thirty-five thousand dollars accumulated during the season. The players earned forty-five hundred dollars, which they divided ten ways.[142] When the team met to split up the money, some frustrations surfaced when the players voted against giving Al Cervi a share of the pot. Fifty-five years after this symbolic rebellion, Earl Lloyd said, "With the passage of time, it was probably not the right decision." Schayes agreed and remembered that it was a "snap decision, foolishly arrived at, even childish, but emotions were running high." If the decision was unwise, Lloyd added that on March 30, 1956, "you couldn't have talked us out of it." The vote was nine to one against Cervi. Lloyd stressed that it was not about the money, but the team wanted to send a message about how they felt about their coach. In particular, Lloyd remembered that Cervi began to think that the team was all about him. When the team won, "it was because of Al," and when it lost, "it was because of us."[143] While the Nats were winning, the players had tolerated Cervi's difficult personality. By the end of the 1956 playoffs, a tipping point had been reached, and only time would tell if the relationship between the players and coach could be repaired. In the short term Danny Biasone tried to soften the blow by writing a check to Cervi for his share of the playoff money.

In what was clearly a difficult season, Dolph Schayes continued to excel. For the first time in his career, Schayes averaged twenty points per game, while leading the team in rebounding. In the eight playoff games, Schayes averaged twenty-two points and almost fourteen rebounds a game.

Despite the controversy at the end of the season, the Nats looked forward to a tour of Europe and the Middle East as part of a goodwill tour sponsored by the State Department. The tour started in late April in Iceland, where Bob Sexton, the team's general manager, said that boys walked miles to watch the Nats play or attend clinics. From Iceland the team flew to Hamburg, Germany, and then Vienna, Austria, where they gave more clinics to enthusiastic students. The Viennese were particularly impressed with the size of the Nats. When two Viennese saw Schayes, Kerr, Rocha, and Lloyd, one said, "Wonder who they are?" His friend replied, "Must be acrobats from that circus we saw advertised." The Nats were received by American ambassador Lewellyn Thompson and the mayor of the city.[144]

From Vienna the next stop was Tehran, where they played on an outdoor court before the shah and queen of Iran. Schayes was particularly struck by the extremes of wealth and poverty in Tehran. He saw Iranians washing their clothes in gutters from water supplied by spring snows. The tour then took the Nats to Beirut, Lebanon, which reminded Schayes of Paris. As a gag the Nats played a team of midgets. The trip ended with stops in Egypt, Italy, and Spain. Schayes remembered that when he told a curious onlooker that the Nats were the 1955 champions of the world, the person replied that he was sure the Harlem Globetrotters were the champions of the world.[145] Earl Lloyd remembered the trip fondly, because wherever the team traveled, the fans were eager to talk with black athletes.[146]

In 1956 the United States and the Soviet Union were locked in the Cold War. The United States hoped that goodwill tours would help cement relationships with other nations. The host countries also welcomed the Americans, because they hoped to learn the techniques that would make them more competitive in international basketball competition. In the 1950s the talent gap between the United States and the rest of the world was enormous. In Olympic basketball competition, which began in 1936, the United States won seven consecutive gold medals until 1972, when the Soviet Union defeated the Americans in the gold-medal game.

The Nats traveled in April and May. By the end of October, the Cold War got hot. In late October, Great Britain, France, and Israel attacked Egypt after it nationalized the Suez Canal. At the same time, the Soviets were brutally suppressing the Hungarian Revolution in Budapest. These Cold War hostilities gave a special edge to the 1956 Olympics, held just a few weeks later in Melbourne, Australia. During the Cold War, the Olympics became another test of the rival political and economic systems. In 1956 the American Olympic basketball team, led by Bill Russell, the University of San Francisco's All-American center, remained undefeated, as they beat the Soviet Union in the gold-medal game. The trip taken by the Syracuse Nationals and others like it, plus the Olympic basketball competitions, can be seen as the seeds of the globalization of basketball that is so much a part of the sport today.

3

Dolph Schayes Rewrites the Record Book

In the fall of 1956, the Nats' roster was slightly different. Red Rocha and Billy Kenville were sent to Fort Wayne, and George King retired. The rookies who would make a contribution during the 1956–57 season were Al Bianchi, six-foot-three guard from Bowling Green; Joe Holup, six-foot-six forward from George Washington; and Bob Hopkins, six-foot-eight center-forward from Grambling. Bobby Harrison, a seven-year veteran guard, came over from the St. Louis Hawks. He and Paul Seymour had been teammates at Woodward High School in Toledo. Another veteran pickup was Togo Palazzi, who had played two years for the Celtics. The core of the team remained Schayes, Kerr, Seymour, Lloyd, and Conlin.

Snapshot

Bob Hopkins

The integration of the NBA was painfully slow. When Syracuse drafted Bob Hopkins in 1956, Chuck Cooper, Nat "Sweetwater" Clifton, Earl Lloyd, Don Barksdale, and Ray Felix were the only black players to have played at least three years in the league. In 1955 Walter Dukes was the only black player drafted who would have a substantial tenure in the NBA. Another 1955 draftee, Maurice Stokes, was the first black player to earn All-NBA recognition, as he was named to the second team in three consecutive years. Therefore, when Bob Hopkins entered the league, he was among the first group of black players to integrate the sport. Among

79

those players joining Hopkins in the 1956 draft class who would have long careers in the NBA were Bill Russell, Willie Naulls, and Sihugo Green.

Born on November 3, 1934, in Jonesboro, Louisiana, Hopkins grew up in the segregated South. By first grade, Hopkins was six foot one and reached his full height, six foot eight, by ninth grade. Because of his size, Hopkins could pass for a teenager, which made it possible for him to make some extra money as a pool hustler. Because of rather flexible rules, Hopkins was able to play varsity baseball in the seventh grade and led his team in home runs and batting average. Hopkins entered high school in 1948. For his first two years of high school, his team played on an outdoor court, which was not unusual for segregated schools in the South. One consequence of playing on this surface was that Hopkins learned to dribble close to the ground. In his junior and senior years, Hopkins's team took a twenty-mile bus ride to Winnfield, Louisiana, where there was a black school with an indoor gym. As a freshman Hopkins averaged 28 points per game, and by his senior year he poured in 39 points per game. The team played run-and-gun basketball.

When Bob Hopkins was growing up in Jonesboro, it was a small town of just under four thousand in northern Louisiana. There was a clear line that divided the white and black communities of the town. Despite the unwritten rules of segregated communities, there was some contact between the races. Black and white kids played basketball on one of the town's playgrounds. Hopkins also remembered shooting baskets with the local judge's son. He also worked for a white woman who had a small library and encouraged him to read. Hopkins was a good student and attended the Boys State program sponsored by states to promote civics education.

After graduating from high school, Hopkins elected to attend all-black Grambling College, about twenty miles north of Jonesboro. Grambling's basketball coach was Eddie Robinson, better known for his record as Grambling's legendary football coach. Robinson was a stickler on conditioning and basketball fundamentals. As a freshman Hopkins was an immediate star, averaging 28 points and 17 rebounds per game. After his freshman year, he spent the summer with his sister in San Francisco. The real attraction was that he could play in the summer leagues around San Francisco with his second cousin Bill Russell, who had just finished his freshman year at the University of San Francisco. Along with K. C. Jones and Russell, Hopkins played with and against the best players in the Bay Area.

In Hopkins's four years at Grambling, the Tigers won two conference titles. Hopkins was a scoring machine who amassed 3,759 points in 126 games for a 29.8 average. He also collected 2,191 rebounds.

In 1956 Syracuse drafted Bob Hopkins in the tenth round. Low draft choices rarely survived the exhibition season, but Hopkins demonstrated excellent basketball skills and athletic ability. At the end of the last exhibition game, Danny Biasone called Hopkins aside and said, "Don't leave town." When Jim Tucker pulled a hamstring muscle, he was cut, and Hopkins had a spot on the final roster. He received a bonus of fifteen hundred dollars and signed a contract for fifty-seven hundred dollars.

Earl Lloyd eased the transition for Hopkins from Grambling to Syracuse. Fifty-five years later, Hopkins said, "I would not have made it without Earl." Lloyd taught Hopkins how to protect the ball, to hand-check on defense, and to be physical. Lloyd stressed, "You have to look out for yourself." Like Jim Tucker before him, Hopkins accompanied Lloyd on his tour of all the great jazz clubs in NBA cities.

Hopkins remembered Dolph Schayes as a perfectionist with excellent skills. No player put in more time after practice than Dolph Schayes. Sometime Hopkins would challenge Schayes to free-throw shooting and remembered that Schayes once beat him by making 116 consecutive free throws.

Hopkins played four years with the Syracuse Nationals. His best year was in 1958–59, when he averaged ten points a game. In one game Hopkins scored forty-four points against the Boston Celtics and Bill Russell. An injury to his left knee after the 1959–60 season cut short what looked like a promising career. Bob Hopkins never played another professional game after 1960.

After leaving Syracuse, Hopkins coached basketball at a number of black colleges. In the late 1970s he was an assistant coach with the Seattle Supersonics and the New York Knicks. In 1977 Hopkins coached the Seattle Supersonics, but he was fired after the team got off to a 5-17 start. Afterward, he returned to college coaching.[1]

The 1956–57 Season

The biggest surprise of the season came in late November when Al Cervi resigned as the team's coach after the Nats won only four of their first twelve games. Jack Andrews quoted Biasone as saying, "I didn't want him to go and I would like to make it clear, once and for all, that it was his own decision." Biasone named Paul Seymour to be his playing coach.

Biasone wrote a statement that said, "I have full and complete confidence in Paul Seymour." Jack Andrews reported that when Dolph Schayes saw the statement, he added, "Me, too—A. Schayes."[2]

Al Cervi had coached the Nationals for eight years. His list of accomplishments included one NBA championship and two other trips to the NBA finals. Cervi was old school, and the Nats were a reflection of his competitiveness. In his desire to win, however, Cervi was unforgiving to those players who fell short of his expectations. When a team is winning,

7. Paul Seymour's 1956–57 Syracuse Nationals. *Front (L–R):* Art Van Auken, Paul Seymour, Bobby Harrison; *back:* Johnny Kerr, Togo Palazzi, Ed Conlin, Earl Lloyd, Father Murray, Al Bianchi, Joe Holup, Dolph Schayes, Bob Hopkins. Courtesy of Gregory Newsome.

the psychological bruises that accompany competitiveness can be pushed under the rug. Losing, however, changes that dynamic. Cervi was not the first or last coach to fall victim to that reality.

After the departure of Cervi, the Nats began to dig themselves out of their early-season hole. In December the Nats played one of their best games in the first half of the season by beating the Celtics. Schayes scored 42, hitting shots from every spot on the court. When asked about Dolph's performance, Naomi Schayes replied, "Dolph only talked about the things he didn't do—the poor shots that he had taken, and how he could improve his next time out." This had been and would remain a trademark of Dolph's approach to the game.[3] As the campaign came to an end, the Nats were fighting for a playoff spot with the Warriors and Knicks. On March 9, at the War Memorial, Dolph Schayes poured in 36 and hit a long shot at the buzzer, as the Nats edged the Celtics, 104–102.[4] The win ensured the Nats a playoff spot. The next night in Boston, Schayes scored 22, and Bobby Harrison heaved in a partial hook shot from in front of Syracuse's bench to give the Nats a 94–92 victory.[5] The Nats finished with a 38-34 record, six games behind Boston, but in second place, one game ahead of the Warriors and two in front of the Knicks, who were eliminated from the playoffs. Syracuse's strong finish set up a first-round clash with the Warriors for the right to play the Celtics.

Philadelphia's chances of beating the Nats were hindered by a leg injury to Paul Arizin, its high-scoring forward, who was not a factor in the series. In the opener at Philadelphia, the Nats topped the Warriors, 103–96, as Johnny Kerr with 25 and Togo Palazzi with 19 sparked the Nats.[6] Two nights later Syracuse eliminated Philadelphia, 91–80, as Kerr, Schayes, and Conlin led the Nats.[7] The victory propelled the Nats into the Eastern Division finals against the Celtics.

The Nats-Celtics series had always been a dogfight. In 1957, however, the Nats faced a different Celtics team. In the 1956 draft the Celtics traded Ed Macauley and Cliff Hagan to the St. Louis Hawks so that Boston could have the second spot in the first round. With that choice Red Auerbach selected Bill Russell, the gifted six-foot-nine center from the University of San Francisco. Russell had led the Dons to consecutive NCAA championships in 1955 and 1956. Along the way the Dons compiled a fifty-five-game

8. Schayes drives hard with the left hand against George Yardley in an early All-Star Game. Courtesy of Gregory Newsome.

winning streak. In the fall of 1956, Russell also led the US Olympic Basketball Team to a gold medal in Melbourne, Australia. Russell's leaping ability, timing, and competitiveness set a new standard for centers. He rebounded, blocked shots, and intimidated offensive players. In thirteen seasons with the Celtics, Russell also averaged 15 points a game and led his team to eleven NBA championships. When Wilt Chamberlain joined the Philadelphia Warriors in 1959, the Russell-Chamberlain rivalry was one of the most storied in NBA history. Because Bill Russell's impact on professional basketball was so profound, the teams that had a crack at Russell looked inept. Rochester's Les Harrison had the first choice and took Duquesne's Sihugo Green. Harrison had Maurice Stokes, an all-pro center who tragically suffered a brain injury in the 1958 playoffs that shortened his career to three years, an outcome that Harrison could not have anticipated. Harrison did have doubts about Russell's star quality and also thought Russell's asking

price would be too high for his wallet. Ben Kerner of the Hawks was convinced that he did not have the resources to sign Russell. In the short term
Kerner did profit from the deal because Macauley and Hagan joined Bob
Pettit and Slater Martin to win five straight Western Division titles and one
NBA championship. The 1957 season was also the first for Tom Heinsohn,
a six-foot-seven forward from Holy Cross, who became only the tenth NBA
player to score more than 1,000 points in his rookie year, with a 16.2 average.[8] Most likely, Bill Russell also would have broken the 1,000-point pla-
teau, but he did not play his first game until December 22, because the
Melbourne Olympics were held so late in the year. Although Russell played
only forty-eight games, he still led the Celtics in rebounds, with 943.

In Boston, Clif Keane, who covered basketball for the *Boston Daily
Globe*, wrote that Dolph Schayes was the player the Celtics had to stop.
The only time the Celtics beat the Nats in a playoff series was in 1953,
when Bob Brannon instigated a fight with Schayes, and, as Keane remembered, "both were ejected." Otherwise, Keane wrote, Schayes "has always
hurt the Celtics." Keane expected Jim Loscutoff, Frank Ramsey, and Jack
Nichols to take turns guarding Schayes.[9] Before 13,292 fans the Celtics outplayed the Nats and took game one, 108–90. Six Celtics scored in double
figures, and Russell grabbed 31 rebounds to go along with 16 points. After
the game Coach Paul Seymour said Russell "really showed me something
out there tonight." Schayes added, "It would be to our advantage if we paid
him off for five years just to get him away from us for the rest of the series."
Red Auerbach assigned Ramsey and Heinsohn to deal with Schayes. They
held Schayes to 20 points, but 14 came from a perfect night on the free-
throw line. "Ramsey is the only man in the league his size (four inches
shorter) who plays me," Schayes said. "He dogs me, I'll say that for him."[10]

Although only down 4 at the end of three quarters in the second game
in Syracuse, the Celtics pulled away in the fourth quarter to win 120–105.
Schayes led the Nats with 31, but Heinsohn countered with 30. After Russell
scored 20 and pulled down another 30 rebounds, Earl Lloyd said, "If that
guy ever learns to shoot, I don't want to be around. He drives you crazy."[11]

A capacity crowd of 13,909 at the Boston Garden watched the Celtics
pull out a narrow 83–80 victory to sweep the series. One writer thought
Syracuse "fought with all its resources to avoid elimination," but could

not overcome key plays by Heinsohn and Russell at the end of the game. The Boston victory meant that for the first time in its history, the Celtics would play in the NBA finals. In an exciting seven-game series, the Celtics defeated the St. Louis Hawks and captured their first NBA crown.[12]

For the season Dolph Schayes's scoring numbers improved to 22.5 points a game, and once again he led the team in rebounding. In the play-offs Schayes continued to sparkle with a 21.4 average. For the fifth time in his eight-year NBA career, Schayes was All-NBA first team. The other three years, he was named to the second team.

Snapshot

Al Bianchi

The rookie who clocked the most minutes in the 1956–57 season was six-foot-three, 185-pound Al Bianchi. Born on March 26, 1932, Bianchi grew up and played high school basketball in Long Island City, New York. He played his college basketball at Bowling Green University, where he earned All-America mention in his senior year, 1954. Drafted by the Minneapolis Lakers in the second round, Bianchi reported instead to the US Army, where he served for two years. In 1956 he was selected to play on the Armed Forces All-Star team that played in the tournament to determine the roster for the 1956 Olympic basketball tournament. In the fall of 1956 Bianchi reported to the Minneapolis Lakers' camp, where he made it to the last cut. Then Bianchi caught a break, when Harry Boykoff, a star at St. John's who played professionally, recommended him to Danny Biasone. Al Cervi liked Bianchi's game, and the New Yorker embarked on a ten-year NBA career.

Dolph Schayes remembered Bianchi as "tough," "feisty," "aggressive," and "great in the locker room." Bianchi observed that Schayes was one of the best passing and rebounding forwards in the game. At the end of games, Bianchi placed Schayes as one of the top-five players he would want to take the last shot. As a rookie Bianchi got the Schayes treatment. He remembered Schayes saying, "Come on, 'rook,' let's have a shooting contest." Schayes took Bianchi outside and added, "If mine hit the rim, they don't count." Schayes would be Bianchi's teammate for seven years and coach for three years. Bianchi considered Schayes "one of the nicest people you would ever want to meet," a great teammate, and a receptive coach.

Al Bianchi spent his entire career in professional basketball. When the NBA granted a franchise to Chicago in 1966, it held a dispersal draft, and Chicago selected Kerr and Bianchi, who were not protected by their teams. Except for the 1965–66 season, when Kerr played in Baltimore, he and Bianchi had been roommates in Syracuse and Philadelphia. The rumor was that Chicago wanted Ray Meyer, DePaul University's legendary mentor, to coach the Bulls. When that effort failed, Chicago named Kerr its first head coach, and Bianchi joined him as his assistant. By 1966 both players were ready to leave the game. Between 1967 and 1969, Bianchi coached the Seattle Supersonics. For the next six years, Bianchi coached in the American Basketball Association, five for the Virginia Squires. His next eleven years were spent as John MacLeod's assistant with the Phoenix Suns. From 1987 to 1991, Bianchi served as the general manager of the New York Knicks, before ending his basketball career by scouting for Phoenix until 2004 and the Golden State Warriors until 2009.[13]

At the end of the 1956–57 season, the NBA experienced another mutation. After nine years in the NBA, Les Harrison moved the Royals from Rochester to Cincinnati. For the previous seven years, the Royals never averaged more than 2,408 fans. Whether it was competition from television or the flight of the wealthy to the suburbs, Les Harrison was swimming in a sea of red ink to the tune of $156,263. The Cincinnati Gardens sat 14,000 fans, and the Queen City's metropolitan population was 50 percent larger than Rochester's. Unfortunately, in their first year, the Royals averaged only 3,700 fans in Cincinnati, leaving Harrison in more red ink. His difficulties at the gate were compounded by the tragic loss of Maurice Stokes, who was permanently paralyzed by an attack of encephalitis after suffering a head injury during the 1958 playoffs. To get out of debt, Harrison sold the franchise to a Cincinnati group for $225,000 and ended his long association with professional basketball.[14]

Several months before Harrison made his move, Fred Zollner decided to move the Pistons from Fort Wayne to Detroit. Zollner's move was one more step in the recognition of the NBA's pioneer owners that the future of NBA basketball was in big markets.[15] In the face of these developments, Syracuse's fans had to wonder how much longer Danny Biasone could survive.

Snapshot

Larry Costello

In the 1957–58 season, the Nats' roster was basically unchanged except for the important addition of Larry Costello, purchased from Philadelphia. As a high school player in Minoa, New York, Costello had been a fan of the Nationals. He played his college ball at the University of Niagara and was drafted by Philadelphia in 1954. After nineteen games in the 1954–55 season, Costello's basketball career was interrupted when he had to enter military service. He returned from the service in 1956 and played seventy-two games for the Warriors and averaged 7.6 points. In October 1957 the Warriors sold Costello to the Nationals, where he became an immediate starter. Costello was quick and a good ball handler, and he played good defense. He averaged double figures for eight straight seasons. During that period Costello played in five All-Star Games. Bob Cousy recalled that Costello played with "animal determination" and considered him the toughest player he played against.[16]

Costello moved with the Nats to Philadelphia in 1963 and retired after the 1965 season. During the summer of 1966, Alex Hannum talked Costello out of retirement, and he played forty-nine games for the 76ers, until he was sidelined with a ruptured Achilles' tendon on January 6, 1967. Costello played in only two of the 1967 playoff games, as the 76ers marched to the NBA championship.

In April 1968 the Milwaukee Bucks made Costello the first coach of the expansion franchise. As a coach, according to Wayne Embry, his general manager, Costello was a stickler for detail and conditioning who expected to win every game. No player worked harder than he did in preparing for practice and games.[17] Dave Gambee, who played with and for Costello, compared Costello's coaching style to the manner of a drill sergeant. In the changing culture of the 1960s and 1970s, Costello's "old-school" approach turned off some players, though this could be overlooked, as long as the Bucks won.[18] In 1971 the Bucks captured the NBA championship with a team built around Kareem Abdul-Jabbar and Oscar Robertson. In 1976, after Robertson retired and Abdul-Jabbar forced a trade, Milwaukee fired Costello when the Bucks got off to a 3-15 start. In 1978–79 Costello coached fifty-six games for the Chicago Bulls, his last professional coaching position. Between 1981 and 1987 Costello coached Utica College for six seasons. On December 13, 2001, Larry Costello died from cancer.[19]

The 1957–58 Season

Perhaps no writer who covered the NBA appreciated the type of basketball Dolph Schayes and the Nats played more than the *New York Times*'s Leonard Koppett. While Schayes usually haunted the Knicks, on December 4, 1957, Dolph had a special game. After beating New York 119–96, a jubilant Schayes believed, "I think that's the best game I've ever played in New York." In addition to scoring twenty-seven points, Dolph added thirteen assists and fourteen rebounds. Schayes was particularly proud of assists and thought, "I've never had that many assists in a pro game." When Schayes called over to Ed Conlin and jokingly said, "You want to go out and play some ball in the school yard," Conlin replied, "You can't beat that school yard basketball." This exchange prompted Koppett to write, "Their banter was very much to the point. Great as Schayes is, the Syracuse success is built on school yard ball—a maximum of five men cooperating, helping out on defense, give and go offense, hustle and teamwork."[20]

In February 1958 Dolph Schayes played another amazing game, one that was part of a bizarre series of events. On Friday, February 7, 1958, the Nats defeated the New York Knicks, 105–102, in the first game of a doubleheader at the Boston Garden. After the game the Nats were scheduled to fly back to Syracuse to play Saturday's 2:00 p.m. nationally televised game against the St. Louis Hawks. The only problem was that a snowstorm had engulfed Boston and the surrounding area. Planes were grounded, no train could get the team to Syracuse in time for the game, commercial buses were stalled, and renting automobiles seemed too dangerous. According to Clif Keane, who wrote for the *Boston Globe*, one Bostonian snickered, "Dolph Schayes should be able to get home in time for the game. He's always walking on the court and should be able to maneuver his way back to Syracuse the same way."[21] Finally, Danny Biasone chartered a bus, and the team started the 330-mile journey to Syracuse. When the bus reached the New York state line, there was total chaos, as the road to Albany and the New York State Thruway (just 16 miles away) was a parking lot filled with trucks and cars. The Nats sat motionless for four hours, but Danny Biasone was determined that his team would not miss its televised date with the St. Louis Hawks. In desperation, he turned to the police for help. The chief of police of Nassau, New York, put together an escort that made it possible for Syracuse's bus to weave its way through the congestion to the New York State Thruway. By the time the Nats made it to the thruway, it was nine in the morning, five hours before game time. When the bus, driving at thirty-five miles per hour, reached the War Memorial, it was an hour before game time, and the rested St. Louis Hawks were waiting for the bedraggled Nats.[22]

Before the game, Togo Palazzi remembered that his "legs felt like rubber." The bus had been very uncomfortable, and the players had very little sleep. When he looked over at Dolph Schayes, he noticed that he was going through his regular pregame ritual. Schayes always got very quiet before games as he prepared to compete. Despite their fatigue, the Nats battled the Hawks for the entire game but lost, 103–102. Throughout the game Schayes had carried the team on his back and finished with 33 points and 23 rebounds, while playing the entire forty-eight minutes.[23]

For Togo Palazzi, Schayes's performance captured the essence of his teammate. As Schayes's roommate on the road, Togo remembered that Dolph had talked about what people could do if they gave 100 percent. Later, when Palazzi coached and gave clinics, young players would ask, "How do I know if I am giving 100 percent?" Palazzi would respond by describing Dolph's performance against the Hawks when it would have been very easy just to show up rather than compete.[24]

As demanding as the two games were, the Nats had to get up on Sunday to play the Boston Celtics, whom they defeated. The two teams then played on Tuesday in Philadelphia as part of a doubleheader, and the Nats won again. The following night in Boston, the Celtics topped the Nats, as

Bill Russell gathered in 41 rebounds. In what was a grueling schedule, five games in six days, the Nats had come out on top in three contests.[25]

The Nats finished the season 41-31, good enough for second place in the Eastern Division. Most disappointing was that attendance dipped to 112,397. A fan wrote a letter to the *Syracuse Post-Standard*, wondering why people did not go to the games. On March 5, 1958, for example, a mere 1,823 turned out for a game, a season low. Of the seven reasons he gave to attend, the fan wrote that Syracuse had Dolph Schayes, "The Babe Ruth of Basketball."[26]

For the third consecutive year, Syracuse and Philadelphia met in the playoffs. In the opening game, played at the State Fair Coliseum, the Nats squeaked out an 86–82 victory before 3,658 fans. Schayes led all Syracuse scorers with 22 points, and Johnny Kerr added 18 to go along with 22 rebounds while holding Neil Johnston to 4 points.[27] The next night the Warriors edged the Nats, 95–93, in Philadelphia. The Nats were particularly bitter about the officiating of Arnie Heft, who they thought cost them the game. Bud Vander Verr of the *Herald-Journal* thought it was unfortunate that the officiating became an issue, because "the play has been terrific." Schayes played all but four minutes of the game and led all scorers with 32 points.[28] For the first time in playoff history, the Warriors beat the Nats in Syracuse, 101–88, to take the series. Bill Reddy, of the *Post-Standard*, reported that Philadelphia simply outplayed the Nats the entire game. Six Warriors scored in double figures, while only three Nats did. Schayes led all scorers with 26, but Reddy thought "the strain of the back-breaking season finally got too big for Dolph. He grew so weary that he needed a pair of rests, and in the fourth period he was missing shots which had given him no trouble through the campaign."[29]

The 1958 season was memorable for Dolph Schayes. On January 12, 1958, he scored 23 points against the Detroit Pistons, which gave him 11,770 career points, eclipsing the old record of 11,764 points set by George Mikan.[30] Schayes averaged 24.9 points per game, his career high. He also led the team in minutes played and rebounds. In March New York's Metropolitan Basketball Writers Association named Schayes the professional basketball player of the year.[31] Once again writers named Schayes to the All-NBA's first team.

#4 Dolph Schayes
drives the lane past
#9 Bob Pettit.
Nats vs. Hawks

9. Dolph Schayes driving against Bob Pettit of the St. Louis Hawks.
Courtesy of Gregory Newsome.

In 1958–59 the Nats' roster had a slightly different look. Earl Lloyd was traded to Detroit, and Bobby Harrison retired. The Nats drafted Connie Dierking, a six-foot-nine center from the University of Cincinnati, in the first round. The steal of the draft came in the second round, when the Nats picked Hal Greer, from Marshall University.

Snapshot

Hal Greer

In 1996 the NBA celebrated its fiftieth anniversary. To commemorate that achievement, the NBA composed a list of the fifty greatest players in that half century. The two Nats selected were Dolph Schayes and Hal Greer. Born on June 26, 1936, in Huntington, West Virginia, Greer was the youngest of nine children. A gifted athlete, Greer led Douglass High School to the Negro State Championship in 1954. Although no African American had played for a major university in West Virginia, change was imminent. In 1955, a year after the *Brown* decision, Martin Luther King Jr. directed a successful boycott of segregated busing in Montgomery, Alabama. Racial barriers were collapsing, and Hal Greer was part of this historical process when he elected to accept an athletic scholarship to play basketball at Marshall University. He was the first black athlete to play at a major university in West Virginia.

Greer's first year at Marshall was also the first year of its new head coach, Jules Rivlin. Between 1937 and 1940, Rivlin had starred in basketball at Marshall. During World War II, Rivlin played basketball at Fort Warren, Wyoming, where one of his teammates was Ermer Robinson, who would enjoy a long career with the Harlem Globetrotters. For two years after the war, Rivlin was a player and coach for the Toledo Jeeps in the NBL. One of his players was Paul Seymour.

The Rivlin-Greer combination worked well. In Greer's sophomore year, 1956, the Thundering Herd won the Mid-American Conference and finished with an 18-4 record. This earned Marshall its first NCAA Tournament bid in the school's history. In the first round, Morehead State eliminated Marshall, 107–92. In Greer's senior year, he averaged 23.6 points, was the conference's MVP, and earned honorable mention on the Associated Press's All-America team.

Before the 1958 draft, Seymour called Rivlin, who told him that Greer would not disappoint the Nats. When Greer arrived at Syracuse, Larry Costello and Al Bianchi were the starting guards. Coming off the bench was new for Greer, but in February Greer caught a break when Al Bianchi injured his ankle. On February 14, Greer had a breakout performance against the Celtics, when he scored 45 points. He did not relinquish his spot in the starting lineup. At six foot two, Greer was fast and quick, and he possessed, Schayes thought, the best midrange jump shot in the league. Greer averaged 11 points per game as a rookie, 13 points per contest in his second year, and just under 20 points per game in his third year. By 1962, when injuries slowed Schayes, Greer became the team's high scorer and remained so when the Nats moved to Philadelphia, until Wilt Chamberlain's first full season with the 76ers in 1965–66. The following season the 76ers ended the Celtics' series of consecutive NBA championships at eight in the Eastern Division finals and won the NBA crown by defeating the San Francisco Warriors. Between 1963 and 1969, Hal Greer was named to the All-NBA second team. Between 1961 and 1970, Greer played in ten All-Star Games and was the MVP in the 1968 All-Star Game. Greer retired after the 1973 season. When Greer was inducted into the Hall of Fame in 1982, Dolph Schayes paid him the ultimate compliment when he said, "Hal Greer came to play. He came to practice the same way, to every team function the same way. Every bus and plane and train, he was on time. Hal Greer punched the clock. Hal Greer brought the lunch pail."[32]

The 1958–59 Season

While the Nats struggled during the season, they strengthened their roster on February 13, 1959, when they were able to trade Ed Conlin to the Detroit Pistons for George Yardley. In 1958 Yardley became the first NBA player to break the 2,000-point barrier. His 2,001 points broke George Mikan's season scoring record of 1,932 points. Yardley also made 655 free throws, breaking Dolph Schayes's single-season record of 625. In the Pistons' second year in Detroit, Yardley struggled with a variety of illnesses, and on January 25 he broke his left hand. On his way to the dressing room, Fred Zollner said, "You're through as far as I'm concerned. I never want to see you again." With a light cast on his left arm, Yardley played the last fifteen games of the season with the Nats.[33]

10. Dolph Schayes shoots over Bob Pettit, demonstrating the form that made his set shot one of the NBA's best. Courtesy of Gregory Newsome.

Yardley helped the Nats and Dolph Schayes. As Schayes explained, "Teams couldn't defend us. If they concentrated on me, George scored 20. If they concentrated on George, I scored 20." Financially, Yardley also helped Schayes. When Yardley was signed by Syracuse, he was making more money than Schayes's fifteen thousand dollars. Danny Biasone immediately raised Schayes's salary so that it would be above the seventeen thousand dollars that Biasone paid Yardley.[34]

Yardley immediately energized the team. Bill Reddy reported that Yardley had "the ability to come into the game and score in clusters." Attendance at home games also increased, as the Nats put together a string of home victories. Reddy explained that the Nats were good before Yardley, but the team was "a better more colorful array now."[35]

The Nats finished the season with a 35-37 record. In the first round of the playoffs, they met the New York Knicks. In the three previous seasons, the Knicks had failed to make the playoffs. The Knicks had run into some bad luck. After they purchased the six-foot-eight Willie Gardner from the Globetrotters for thirty thousand dollars, it turned out that a heart condition prevented him from playing. When New York acquired Mel Hutchins, a knee injury ended his career. In the summer of 1958, Vince Boryla resigned as New York's coach to devote more time to commercial real estate interests in Denver. Ned Irish retained Boryla as a scout.

To replace Boryla the Knicks hired Andrew "Fuzzy" Levane, who starred collegiately with St. John's University and played professionally with Rochester and Syracuse.[36] Levane's Knicks finished in second place with a 40-32 record. Carl Braun was the only connection to the New York teams that made it to the finals between 1951 and 1953. Richie Guerin was a fine guard from Iona, and Ken Sears, Willie Naulls, and Ray Felix gave the Knicks size in the front court. The Knicks had won nine of the twelve regular-season games with the Nats, but in early March the Nats won their last two meetings with the Knicks. In the first playoff game at the 69th Regiment Armory, the Nats played flawlessly and edged the Knicks, 129–123, before a capacity crowd of 5,000. Schayes continued to haunt the Knicks, as he scored thirty-five points, twenty-five in the first half, and Yardley followed with twenty-two.[37] The Knicks' loss left the New York press corps reeling. With the second game scheduled two days later in

Syracuse, Warren Pack of the *New York Journal-American* wrote, "If you want to sit in on the funeral, the services will be held at 2:30 tomorrow, with local mourners able to watch on Channel 4. . . . Black ties, please." Sid Gray in the *Herald-Tribune* chimed in, "For die-hard Knick fans announcement please: in the event of a third game, it will be held at the Garden Monday night. Word of advice; don't cancel any bridge dates."[38] As it turned out, the press corps' pessimism was justified, as the Nationals wrapped up the series in Syracuse by thumping the Knicks, 131–115, before 7,434 fans. Johnny Kerr had a monster game with thirty-four points, followed by Yardley's twenty-four and Schayes's twenty.[39]

The Syracuse victory set up a seven-game series for the Eastern Division title with the Boston Celtics. The rivalry between the two teams was one of the most heated and physical in the NBA. On February 20 three fights broke out in a game at Syracuse won by the Nats, 113–105. Referee Sid Borgia tangled with Eli Roth, one of Syracuse's more avid fans, after he verbally attacked the official near the end of the game. Then Bill Russell and Frank Ramsey of the Celtics mixed it up with George Dempsey of the Nats. Finally, Boston's Tom Heinsohn and Dolph Schayes started swinging at each other following a shoving match while fighting for position during a free throw. When Paul Seymour jumped into the melee, the fans followed, and it took the police and ushers five minutes to clear the floor.[40]

Although Boston was the favorite to win the series, Syracuse was confident it could take the Celtics. During the regular season, the two teams played evenly, as the Celtics took seven of twelve games. In their last game, the Nats had trounced the Celtics, 142–118. Dolph Schayes thought this Syracuse team was the best one that he played on during the course of his career. Both teams had difficulty winning on their opponent's court. Boston's players were candid about not liking to play in Syracuse. Frank Ramsey, Boston's star sixth man, said, "There's all kinds of yelling go on, and it's tough beating them up there."[41] Bill Sharman, Boston's sharpshooting guard, chimed in, "It's the people mostly. They can really get under your skin." Clif Keane, who covered the Celtics for the *Boston Evening Globe*, wrote, "They're all Americans up in that area, but even if they're related to you, people from Syracuse somehow detest everyone connected with the Boston Celtics." Because the baskets are ten feet high on all courts, Keane, in theory, found the home-court advantage a bit mysterious. The reality, Keane observed, was that "of all the places the Celtics are forced to travel each season, they seem to resent Syracuse more than any other arena."[42]

The outcome of the first six games was predictable. In the three games in Boston, the Celtics' margin of victory was at least 20 points in every game. The Nats won all three games in Syracuse. The closest was the first game, which the Nats won, 120–118. Schayes had 34 and Yardley 27 to lead Syracuse. Jack Barry of the *Boston Globe* observed that the "Syracuse fans were sportsmen all the way."[43] The margin of victory in Syracuse's other wins was 12 points. In those two games Schayes had 28 and 39, respectively. On Boston's inability to beat the Nationals in Syracuse, a puzzled Bill Russell observed, "It's two different teams in Syracuse when we play. We just don't seem to play good ball and they play very well."[44] Clif Keane noted, "The Celtics simply act like they are mesmerized on the War Memorial Court."[45]

Going into the deciding game of the series, the Nats were confident. George Yardley captured the Syracuse style of play when he observed, "When you pass the ball to someone here, a shot will be taken and chances are a basket will be scored. It's wonderful to be with a team that has the spirit of Syracuse."[46] Clif Keane of the *Boston Globe* wrote amusingly, "It was difficult to draw any controversy from the Syracuse members. Used to be that they would come into Boston with a dozen chips on their shoulders." On the eve of the big game, Bill Russell observed, "Well, a lot of people are going to be very tight in here tomorrow evening. And I'm going to be one of those players believe me. I think right now that I am going to play the best game of basketball I ever played in my life." After six games, Dolph Schayes led all scorers with a 27.3 average. He had played through the flu, headaches, and an injured big left toe. Schayes told the press that he had a premonition that "someone on the bench will win it for us."[47]

In a game that lived up to all expectations, the Celtics edged the Nats, 130–125, before a sellout crowd of 13,909. Although the Nats were up by 16 in the second period, the Celtics narrowed the lead to 8 by the half. Up by 1 at the end of three quarters, the Nats and the Celtics exchanged leads in the fourth quarter until the Celtics prevailed. Schayes led all players with 35 points, followed by Yardley's 32. Ramsey with 28 and Cousy with 25 led the Celtics, who had five other players in double figures.[48] Bill Russell had an astounding 32 rebounds to go with 18 points. Russell said, "That was the best game I've ever seen Syracuse play." Sharman called the finale "the greatest game of basketball I've ever seen."[49] In the Syracuse locker room, Yardley agreed with Sharman that "it was quite a basketball game. I don't think anyone disgraced himself out there tonight."[50] After eliminating the Nats, the Celtics won their second NBA title by defeating the Minneapolis Lakers, 4–0.

In 1958–59 Schayes averaged 21.3 points per game, and the writers placed him on the All-NBA's second team. In the nine playoff games, Schayes truly excelled. He averaged 28.2 points and 13 rebounds per game. Schayes also made 98 of his 107 free-throw attempts. In May 1959 Schayes turned thirty-one and looked forward to his twelfth year of professional basketball.

In 1959 the NBA was looking increasingly more stable. The *New York Times* reported that the average salary was $10,197. Bob Cousy's estimated $28,000 led all players.[51] The infusion of new talent continued to make the NBA more attractive. The remarkable Elgin Baylor led the Lakers to the NBA finals in April 1959 and earned a spot on the All-NBA first team. In the fall of 1959, Wilt Chamberlain made his much-anticipated debut with the Philadelphia Warriors. The NBA reported that 2 million fans paid to see the pro game, an 8 percent increase over the previous year. Accompanying the growth of attendance were rumors of expansion to Chicago, Los Angeles, and San Francisco.

Snapshot

Dick Barnett

The Nats lost none of their key players for the 1959–60 season. The only rookie to make the team was Dick Barnett, a six-foot-four guard who played for future Hall of Fame coach John McLendon at all-black Tennessee A&I (now Tennessee State) in Nashville. Barnett had been a high school star at Gary, Indiana's Roosevelt High School, which fell to Oscar Robertson's Indianapolis Crispus Attucks in the 1955 Indiana state basketball finals. Attending A&I was a transformational experience for Barnett. Initially, McLendon struggled to get Barnett to fit into his system. After some very rough patches in which Barnett and McLendon locked horns, Barnett accepted the structure demanded by McLendon. The one thing that McLendon did not touch was Barnett's unorthodox jump shot. The left-hander shot with bent knees that he would thrust back in the act of shooting so that he always looked off balance.

At Tennessee A&I Barnett was a part of history. Until 1953 black colleges were denied the opportunity to compete in postseason national basketball tournaments. The National Association of Intercollegiate Athletics (NAIA) broke with that tradition in 1953. In 1957 Tennessee A&I became the first black college to win a national basketball tournament. In 1958 and 1959 A&I won two more titles, making McLendon the first college coach to win three consecutive national championships. Barnett was the tournament MVP in 1958 and 1959. John Barnhill and Ben Warley were two future NBA players who played alongside Barnett.

By 1959 the NBA was scouting the NAIA, and Syracuse made Barnett its first-round selection. Dolph Schayes did not see Barnett until the rookie joined the Nats for an exhibition game at Upsala College in New Jersey while Barnett was stationed at nearby Fort Dix. In this exhibition game, Schayes remembered that Barnett hit jump shots from all over the court. While Schayes thought Barnett was a terrific player, the rookie was not too happy with his minutes played or living in Syracuse. Nonetheless, in his rookie year Barnett dislodged Al Bianchi as the first guard off the bench and averaged 12.4 points per game. In Barnett's second year with the Nats, he was one of six players to log more than two thousand minutes and averaged 16.9 points per game. That year Schayes remembers that he, Barnett, and a few other players were at a restaurant rehashing a game with Alex Hannum, who had replaced Paul Seymour as coach in 1960. In preparing for the next game with the Celtics, Hannum said, "We need somebody to guard Sam Jones [the Celtics' fine-shooting guard]." Barnett popped up and said, "Let me play him." Barnett's one plea to Hannum was that he keep him in the game for ten minutes at a stretch rather than yanking him in and out every two minutes. Hannum agreed, and the confident Barnett contained Jones in their next meeting.

After the 1960–61 season, Barnett jumped to the American Basketball League (ABL), a short-lived league organized by Abe Saperstein, the founder of the Harlem Globetrotters. There were several reasons Barnett elected to leave Syracuse. He was not fond of Syracuse's winters and wanted to live in a bigger city. Moreover, he wanted more playing time and was assured of doing so in Cleveland, where Barnett averaged 26.2 points a game. Finally, the move would reunite him with Johnny McLendon, now the first black professional basketball coach. The owner of the Pipers was a youthful George Steinbrenner, whose tempestuous personality created all sorts of difficulties that ultimately led to McLendon's resignation. While the Pipers won the ABL championship in 1962, the league folded on December 31, 1962. Barnett was not around to see the lights go out. From the beginning, Biasone claimed that Syracuse owned Barnett's contract, and ultimately he won that argument in an Ohio court. On September 5, 1962, Syracuse sold Barnett to the Los Angeles Lakers. For three years Barnett flourished in LA, before he was traded to the New York Knicks for Bob Boozer on October 14, 1965. An immediate hit with New York's fans, Barnett averaged a career high 23.1 points per game. Four years later Willis Reed, Walt Frazier, Dave DeBusschere, and Bill Bradley joined Barnett, and the Knicks won their first NBA championship. In 1973, Barnett's last campaign, the Knicks won their second NBA title.

While playing with the Lakers, Barnett completed his bachelor's degree at California Poly Pomona. He then earned a master's degree from New York University and his doctorate in education from Fordham. His major research interest was writing about the intersection of sports and society with an emphasis on the role and responsibilities of black athletes in American society.[52]

The 1959–60 Season

With Yardley playing a full year, the Nats finished the 1959–60 season with a 45-30 record, ten games better than the previous season. Though playing well, the Nats had to settle for third place in the Eastern Division.

The Celtics finished first, amassing fifty-nine wins against sixteen losses. With Chamberlain averaging an unbelievable 37.6 points per game, Philadelphia finished second, with forty-nine wins, ten behind the Celtics. The New York Knicks were consigned to last place, where they would remain until the 1966–67 season. In the Western Division, Bob Pettit, Cliff Hagan, and Slater Martin led the St. Louis Hawks to a Western Division title, but no other team in the West had a winning record.

As the level of NBA play improved, Dolph Schayes continued to set records. On January 12, 1960, as part of a doubleheader at Philadelphia's Convention Hall, Schayes scored 34 points against Boston, which made him the first NBA player to score more than 15,000 career points.

Fittingly, Schayes's 15,000th point came after he sank a long set shot. One writer noted that "the Schayes fist shot up with more vehemence than usual." At that point officials stopped the game and presented the ball to Schayes, while a capacity crowd gave him a standing ovation. If Schayes was hot, George Yardley was blazing. He scored 47 points, 30 in the first half, a Convention Hall record. At one point Yardley made twelve consecutive shots from the floor, and his twenty-one field goals was also a Convention Hall record. The Schayes-Yardley outburst spearheaded a 127–120 victory over the Celtics. After the game Schayes acknowledged that "the ovation was a great feeling."[53]

The attention given to Schayes on breaking the 15,000-point barrier gave him an opportunity to reflect upon himself and the game he played. "My ambition," Schayes said, "has always been to walk down the street and hear someone say, 'There goes the greatest basketball player there is.'" Schayes also thought that basketball should have a line beyond which a player earned 3 points. "It takes more skill to score from farther out," Schayes thought, "and it ought to be rewarded." He would give tip-ins just 1 point. Schayes laughed that if his system was used, he would have had 37 rather than 34 points since he hit four long set shots and had just one tip-in. Eventually, basketball at all levels would draw that 3-point line.[54]

Ten days later the East All-Stars beat the West All-Stars, 125–115, before a capacity crowd of 10,421 at Philadelphia's Convention Hall. Schayes had 19 points, but Chamberlain, with 23 points and 25 rebounds, was the game's most valuable player.[55]

11. On January 12, 1960, Dolph Schayes was the first NBA player to score fifteen thousand points. Courtesy of Gregory Newsome.

The Nats met the Philadelphia Warriors in the first round of the play-offs. Along with Chamberlain, Philly had Paul Arizin and Woody Sauldsberry at forwards and Guy Rodgers and Tom Gola at guards. In the series opener in Philadelphia, the Warriors won easily, 115–92. The Nats evened the series in Syracuse by edging the Warriors, 125–119, before 6,108 and a national television audience. In one of his best postseason games, Schayes scored 40 points, collected 22 rebounds, dished out 4 assists, and played all forty-eight minutes of the game. The next night, back in Philadelphia, Wilt Chamberlain set a new NBA playoff record by tossing in 53 points, as the Warriors won the series, 132–112. When Coach Neil Johnston took him out of the game with a minute to play, the 9,428 fans at Convention Hall gave Chamberlain a two-minute ovation. Schayes led the Nats with 31 points, which gave him 1,700 career playoff points and eclipsed the old record of 1,680 points set by George Mikan.[56]

At the end of his twelfth professional season, Dolph Schayes owned most of the NBA's records. Besides most career and playoff points, Schayes led all players in rebounds, free throws made and attempted, and games played. For the fifth straight season, Schayes averaged more than 20 points per game.

In 1960–61, for only the second time in its NBA history, Syracuse made a coaching change. After four years as the head coach of the Nats, Paul Seymour decided to take a similar position with the St. Louis Hawks when Ben Kerner offered him more money than Biasone could afford to pay. Seymour had been Dolph Schayes's teammate, coach, and friend since 1948. Together they had been the heart and soul of the franchise.

To replace Seymour, Danny Biasone turned to Alex Hannum, who had played for the Nats in 1950 and 1951. In 1957 Hannum became the player-coach of the St. Louis Hawks and directed his team to the NBA finals, which the Hawks lost in double overtime to the Celtics. The following year, Hannum's Hawks defeated the Celtics in seven games to win their only NBA championship. After a contract dispute with Ben Kerner, St. Louis's owner, Hannum resigned. Jack and Jim Vickers of the Vickers Petroleum Company quickly moved in and signed Hannum to coach their Wichita Vickers in the National Industrial Basketball League. In 1959 Hannum coached the Vickers to a National AAU championship, then held in Denver, Colorado. After the 1960 season, Jack and Jim Vickers dropped their basketball program, which made Hannum available for the Syracuse job.[57]

The team that Hannum inherited lost George Yardley, who decided to retire. Although Yardley was not happy with his performance in the 1960

12. Alex Hannum, Syracuse's last coach, shows his displeasure with an official's call. Danny Biasone sits to his right. Courtesy of Gregory Newsome.

season, he still averaged 20.2 points per game. For Yardley, the decision to retire involved pursuing business interests in California and stabilizing his family life.[58] The Nats also lost Bob Hopkins, who had been a solid player for four years. After two years with Syracuse, Connie Dierking was also gone. The most significant addition was Dave Gambee, a six-foot-six forward with two years of NBA experience. From the Wichita Vickers Alex Hannum brought Harvey Wade "Swede" Halbrook, a seven-foot-three center with five years of AAU experience. Joe Roberts, a six-foot-six forward from Ohio State's 1960 NCAA championship team, was the only true rookie. Roberts was the third African American on the team, joining Dick Barnett and Hal Greer.

Syracuse's transformation paled against that experienced by the NBA itself. The biggest business news was Minneapolis's decision to move the Lakers to Los Angeles. With a new arena that sat fourteen thousand, fans poured into the facility to watch Elgin Baylor and Jerry West, a rookie from West Virginia. The NBA's biggest new star, however, was Oscar Robertson, with the Cincinnati Royals. As a rookie, Robertson averaged 30.5 points, 10 rebounds, and 9.7 assists. Higher salaries and the increasing cost of travel led to an expansion of the schedule to seventy-nine games from the seventy-five in 1960 and seventy-two in 1959.[59]

Snapshots

Harvey Wade "Swede" Halbrook and Dave Gambee

Wade "Swede" Halbrook was certainly one of the most enigmatic players of his time. At seven foot three, Halbrook's towering height seemed both a blessing and a curse. Born on January 30, 1933, in Dresden, Tennessee, Halbrook made his first impact as a basketball player at Lincoln High School in Portland, Oregon, where he enrolled as a sophomore in 1949. In 1952 Halbrook led Lincoln to the state high school basketball championship. As a senior Halbrook averaged 38.3 points per game and established a single-game tournament high with 51 points. He briefly held Oregon's single-game scoring record, with 71 points.[60]

In the fall of 1952, Halbrook entered Oregon State College in Corvallis (now Oregon State University), where he played for Amory "Slats" Gill. Because freshmen were not eligible for varsity competition, Halbrook had to wait for the fall of 1953 to play his first varsity game. In anticipation of the Halbrook era, Oregon State College sold four hundred more season tickets and anticipated sellouts for its fourteen home games. Halbrook lived up to all expectations on the court. As a sophomore he broke Cliff Crandall's season scoring record by scoring 614 points and led Oregon State to the Northern Division title in the Pacific Coast Conference. He was a unanimous choice on the All–Northern Division's first team. The University of Southern California defeated Oregon State in a three-game playoff to determine the Pacific Coast champion. In addition to on-court success, *Life* gave Halbrook national exposure by featuring him in its January 18, 1954, issue entitled "The World's Tallest Basketball Player."[61]

Unfortunately, there was a darker side to the Halbrook story. He fell into a pattern of missing classes and disappearing from view. Academically ineligible in the fall of 1954, Halbrook returned to competition in the spring of 1955. Gill had to suspend Halbrook once for falling back into his bad habits, but Halbrook returned and led Oregon State to the Pacific Coast Conference championship and a bid to the NCAA Tournament. After beating the University of Seattle easily, Oregon State met the University of San Francisco Dons, led by Bill Russell, on the Beavers' home floor. In a memorable game, the Dons escaped with a 57–56 victory on San Francisco's way to its first NCAA championship. This matchup was Halbrook's last college game. When Coach Gill told Halbrook that he would have to attend class and follow team rules, the big center replied that he could make no promises, which ended his collegiate career.[62]

For the next five seasons, Halbrook played for the Wichita Vickers in the National Industrial League. During those years the highlight of the season was the national Amateur Athletic Union tournament, held in Denver. Halbrook never made the AAU All-America team. In 1959 Wichita won the AAU tournament, but Halbrook was injured and did not play. Unfortunately, his personal behavior remained erratic, and periodically he would disappear.[63]

After the 1960 AAU tournament, the Wichita Vickers dropped its basketball program. In the summer of 1960, when Hannum agreed to coach the Syracuse Nationals, he took Halbrook with him to Syracuse, where Swede played two seasons and averaged 5.5 points per game. In the 1961 playoffs against the Philadelphia Warriors, Halbrook managed to shine and make a difference. Was there a basketball player buried in that seven-foot-three frame? Alex Hannum thought, "He could have had a worthwhile career if he had taken care of himself." After Syracuse cut him in 1962, Halbrook returned to Portland and lived by doing odd jobs. He died of a heart attack on April 5, 1988, at the age of fifty-five.[64]

If Halbrook had played his senior year, he and Dave Gambee would have been teammates in the latter's sophomore year. Gambee starred at Corvallis High School and, after considering the University of Washington, decided to stay at home and play for "Slats" Gill at Oregon State. By 1954–55, Gambee's freshman year, Gill had coached Oregon State for twenty-six years. Gambee thought of him as a rather stern father figure. As a coach Gill insisted that all of his players shoot their free throws underhanded—a throwback to Gill's playing days. Gambee worked on this shot so that when he entered the NBA, he was one of the last of the pros to employ the underhanded free throw. At six-foot-six and 215 pounds, Gambee played the forward position.

In 1958 the St. Louis Hawks drafted Gambee in the first round. There still were no agents to represent players, so Gambee negotiated his contract with Ben Kerner, the owner of the Hawks. Gambee wanted a no-cut contract, which Kerner agreed to, provided Gambee accept a smaller salary. Gambee signed for around nine thousand dollars and figured that the no-cut contract cost him about a thousand dollars.

After two games in the 1958–59 season, Gambee suffered an attack of appendicitis. When he returned, he practiced with the team but did not play another game. In the middle of the 1959–60 season, St. Louis sold Gambee's contract to the Cincinnati Royals, where he finished the season. The Hawks reacquired Gambee and then sold him to Syracuse.

Gambee's move to Syracuse was the best thing that happened to his basketball career. He immediately played more minutes and averaged double figures in scoring for the next five years. His first year in Syracuse also coincided with Hannum's return to Syracuse as the team's coach. Gambee had high praise for Hannum, who had the ability to "extract from each player their best talents without offending them." If Alex got on a player during the game, he usually followed up by explaining himself after the game over a beer at his favorite bar.

When Syracuse moved to Philadelphia, Gambee played there for four years. He was a member of the 1967 NBA champions. In Gambee's last three years in the NBA, he played on four different teams and retired after the 1969–70 season, after twelve years in the league.

Following every season Gambee and his wife, Joyce, whom he met at Corvallis High School, returned to Oregon. With his basketball days behind him, Gambee returned to Portland and got into the wholesale building-product business. Today Gambee, with two of his sons, owns the Shamrock Building Company, which employs fifty people and buys and sells steel and lumber.[65]

The 1960–61 Season

As the 1960–61 season evolved, Dolph Schayes picked up more honors. In November 1960 the Jewish Basketball League Alumni of Philadelphia honored Schayes as "the outstanding Jewish athlete in the United States." On January 1, 1961, writers and broadcasters placed Schayes on the East's starting five in the eleventh annual All-Star Game, which was played in Syracuse on January 17. The West routed the East, 153–131, as Oscar Robertson scored 23 points to go along with 9 rebounds and 14 assists to win MVP honors. Schayes did not disappoint the hometown fans, as he scored 21 points.

Later in the month Schayes passed the 17,000-point mark for his career. The Nats finished the season with a 38-41 mark for a third-place finish in the East, nineteen games behind Boston and eight behind Philadelphia.[66]

In the first round of the playoffs, the Nats surprised all the experts by eliminating the Warriors, 3–0. In the first game in Philadelphia, Syracuse nipped Philly, 115–107. Six Nats scored in double figures, with Larry Costello and Hal Greer paving the way with 28 and 25 points, respectively. Chamberlain led all scorers with 46 points, but Guy Rodgers with 22 points and Paul Arizin with 16 points were the only other Warriors in double figures. A key player for the Nats was Swede Halbrook, who scored 15 points and snared 15 rebounds in thirty-one minutes. Although Chamberlain had a big night, Bill Reddy wrote that Halbrook kept Wilt "frustrated a good share of the night." The Philly fans even gave him a "rousing cheer" when he left the game. Two days later the Nats squeezed by the Warriors, 115–114, at the War Memorial in what Jack Andrews called "one of the most exciting games in the history of the NBA playoffs." Playing in

13. Schayes drives the lane for a basket in the 1961 NBA All-Star Game played in Syracuse. Jerry West (44) and Walter Dukes (23) watch for the West. Courtesy of Gregory Newsome.

his thousandth game, Schayes, who had been held to 10 points in the first game, tallied 24 points but fouled out with almost eight minutes left to play and the Nats leading 101–88. Jack Andrews reported that the Nats, who had built up double-digit leads "on fast moving plays, slowed down their attack in favor of careful ball-handling and that was a mistake." Led by Guy Rodgers, who scored 10 points on a variety of different shots in a few minutes, the Warriors rallied to tie the game at 108. At this point Costello, Halbrook, and Greer hit free throws to secure the victory. Besides Schayes, Hal Greer with 26 and Larry Costello with 24 also topped the 20-point mark. Again the play of Swede Halbrook, called the "People's Choice" by Jack Andrews, grabbed attention. Halbrook scored 12 points, and Andrews called him "a defensive star against the great Wilt Chamberlain." The Warrior center had 32 points, followed by Rodgers with 26 and Arizin with 21. The Nats and Warriors met at the University of Pennsylvania's Palestra for the third game of the five-game series. Before a crowd of 6,389, the Nats shocked the Warriors by sweeping the series, 106–103. Down by five after three periods, 82–77, the Nats rallied to take a 93–92 lead with less than seven minutes left, which they never relinquished. One of the keys to the win was that the Nats outrebounded the Warriors, 83–58. While Chamberlain led all rebounders with 23, Kerr with 18, Schayes with 15, and Halbrook with 11 more than neutralized him. As important was Syracuse's superior free-throw shooting. The Nats made 24 of 29 attempts, while the Warriors made just 23 of 49 opportunities. Schayes hit all 7 of his free throws, while Chamberlain made 7 of his 14 chances. Costello's 20 points led a balanced scoring attack, as five other Nats were in double figures. Chamberlain led Philadelphia with 33, followed by Arizin's 30, but the Nats limited Rodgers to 5 points.[67]

The Eastern Division playoffs began in Boston, just fifteen hours after the Nats had eliminated the Warriors. Before 7,728 at the Garden in a game televised nationally, the Celtics dispatched the Nats, 128–115. Schayes led all players with 26 points, while Greer and Barnett each tallied 20 points. Ramsey, Cousy, Russell, and Heinsohn all poured in 20 or more points for the Celtics.[68]

Three days later the Nationals bounced back in Syracuse and posted a 115–98 victory over the Celtics, before 6,657 fans. After the game Hannum

14. Bill Russell blocks Dolph Schayes's hook shot. "Swede" Halbrook (11) and Hall Greer (15) look on for the Nats. Tommy Heinsohn screens out Halbrook. Courtesy of Gregory Newsome.

said, "Every single guy on our club was great tonight." Schayes led all players again with 32. Hannum observed that Schayes "was getting driving
shots, outside shots, everything, and he really crashed the boards. This
game was a lasting tribute to the guy." Dick Barnett, Hannum thought,
played "an absolutely sensational game. He played a tremendous defensive
game." Danny Biasone chimed in, "He chased everyone dizzily." Johnny
Kerr matched Bill Russell's 17 points, which was another key to the victory. Finally, Larry Costello outscored Bob Cousy, 15–11.[69]

The Celtics grabbed a 2–1 lead in the series as they dominated the
Nats, 133–110, before 11,754 fans at the Boston Garden. Bill Sharman hit
for 30 points, and Tom Heinsohn picked up 24 points. Tom "Satch" Sanders, Boston's defensive specialist, limited Dolph Schayes to 18, as Dick
Barnett led the Nats with 22. In the fourth game, the home-court magic
failed, as Syracuse lost, 120–107. When the series returned to Boston the
Celtics captured the Eastern Division playoff, 123–101. For three quarters only a few points separated the two teams. At the beginning of the
fourth quarter, the Celtics outscored the Nats 14–3 and cruised to victory
from that point. Sharman led all scorers with 27 points, and Russell added
25 points plus an eye-popping 33 rebounds. Schayes fouled out with 17
points, second to Barnett with 25 points.[70] The Celtics won their fourth
NBA title, by easily beating the St. Louis Hawks.

Dolph Schayes finished the regular season with 23.5 points per game.
The writers placed Schayes on the All-NBA second team. It was the
twelfth time that Schayes had earned a spot on the All-NBA first or second team. For thirteen straight years, Schayes had led Syracuse in points
and rebounds.

Before the 1961–62 season, the NBA expanded to Chicago, which
had not had a team since 1950. It was the first time the NBA had nine
teams since Baltimore dropped out in 1954. Expansion had its own set of
problems. At the end of the 1960–61 season, the New York Knicks were
clearly the worst team in the NBA. For the health of the league, a strong
team at Madison Square Garden made sense. Unfortunately, in 1961 Walt
Bellamy, a six-foot-eleven center from the University of Indiana, was the
only player coming out of the college game who could possibly make a difference for the Knicks. Instead, the NBA awarded Chicago the first pick,

and the Packers took Bellamy. The result was that the NBA had two weak franchises—Chicago and New York.[71]

Another irritant for the NBA was that Abe Saperstein, the owner of the Harlem Globetrotters, formed the American Basketball League to compete with the NBA. Saperstein's motivation was grounded primarily in resentment. As early as March 1959 Saperstein was annoyed with Eddie Gottlieb for luring Wilt Chamberlain away from the Globetrotters to play for his Warriors. Saperstein began to take steps to form a new league, which might have been headed off by the NBA if it had given him an NBA franchise. In the 1950s the Globetrotters frequently agreed to play games as part of a doubleheader with NBA teams. Often fans came to see the Globetrotters, and the NBA hoped that they would stick around to see its teams. Because Saperstein had helped the NBA, he thought it owed him a franchise now that it was making money. When it did not happen, Saperstein proceeded to form his own league, which, as noted, folded in the middle of its second season in a sea of red ink.[72]

Snapshot

Lee Shaffer

The Nats added two players for the 1961–62 season, Lee Shaffer, a six-foot-seven forward from the University of North Carolina, and Paul Neumann, a six-foot-one guard from Stanford. While Neumann would average 6 points off the bench, Shaffer was an immediate starter at the forward position, opposite Dolph Schayes, and established a club scoring record for rookies by chalking up 16.9 points a game. Shaffer came to the Nats in a roundabout way. In 1960 Shaffer was a consensus second-team All-America selection at North Carolina and the Atlantic Coast Conference Basketball Player of the Year. The Nats made Shaffer the fifth overall pick in the first round of the 1960 draft, which included Oscar Robertson, Jerry West, Lenny Wilkens, and Tom Sanders, all future Hall of Famers. Rather than signing with the Nats, Shaffer signed with the New York Tuck Tapers in the National Industrial League. Paul Cohen, the president of the Technical Tape Company, offered Shaffer a package worth $25,000 for two years and the promise of future employment in the company. After the 1960–61 season Cohen disbanded the team and gave up on any dreams of entering professional basketball.

When Danny Biasone learned of the dissolution of the Tuck Tapers, he called Shaffer and told him that the Nats needed him. He offered Shaffer $12,500, which matched his salary with the Tuck Tapers, and threw in $1,000 for moving expenses. Biasone also signed Paul Neumann, who had been Shaffer's teammate with the Tuck Tapers. The Nats had drafted Neumann in 1959, but he elected to play AAU ball until signing in 1961.

In the late summer of 1961, Dolph Schayes invited Lee to work as a counselor at his basketball camp. After one of the scrimmages, Shaffer remembered that Dolph came up to him and said, "You can help us." During Shaffer's first year, he and Dolph were roommates on the road, and Shaffer remembered that Dolph could not have been more helpful. When Shaffer was frustrated by a lack of playing time, Dolph reminded him to be patient, take care of himself, and remember that it was a long season. As he did with so many of his teammates, Dolph challenged him to a free-throw contest, where the veteran insisted that they could only count perfect swishes as made free throws. Shaffer wondered how such a big guy could have such a soft touch.

Shaffer also got the Alex Hannum treatment. In a game at San Francisco, Hannum took Shaffer out of the game, and Lee began throwing towels and generally showing his disgust with the coach's decision. Alex, who would back down to nobody, responded in a vintage Hannum way. He came over to Lee and said, "If you don't settle down, I am going to kick the bleep out of you before the entire arena." After the game, Alex and Lee went out for a few beers and resolved their differences.

Shaffer loved the Nats' style of play. It was still the New York style, with the floor balanced, everybody touching the ball, and running the court. In 1961–62 seven players scored in double figures, which was testimony to Syracuse's team play. Al Bianchi told me that at the end of games when the Nats were ahead, the team's goal was to make sure that as many players as possible finished in double figures.[73] In his second year with Syracuse, Shaffer averaged 18.6 points per game and played in the 1963 NBA All-Star Game, scoring 12 points in the East's victory. Although the franchise was nearing the end of its tenure in Syracuse, the Nats remained a family on and off the court. Shaffer recalled that everybody loved Biasone, thought that Hannum was a great leader, and enjoyed informal gatherings, often at Schayes's home, where Naomi would prepare the food, all of which created an atmosphere that would be difficult to reproduce today.[74]

Shaffer was involved in the biggest trade in the early history of the NBA. On January 13, 1965, the Philadelphia 76ers traded Connie Dierking, Paul Neumann, and Lee Shaffer to the San Francisco Warriors for Wilt Chamberlain. The trade would have reunited Shaffer with Alex Hannum, who had become San Francisco's coach in the 1963–64 season. There was a catch. Shaffer had not signed a contract to play with the 76ers for the 1964–65 season. When San Francisco offered Shaffer forty thousand dollars, an excellent salary in 1965, he turned the Warriors down. The offer could not compete with a golden business opportunity offered to Shaffer by Frank H. Kenan, a successful North Carolina entrepreneur and one of the University of North Carolina's major benefactors. Shaffer had worked for Kenan in the summers while attending UNC and playing for the Tar Heels. In 1964 Kenan offered Shaffer a 10 percent share of the business, if he would join the Kenan Transport Company, already the Southeast's largest petroleum hauler. When Shaffer told Irv Kosloff that this business opportunity was too good to pass up, the 76ers' owner understood his position. In 1970 Shaffer became the chief executive officer of Kenan Transport Company and in 2001 became the chairman of the board.[75]

The 1961–62 Season

The season started well for Schayes. On November 15, 1961, Arthur Daley of the *New York Times* reported that Schayes had just played his 683rd consecutive game, establishing a new record for endurance. After watching Schayes, Daley thought he could "continue indefinitely as the dribbling counterpart of Lou Gehrig, the original Iron Horse."[76] On November 14 the New York University Varsity Club presented Schayes and Sam Mele with the first Violet Award, recognizing the alumni of the year in sports. Mele played baseball and basketball at NYU before playing eleven years and managing in the major leagues.[77] On December 22 writers and broadcasters named Schayes to the Eastern Division's All-Star starting lineup for the twelfth consecutive time. Schayes had missed just one All-Star Game because of an injury. In ten All-Star Games, Schayes had scored 138 points. Only Bob Pettit of the St. Louis Hawks, with 142 points, had scored more than Schayes.[78] Three days after his selection to the East's All-Star squad, Schayes fractured his cheekbone in a collision with Al Attles of the Philadelphia Warriors while the two players were fighting for a loose ball. Schayes's streak of consecutive games ended at 705, 764 if playoff games were added to the regular-season games. Syracuse's star had not missed a game since February 17, 1952.[79]

Schayes missed 13 games and by February was playing sparingly with a protective mask. The mask was heavy and poorly designed, and it limited Dolph's peripheral vision.

Consequently, Schayes's effectiveness was diminished. To fill in for Schayes, Syracuse purchased the contract of Joe Graboski, an eight-year veteran with the Philadelphia Warriors. Adding to Syracuse's woes, Larry Costello broke his wrist on January 7. Then Graboski fractured his elbow in a game with Philadelphia. As Schayes recovered from his facial injury, fluid began to collect in his left knee, and he was forced to wear a cumbersome knee brace. The combination of the two injuries cost Schayes 24 games. As the season neared its end, Hal Greer suffered a thigh injury, and Swede Halbrook injured his knee. Despite all the injuries, Alex Hannum managed to keep the team competitive, and Syracuse finished with a 41-39 record, good for a third-place finish in the NBA's Eastern Division.

Once again the Nats met the Philadelphia Warriors in the first round of the Eastern Division playoffs. The two teams had split the 12 games they played in the regular season. In Wilt Chamberlain's three seasons with the Warriors, Philadelphia and Syracuse had split 44 games. During the regular season Chamberlain scored 4,029 points and averaged an unheard-of 50.4 points per game. This amount was twice as many as George Yardley had scored in 1958. As the Nats entered the playoffs, they reminded their fans of 1954's "Bandage Brigade," as Greer, Halbrook, Schayes, Costello, Bianchi, and Graboski had all been injured at one time or another in the season. On the eve of the first playoff game, Hannum reported that Hal

15. Wearing a protective mask, Schayes drives to the basket against the
New York Knicks. Courtesy of Gregory Newsome.

16. Wilt Chamberlain rebounds over Dolph Schayes in the 1962 play-offs. Johnny Kerr (10) and Larry Costello (21) look on for the Nats. Tom Meschery (14) and Paul Arizin (11) watch for Philadelphia. Courtesy of Gregory Newsome.

Greer, who had led the Nats in scoring with a 22.8 average, could see only limited action with a thigh injury.

In the opener at Philadelphia's Convention Hall, the Warriors topped the Nats, 110–103. Two days later the Warriors stunned the Nats, 97–82, in Syracuse. The following night the Nats surprised the Warriors, 101–100, in Philadelphia. Lee Shaffer led the Nats with 30 points, and Schayes came off the bench to score 22 points. In their third game in three days, the Nats evened the series with a 106–99 squeaker in Syracuse. Johnny Kerr outrebounded Chamberlain, 22–20, and had 27 points, just 1 less than Chamberlain. Five Nats were in double figures, including Schayes with 14 points. Two nights later in Philadelphia, the Warriors outscored the Nats, 121–104, to take the series. Wilt Chamberlain set a new NBA playoff scoring record by tallying 56 points.[80]

The Warriors forced the Celtics to the seventh game of the Eastern Division finals, which Boston won, 109–107. Then the Celtics won their fifth NBA crown by edging the Los Angeles Lakers in 7 games, the last game a 110–107 overtime victory.

The 1962 season was a disappointment for Schayes. The broken cheek bone followed by a knee injury limited Schayes to 56 games. For the first time he was not his team's leading scorer and rebounder. Even with reduced playing time, Schayes finished with a respectable 14.7 average.

Snapshot

Chet Walker

In the spring of 1962 Syracuse's top-two draft choices were Len Chappell and Chet Walker. Of the two Chet Walker would quickly turn out to be a star. Walker was born in Bethlehem, Mississippi, on February 22, 1940, to Regina and John Walker. When Walker was ten years old, his mother took him and two brothers to Benton Harbor, Michigan, to escape an abusive relationship with her husband and to find a new life. She chose Benton Harbor because one of her sons had run away from home and settled there. On the playgrounds of Benton Harbor, Chet

Walker discovered that he possessed marvelous basketball skills. By his senior year of high school, Walker led his team to the 1958 state finals at Jennison Fieldhouse on the campus of Michigan State University. In one of the most memorable games in Michigan high school basketball history, Benton Harbor lost 71–68 to Detroit's Austin High School, led by Dave DeBusschere. Four years later Walker and DeBusschere would be dueling in the NBA.

Walker played his college basketball at Bradley University in Peoria, Illinois. One of the highlights of his collegiate career came in 1960, when Bradley won the National Invitational Tournament at Madison Square Garden. In 1962 the *Sporting News* placed Walker on its All-America first team. Syracuse selected Walker in the second round of the 1962 draft, and he immediately fitted into Syracuse's team concept. Walker liked Alex Hannum and admired Syracuse's passing game and the veterans who played it. As a rookie Chet Walker averaged 12.2 points per game. When Syracuse moved to Philadelphia and became the 76ers, Walker continued to average double figures. In 1967 he was the starting forward on the 76ers team that won the NBA championship that ended Boston's streak of eight straight championships. In 1969 the 76ers traded Walker to the Chicago Bulls, where he played until he retired in 1975. Walker played in seven All-Star Games and finished his thirteen-year career with an 18.2 average. In 1988 Chet Walker earned an Emmy for producing *A Mother's Courage: The Mary Thomas Story*. Mary Thomas was Isiah Thomas's mother.[81] In 2012 Walker was inducted into the Basketball Hall of Fame in Springfield, Massachusetts.

The 1962–63 Season

On May 13, 1962, the *Syracuse Post-Standard* announced that Dolph Schayes had signed to play his fifteenth season for the Nationals. The announcement came one day before the Chamber of Commerce met to unveil a new ticket plan designed to lure fans to the games. Beginning with the 1957–58 season, Syracuse's attendance never exceeded 112,000, placing it near the bottom in the NBA. Syracuse had always struggled financially, and escalating travel costs and upward pressures on salaries left the franchise in a precarious position.[82] Meanwhile, Eddie Gottlieb sold the Warriors to a group from San Francisco for $850,000, leaving Philadelphia without an NBA basketball team. With the San Francisco Warriors moving into the Western Division, Cincinnati moved from the Western to the Eastern Division.[83]

The 1962–63 season was the last for Syracuse in the NBA. The team played extremely well, finishing the season with a 48-32 mark for a second-place finish. On January 22, 1963, Schayes played in his 1,000th regular-season game, before 15,034 fans at Madison Square Garden. In a ceremony after the game, Schayes told the cheering crowd, "The first 1,000 were tough; the second 1,000 should be tougher." As Schayes reflected upon his career, he added, "Imagine a big guy like me and all those points and I never dunked a shot." Because Schayes had played only fifteen minutes in this game, writers asked him if he planned to retire after the season. Schayes said that the answer to that question depended on how his left knee responded in the remaining games of the season. "If I can't help the team," Schayes concluded, "I won't linger on."[84] A month later Schayes scored the 19,000th point of his professional career.

On March 3, in Syracuse, Maurice Podoloff presented Dolph Schayes with a color television set in celebration of the Syracuse star's 1,000 games, 19,000 points, and 3,000 assists. Podoloff concluded his tribute by saying that Schayes was "a credit to yourself, to your adopted city of Syracuse, and to the league." Dolph replied that while the game had changed significantly since 1948, "Danny Biasone and Maurice Podoloff have had the same type of monumental character—and Syracuse fans have remained, as you were in 1948 . . . the greatest fans in the world."[85]

While Schayes's future was up in the air, the same was not true for Bob Cousy, who had announced that he would retire and become the head basketball coach at Boston College. On March 16 Cousy played his last game in Syracuse, and Schayes presented him with a silver service. In thirteen seasons they had played against each other in more than 150 games. Schayes told Cousy that he had the unique ability "to perform the impossible, coming up with plays game after game." Cousy repaid the compliment by telling the fans, "You have been fortunate in having

17. On March 3, 1963, Maurice Podoloff presents Dolph Schayes with a television to mark his one thousand games, nineteen thousand points, and three thousand assists. Courtesy of Gregory Newsome.

a player like Dolph, who has personified everything good that there is in this game. He has never given anything but his best." Just over 7,000 fans gave Cousy a two-minute standing ovation.[86]

Ironically, on the very next day, St. Patrick's Day, the Boston Celtics honored Cousy, and the Nats were their opponents. Schayes remembered that after all the proclamations were read and the speeches were made, Cousy was asked to speak. With tears in his eyes, Cousy struggled to find the right words when, Schayes remembered, the fans started to chant, "Cousy, Cousy, Cousy." When Dolph saw that even the officials were teary eyed, he thought to himself, "We are in trouble."[87]

One venerable sports cliché is that "records are made to be broken." When Dolph Schayes played his 1,000th regular-season NBA game, he had scored more points and gathered in more rebounds than any other player in NBA history. The latter record was about to be broken by Bill Russell in his seventh season of play. Bill Reddy, sports editor of the *Post-Standard*, was not unconditionally ready to surrender the record to Russell.

Bob Cousy with Dolph Schayes. Cousy's final game in Syracuse's War Memorial. March 16, 1963

18. On March 16, 1963, Dolph Schayes congratulates Bob Cousy as the Nats honor the Celtics star on his last game in Syracuse. Courtesy of Gregory Newsome.

He pointed out that in the first two years that Schayes played in the NBA, the league did not keep rebounding statistics.[88]

In the first round of the NBA playoffs, the Nats met Oscar Robertson and the Cincinnati Royals. Because the Nats had finished 6 games ahead of the Royals, they had the home-court advantage in the 5-game series. In the opener 4,335 fans watched the Nats edge the Royals, 123–120. In the first half Schayes helped keep the Nats in the game by scoring all of his 17 points. In the second half Hal Greer scored 23 points of his game-high 32 to secure the victory.[89] The second game, played in Cincinnati, was the 100th playoff game for Schayes, which established a new record for playoff appearances by an NBA player. The Royals evened the series with an easy 133–115 win.[90] The Nats jumped to a 2–1 lead in Syracuse by winning a squeaker, 121–117.[91] When the series returned to the Queen City, the Royals prevailed, 125–118.[92] The deciding game was played before a capacity crowd of 7,418 at Syracuse's War Memorial, and the hometown fans watched the Royals capture the series, as they edged the Nats, 131–127, in overtime. Oscar Robertson led the Royals with 32 points, followed by Jack Twyman's 24 points and Bob Boozer's 20 points. Lee Shaffer led all scorers with 45 points for the Nats.[93]

Playing on a bad knee, Schayes missed 14 regular-season games and averaged a career-low 9.5 points per game. For the second year Hal Greer led the Nats in scoring by averaging 19.5 points per game. Lee Shaffer finished just behind Greer with an 18.1 average, and Chet Walker, at the other forward, had a solid rookie season with a 12.2 average.

Despite playing well during the season and in the playoffs, the Nats drew only 102,209 fans. This figure was a significant increase over the 73,946 of the previous year, but not enough to keep the team in Syracuse. In May 1963 Danny Biasone sold his franchise for $500,000 to two Philadelphia businessmen, Isaac "Ike" Richman and Irv Kosloff. Richman and Kosloff were longtime friends who graduated from the same Philadelphia high school in 1930. Richman graduated from Temple University and its law school in the mid-1930s. While Richman was lawyering, Kosloff was building the Roosevelt Paper Company. One of Richman's clients was Eddie Gottlieb, also a family friend. In 1959 Richman was instrumental in persuading Wilt Chamberlain to sign a contract with the Philadelphia

Warriors. Gottlieb had coveted Chamberlain ever since Wilt had starred at Philadelphia's Overbrook High School. In the summer of 1962, Eddie Gottlieb sold the Philadelphia Warriors to a small group of San Francisco investors for $850,000. This move left Philadelphia without a team. Gottlieb knew that Danny Biasone would be receptive to an offer to sell the Nats and urged Richman to make a bid. Richman persuaded Kosloff, who had deeper pockets, to join him in bringing basketball back to Philadelphia.[94]

The sale of the Nats caught Dolph Schayes by surprise. Naomi Schayes remembered that the experience was very emotional, and for two days she suffered from a migraine headache. She was cool to the idea of moving to Philadelphia and remembered that her father said she had no choice.[95] In its seventeen-year history, Biasone had run the franchise on a shoestring, but it had always survived. The Nats had been an asset to the business community of Syracuse. Mutual of New York, an insurance company, had just moved to Syracuse and cited the Nats as one of the city's attractions, along with the schools, symphony, and hospitals. Because Biasone had kept the negotiations close to his vest, he did not give other Syracuse business interests an opportunity to rescue the team. Biasone claimed to have lost $20,000 in the 1962–63 season and expected to lose $100,000 the following year. The increasing cost of air travel, upward pressures on salaries, and the cost of leasing the War Memorial were reasons offered for the sale. Of today's American professional sports franchises, the Green Bay Packers are the only small-market team to have survived. Syracuse was the last of the small-market teams to compete in the NBA. Given the economic challenges, only some combination of local big investors could have saved the franchise. While the Syracuse fans who attended were rabid, they simply did not come in sufficient numbers. Between 1958 and 1962, the Nats never drew more than 112,486 fans in a season. During that period Syracuse was near the bottom or at the bottom in league attendance. Syracuse was the smallest city in the NBA and not growing. Like Les Harrison before him, Danny Biasone simply succumbed to reality.

Jack Andrews had covered the Nats for seventeen years and thought that Biasone finally "ran out of miracles, and financial common sense finally over-balanced his stubborn aim to keep the flag flying here." As

Andrews reviewed the history of the Nats, he reserved his highest praise for "the greatest of them all, a basketball immortal as he observes his 35th birthday today—Dolph Schayes." Despite all his records, Andrews stressed, "Dolph would be the first to tell you the Nats were never a one-man show." In seventeen years the Nats won 714 and lost 575. Only the Celtics had won more games than the Nats. Syracuse had never missed the playoffs in its seventeen-year history. More than 2.3 million fans watched them play. Jack Andrews ended his brief overview of the team's history by writing, "Farewell Nats, we had a wonderful time together."[96]

Along with the sale of Syracuse, the struggling Chicago franchise moved to Baltimore. The summer of 1963 was also notable in NBA history because it marked the retirement of Maurice Podoloff, the league's commissioner since its formation in 1946 as the Basketball Association of America. After seventeen years the NBA was clearly major league and here to stay. To replace Podoloff, the NBA hired Walter Kennedy, who had a varied career in public relations in sports at Notre Dame, his alma mater, and the Basketball Association of America, before establishing his own public relations firm, which had the Harlem Globetrotters as a client. In 1959 he was elected mayor of Stamford, Connecticut, where he grew up and coached high school basketball briefly in the 1930s.[97]

4

The Transition Game

From Player to Coach

In May 1963 Dolph Schayes celebrated his thirty-fifth birthday. For the last season and a half, Schayes's knee problems had reduced his effectiveness. Finally, Schayes decided to have surgery on his left knee. His surgeon got rid of the arthritis and calcium deposits that had given him so much pain. It left him pain free. Dolph remembered that he felt fantastic.

He had scored 19,115 points in regular-season play and in one good year could surpass the coveted 20,000 mark. Then events intervened. Alex Hannum decided he would not accompany the team to Philadelphia, and Ike Richman, who assumed the duties of general manager, offered the coaching position to Schayes. In considering this offer, Naomi Schayes recalled that she "practically begged" Dolph not to coach and told him that he would be miserable. Despite her advice, on July 15, 1963, he signed a two-year contract to coach the Philadelphia 76ers. Later Dolph admitted that Naomi was right and called the decision to coach the worst of his professional career. Years later he reflected that he was not prepared to coach and still wanted to be a full-time player. Playing coaches, however, had been fairly common in the early history of the NBA.[1]

Publicly, however, Schayes had to answer questions about his approach to coaching. Not surprisingly, Schayes fell back on what had worked for him in the school yards of the Bronx, at New York University, and with Syracuse. "Our style of play is the only way to play the game," Dolph said. He added, "We'll still use the give-and-go, everyone getting into the act." Schayes traced the Syracuse style back to Al Cervi and, with some refinements, continued by Paul Seymour and Alex Hannum. Schayes also

128

revealed another part of his personality, which was an offbeat sense of humor. Contemplating the possibility of preseason training in Hawaii, Schayes joked, "I hope they train. If they don't, I'll hit 'em over the head with a pineapple."[2]

Schayes found it difficult to focus on both tasks. As it turned out, he played in only 24 games and scored 134 points. Besides holding an array of offensive records, Dolph Schayes had one more distinction when he retired as a player. Going back to 1949 when the NBA opened play, Dolph Schayes was the only player to compete in every one of its first fifteen seasons. As professional basketball evolved during this period, Schayes always managed to perform at a high level. As the NBA eventually established itself as one of America's major professional sports, Dolph Schayes has to be included as one of those players who made it all possible.

The transition to Philadelphia for the Nats was very difficult. The attendance was abysmal, as Philly fans seemed unwilling to support players they had rooted against for so many years. Another reason for the poor response was that the *Philadelphia Inquirer* and *Philadelphia Daily News* refused to cover the games. Walter Annenberg, a wealthy businessman, owned both papers and seemed determined to see the 76ers flop. The 76ers' management could only speculate on Annenberg's motives, as he would not talk with them. One theory was that Annenberg was annoyed with the 76ers because Richman wanted to make Les Keiter, a popular sports broadcaster under contract with WIFL, owned by Annenberg, the general manager of the team. Schayes believed that another possible explanation was that Annenberg did not like Eddie Gottlieb and thought that he was part of the 76ers' operation. The sale of the Warriors did not endear Gottlieb to Philly basketball fans. While the NBA hired Gottlieb to make the schedule, he spent a lot of time in the 76ers' offices, which may have encouraged his critics to conclude that Gottlieb was part of the management.[3]

If Philadelphia did not show much brotherly love, it did not help that the 76ers were an average team that first year and struggled to make the playoffs. Before the 1963–64 season, Philadelphia failed to add a significant player. The 76ers released Tom Hoover, their first-round draft choice, just before the season, and then they sold Len Chappell to the Knicks.[4]

Injuries followed, cutting into the team's depth. Dave Gambee suffered a foot injury in late November.[5] Then Lee Shaffer went down with an injury. On January 29, 1964, Larry Costello suffered an ankle injury that kept him out of more than 19 games. The one bright spot in the season was the play of Hal Greer. On the last two nights of November, Greer had back-to-back 43-point games. On February 21, Greer hit a career high of 50 points, as the 76ers routed Boston, 144–119.[6] In his sixth year in the NBA, Greer averaged 23.3 points per game, the first of seven years in which he would average more than 20 points per game.

During the season Schayes saw two of his records broken. On December 28, 1963, Johnny Kerr played in his 707th consecutive game in the NBA, one more than Schayes's streak. Kerr had not missed a game since he started playing with Syracuse in 1954.[7] On February 8, 1964, Bob Pettit of the St. Louis Hawks scored his 19,215th point in the NBA to pass Schayes, who had 19,209 points.[8]

The 76ers finished the season in third place with a record of 34-46. Boston won the Eastern Division with 58 wins, and the Cincinnati Royals were 4 games behind with 54 wins. For the second straight year the Royals and 76ers squared off in a 5-game series to determine who would play the Celtics. The Royals were led by the incomparable Oscar Robertson, who was setting a new standard for guard play in the NBA. Jerry Lucas, Arlen Bockhorn, and Jack Twyman gave the Royals three scoring threats, and Wayne Embry provided solid play at the center position. Tom Hawkins provided punch off the bench. The 76ers surprised all the experts by splitting the first 4 games of the series and pushing the Royals to a fifth game in Cincinnati. In that crucial game Robertson scored 32 points, as the Royals squeaked by the 76ers, 130–124. Robertson made all nine of his field-goal attempts in the second half, as he put on a brilliant shooting display. Johnny Kerr led the 76ers with 31 points, followed by Chet Walker's 27 and Paul Neumann's 22.[9]

Despite making the playoffs, Schayes's transition to coaching was not an easy one. Philadelphia's cool reception to the team, the newspaper blackout, and injuries to key players were all hurdles that Schayes had to overcome. Moreover, there was the challenge of coaching players who had been his teammates and friends. In an interview Schayes said, "I figured these players were my friends, that they wouldn't let me down—and they didn't. They worked hard for me." While the effort was there, Schayes said, "They weren't always doing things the way I asked them. Finally I had to make them pay attention."[10]

As Schayes and the 76ers looked to the future, some of the pieces of the puzzle were in place. Hal Greer had established himself as one of the premier guards in the NBA, and Chet Walker averaged 17.3 points per game in his second year in the league. In the summer of 1964, the 76ers' first-round draft choice was Lucious "Luke" Jackson, a six-foot-nine, 240-pound center from Pan-American, who would become a force at power forward.

While Dolph Schayes, Ike Richman, and Irv Kosloff were figuring out their next moves, the NBA and the United States were in the throes of significant change. On the bright side, the NBA experienced a 20 percent increase in attendance, reaching a new high of 2.5 million paying customers. In 1963–64 the NBA did not have a television contract, but in the summer of 1964 Walter Kennedy negotiated a $650,000 deal with ABC for Sunday-afternoon games. In the third year ABC paid out $1 million. Perhaps the best indicator of the NBA's new status came in 1965 when Bob Short sold the Lakers to Jack Kent Cooke for $5 million. The game was faster, the players more athletic, and the fans obviously loved it.[11]

The growing popularity of professional sports, especially football and basketball, took place against a background of profound social change. For young America Bob Dylan captured it best in "The Times Are a-Changin'" when he pronounced, "The old order is changin'." The establishment was under attack. On August 28, 1963, several hundred thousand marched on Washington and heard Martin Luther King's "I Have a Dream" speech. On June 11, 1964, Congress passed the Civil Rights Act, the most far-reaching civil rights legislation in the nation's history. In the fall of 1964, a "Free Speech Movement" paralyzed the University of California at Berkeley. By August 1965 the Voting Rights Act ended literacy tests in the South.

On January 14, 1964, the NBA players staged their own protest. The occasion was the fourteenth annual All-Star Game, held at the Boston Garden. For this game the NBA formed its own TV network to increase its exposure and project the star quality of the league. While the fans watched an old-timers game, the All-Stars threatened a strike unless the owners recognized the right of the players' association to bargain and agreed to develop a pension plan. Maurice Podoloff had stalled the players for years, but on January 14 the All-Stars had a lot of leverage. Thirty minutes before tip-off, Walter Kennedy met the All-Stars and promised them he would make a good-faith effort to persuade the owners to meet their demands. The players, taking Kennedy at his word, relented and took the floor, saving the NBA much embarrassment. While the East All-Stars posted a 111–107 victory, the game was almost anticlimactic, given the drama that preceded it. Leonard Koppett, the dean of basketball writers at the time, believed that the crisis had come to a head because of the shortsightedness of the NBA owners. Nonetheless, the threatened strike was a portent of the future, as labor relations became more prominent in the future of professional sports. After the season Kennedy succeeded in persuading the owners to agree to a pension plan.[12]

From the beginning the owners had their defenders. Arthur Daley, sports columnist for the *New York Times*, thought that part of the problem was that the NBA was "trapped by its pretense that it's a big-league, thriving organization." Although Daley agreed with Koppett that "the owners had been dragging their feet for many years," it irked him that the "underprivileged athletes evoked considerable sympathy in their battle against their capitalistic exploiters, the owners."[13] But just as the players were changing, so were the owners. By 1967 Danny Biasone, Les Harrison, and Eddie Gottlieb were gone. The future of ownership was shifting to owners and corporations, who would see their teams as components of their larger business portfolios. In the dance between owners and players, each side tried to convince the public that the preponderance of greed rested with the other side.

As the battle for civil rights raged, *Ebony* reported that in 1964 48 percent of NBA players were black, the highest percentage in any of the major sports in the United States. In 1966 the Boston Celtics named Bill Russell its player-coach, the first African American to coach an NBA team.[14]

In the fall of 1964 Dolph Schayes was strictly a bench coach. By the All-Star Game, played on January 6, 1965, the 76ers were a respectable

20-18. The Celtics were in first place with a sparkling 34-7 record. Reflecting the growing popularity of professional basketball, a record-breaking crowd of 16,713 poured into the St. Louis Arena and watched the East All-Stars beat the West All-Stars, 124–123. At intermission the NBA honored Danny Biasone, Eddie Gottlieb, Maurice Podoloff, and Walter Brown posthumously. Brown, the original owner of the Celtics, died on September 17, 1964.

Biasone called "basketball the greatest game going. We have the game just about where we want it now."[15] The biggest buzz at the game, however, was a rumor that Wilt Chamberlain was about to be traded. The rumor was true.

Snapshot

Wilt Chamberlain

On January 13, 1965, after the All-Star Game, the San Francisco Warriors traded Wilt Chamberlain to the Philadelphia 76ers for Connie Dierking, Paul Neumann, the rights to Lee Shaffer (who had not signed a contract), and $150,000.[16] When the Warriors moved to San Francisco, the franchise struggled. Paul Arizin and Tom Gola refused to follow the team, so in 1962–63 the Warriors failed to make the playoffs or to excite fan interest. Chamberlain, however, averaged 44.8 points per game to lead the NBA in scoring. The following season San Francisco hired Alex Hannum, and, with a stronger supporting cast, the team rebounded to win the Western Division, as Chamberlain won the scoring crown with a 36.9 average. In the playoffs the Warriors reached the finals by beating St. Louis in seven games, but fell to Boston in the championship series, four games to one.

In the fall of 1964 Chamberlain was suffering from pancreatitis, and the Warriors got off to a slow start. Since the attendance at Warrior games was abysmal, the owners decided that their best business strategy was to get rid of Chamberlain and his salary. With the $150,000 from Philadelphia, the Warriors almost had enough money to take care of their payroll. Ike Richman and Irv Kosloff thought that Chamberlain would draw fans and make the 76ers more competitive. From Hannum's perspective the key to the trade was Lee Shaffer, but, as observed earlier, he left professional basketball to pursue a business opportunity.[17]

When Schayes responded to questions from the press about Chamberlain, he was extremely positive and was quoted as saying, "I think I'm dreaming."[18] Schayes thought Chamberlain was coachable, despite conflicting evidence. Although it was too late to catch the Celtics, the 76ers were now a playoff threat. Chamberlain also energized Philly basketball fans. In their first fourteen games, the 76ers drew just under 50,000 fans. With Chamberlain the 76ers had capacity crowds in Wilt's first three home appearances, attracting 26,857 fans.[19]

In his first year in the NBA, Chamberlain set a new scoring record by averaging 37.6 points per game. He was the rookie of the year and most valuable player. Chamberlain continued to lead the league in scoring for the next four seasons. In 1961–62 he averaged 50.4 points per game and scored 100 points against the Knicks on March 12, 1962, in Hershey, Pennsylvania.[20] The day after the trade, Leonard Koppett wrote that "Wilt is certainly the biggest name in his sport" and "the highest paid." But, Koppett continued, "Wilt was not popular." Part of Chamberlain's problem was that he broke records so easily that his critics credited it to his physical advantages rather than skill. Along with diminishing his achievements, his critics repeatedly pointed out that Chamberlain had not taken any of his teams to an NBA title. While Koppett had sympathy for Chamberlain, he acknowledged that "Wilt's undeniably abrasive personality made matters worse." As Koppett looked into the future, he wondered how Wilt would fit into the 76ers' "style of integrated basketball totally at variance with Wilt's habits." Would Dolph Schayes succeed in getting Wilt Chamberlain to fit into the coach's style of play? For Koppett, it was an intriguing question and made the trade "the most important . . . in pro basketball's modern era." Here was a story that the fans could follow, and, he concluded, "There's nothing more desirable for a sport than a continuing story."[21]

After the initial euphoria, the reality was that Chamberlain and Schayes were going to have a strained relationship. Unfortunately, Schayes and Chamberlain did not begin with a clean slate. In 1963 Jim Schottelkotte, who covered basketball for the *Cincinnati Enquirer*, wrote that

Dolph Schayes "had not been a controversial man in his career."[22] But, while Schayes had successfully avoided controversy and kept his opinions to himself, he made an exception with Chamberlain when, after his rookie season, Chamberlain claimed that officials applied a double standard in officiating his games. Chamberlain argued that tactics such as shoving and elbowing that were normally fouls were ignored when he was the target. Rather than taking this abuse, Chamberlain floated the idea that he might just leave the NBA. In an article in *Sport*, Schayes took issue with Chamberlain's assertions and argued that Wilt "was pampered, not picked on. He shot more fouls than anybody in the history of the league." Schayes added that Chamberlain used his elbows and often committed charging fouls that were not called when he attacked the basket. Before Chamberlain came along, Schayes recalled, Bob Pettit and George Mikan absorbed a lot of punishment. Chamberlain "knew we played rough," Schayes added, "and he even made jokes about it." Although Chamberlain set new scoring records in his first year, Schayes thought that "he's capable of doing even more. By simply improving his poor foul shooting, Wilt can score from five to ten points more a game."

In trying to understand Chamberlain, Schayes reminded his readers that Wilt was only twenty-three years old and still growing up. He had been drawing national attention since he was a teenager. Basketball experts, Schayes noted, argued that Wilt "was good enough to play in the pros" directly out of high school. Chamberlain's emotional development, Schayes suggested, had to catch up with his physical abilities.

Schayes correctly believed that Chamberlain would not retire from the NBA because the financial incentives were too great for an early exit. Schayes readily conceded, "The NBA, most of us agree, is a better league with him. But it will continue to grow with or without him."[23]

Two years later, in 1963, Schayes criticized Wilt's style of play and was quoted as saying, "Wilt doesn't help them [his teammates]. They're pawns."[24] Schayes told Jim Schottelkotte that Wilt was still not "benefitting the game very much."[25]

When Chamberlain joined the 76ers, Schayes was determined to solve Chamberlain's foul-shooting problems. But Chamberlain's results were still the same. While he made free throws in practice, Chamberlain simply froze up in the games. He never shot better than 61 percent from the foul line in any year of his career. In his book *A View from Above*, Chamberlain was annoyed that before he joined the 76ers, Schayes had stated that "anyone can make foul shots if they just practice." Wilt believed that his free-throw woes were not the result of a lack of effort.[26]

Still another point of conflict between coach and player was that Schayes was a great practice player who regularly stayed afterward to perfect his game. Wilt, by contrast, did not like practices and could disrupt them. Al Bianchi even suggested that Schayes could solve this problem by keeping Chamberlain on the sidelines during scrimmages. But this idea was too unconventional for Schayes. Oddly, Chamberlain's nemesis, Bill Russell, often avoided scrimmages and did just enough to keep his timing. Finally, Wilt shot a fade-away jump shot, which meant that he could not follow up his missed shots. It was as if he needed to show there was more to his game than size and coordination. Al Bianchi also thought that by shooting the fade-away jump shot, Chamberlain would be less likely to be fouled and therefore reduce his trips to the free-throw line and chances of getting beaten up by the defense. There were just too many points of conflict to make the relationship between Schayes and Chamberlain work. Although Schayes liked Chamberlain, he described their professional relationship as an "uneven peace."[27] It was a polite way of saying they did not get along.

The 1965 Playoffs

The 76ers finished the season with a 40-40 record, good enough for a third-place finish and another trip to the playoffs. For the third consecutive year, a Schayes team met the Cincinnati Royals in the first round of the playoffs. In the first game Al Bianchi hit a shot from behind the free-throw circle with eleven seconds left in overtime, and Chamberlain made two free throws seven seconds later to give the 76ers a 119–117 victory. Greer led all scorers with thirty-seven points, followed by Chamberlain's twenty-six and Walker's twenty-two.[28] When the series returned to Philadelphia, Oscar Robertson put on a scintillating offensive display, as he scored forty points and dished out thirteen assists as the Royals nipped the

76ers, 121–120. Chamberlain had thirty points, while Greer and Walker each tallied twenty-two for the 76ers.[29] Defying the home-court advantage once again, the 76ers pulled away in the second half to beat the Royals, 108–94, in Cincinnati to take a 2–1 lead in the series. Five 76ers, led by Greer's thirty points, were in double figures.[30] The 76ers wrapped up the series in Philadelphia, 119–112, as Chamberlain scored thirty-eight points, blocked eleven shots, and grabbed twenty-six rebounds.[31]

The victory set up the much-anticipated clash between the 76ers and the Celtics, Chamberlain versus Russell. Before a sellout crowd of 13,903 at the Boston Garden, the Celtics won the opener rather easily, 108–98. Tom Heinsohn led the Celtics with twenty-three points, and Russell grabbed thirty-two rebounds, one more than Chamberlain, who outscored the Celtic center 33–11.[32] The 76ers knotted up the series in Philadelphia before 9,790 fans by a score of 109–103. Chamberlain pulled down thirty-nine rebounds and scored thirty points, while limiting Russell to sixteen rebounds and twelve points. Greer with twenty-nine points and Walker with twenty-three also had big games. Boston's Sam Jones exploded for forty points to keep the game close.[33] Before another sellout crowd at the Boston Garden, six Celtics scored in double figures, as the Celtics won easily, 112–94. In their personal duel Chamberlain again prevailed by scoring twenty-four points and grabbing thirty-seven rebounds, while Russell tossed in nineteen points and hauled down twenty-six rebounds.[34] In the fourth game, before 9,294 hysterical Philly fans, the home-court advantage continued to hold, but barely. Just before the buzzer sounded at the end of regulation time, Hal Greer popped in a thirty-five-foot turnaround jump shot off the backboard to send the game into overtime, which ended with a 134–131 76ers victory. The big three for Philadelphia were Chamberlain with thirty-four, Walker with thirty-one, and Greer with twenty-seven. Sam Jones led all scorers with thirty-six, and five other Celtics were in double figures.[35]

Accompanying the thrilling victory was an off-the-court controversy. As the newspapers reported the score, they also carried a story that *Sports Illustrated* was about to publish a two-part series entitled "My Life in a Bush League" by Wilt Chamberlain and Bob Ottum. The first article was titled "I'm Punchy from Basketball, Baby, and Tired of Being a Villain."[36]

In a stream-of-consciousness style, Chamberlain took shots at everybody, including Dolph Schayes, who never read the story. Obviously embarrassed, Chamberlain responded by protesting, "I would have to be out of my mind to approve the title placed above my byline by the magazine." He said the article included many "unauthorized thoughts" that have "subjected me to uncalled for embarrassment and humiliation."[37]

Whatever Chamberlain could have been thinking, the series marched on, and once again the Celtics prevailed in Boston, 114–108. Although Chamberlain outscored Russell 30–12, Russell had the rebounding edge, 28–21.[38] Nonetheless, the 76ers remained resilient. In Philadelphia before a packed house of 11,182, the 76ers fought off a fourth-quarter Celtic rally to force a seventh game by a margin of 112–106. Chamberlain had thirty points and twenty-six rebounds, while Greer with twenty, Walker with twenty-two, and Jackson with twenty-three also had great games. Russell posted twenty-two points and twenty-one rebounds. Chamberlain, who had never fouled out of a game, played the last 11:42 minutes of the fourth quarter with five fouls.[39]

The stage was now set for the dream game. It was the stuff of high drama. Wilt Chamberlain had decimated all NBA offensive scoring records, but as any knowledgeable basketball fan on the planet knew, he had not won an NBA championship. After the sixth game he said, "Only when we win the seventh game can I rejoice. I can't feel like rejoicing now. I have great personal stakes in the seventh game in Boston."[40] In 1964 his San Francisco Warriors lost to the Celtics in five games in the NBA finals. Two years earlier his Philadelphia Warriors lost to the Celtics in the seventh game of the Eastern Division finals. Was Chamberlain's fate to be a bridesmaid but never a bride?

In sports as in life, reality often fails to match expectations, but the seventh game in Boston did not disappoint the sports world. The Celtics jumped out to an eighteen-point lead in the first quarter, but the 76ers fought back to take a 62–61 lead at halftime. In the third period the Celtics came back and entered the fourth period ahead, 90–82. With five seconds left in the fourth quarter, the Celtics allowed Chamberlain to score an uncontested basket, leaving the Celtics with a one-point lead, 110–109. With Russell taking the ball out, the game was apparently over, but then the unexpected happened. As Russell attempted to inbound the ball, it hit the guide wire supporting the backboard, turning the ball over to the 76ers. Pandemonium broke out in the Boston Garden. As the Celtics walked back to the bench, an outraged Red Auerbach was arguing with the officials, claiming that the 76er guarding Russell had reached over the baseline. Dolph Schayes vividly remembers that all of his players were excited and shouting out ideas when Ben Warley screamed, "Will everybody shut the bleep up and let Dolph talk." Schayes decided that Hal Greer would take the ball out and pass it to Walker, who would then look for Greer coming off a screen set by Johnny Kerr. Unfortunately for the 76ers, John Havlicek anticipated the pass and tipped it to Sam Jones, and the game was over.

Chamberlain scored thirty points and captured thirty-two rebounds, while Russell tallied fifteen points and snagged twenty-nine rebounds. Gordon S. White Jr. of the *New York Times* observed that Chamberlain "worked hard tonight, possibly harder than he did in any of the three victories the 76ers gained in this series." Sam Jones, who had a great series, scored thirty-seven points, while Havlicek tallied twenty-six for the Celtics. The game's dramatic ending raised a question that cannot be answered definitively. In drawing up the last play, Johnny Kerr told an interviewer that Wilt's teammates were yelling to get the ball to Wilt, but Chamberlain rejected the idea, fearing that he would be fouled and forced to go to the free-throw line. Schayes never heard Chamberlain say that he did not want the ball. Chamberlain said he wanted the ball at the end of every close game, and game seven was no different. Guessing that the Celtics would focus on Wilt, Schayes instructed the team to use a play to get the ball to Greer. In retrospect, Schayes agreed that a play requiring two passes with five seconds left was the wrong approach. In a moment ripe for second-guessing, if Schayes could do it again, he would have tried to let Chet Walker go one-on-one and either score or draw a foul. While we will never know what another play would have produced, we do know that everybody who saw those final moments witnessed one of the great games in NBA playoff basketball history.[41] For Chamberlain, the story line remained the same. After six years he still did not have a championship ring.

After the disappointing loss, Schayes, Richman, and Kosloff did not agree to a one-year contract extension until July 6. In the meantime, Schayes led a group of NBA players on a State Department tour of five European countries in May. Hal Greer, Dave Gambee, and Larry Costello of the 76ers were joined by Nat Thurmond and Tom Meschery of the San Francisco Warriors, Don Ohl and Bailey Howell of the Baltimore Bullets, and Wayne Embry of the Cincinnati Royals. After playing games in Bologna and Rome, Italy, the team traveled to Romania, where they played games and gave clinics in Bucharest and Timisoara. After Romania the NBA players made stops in Yugoslavia and Bulgaria. The trip was designed to spread goodwill between the United States and the Eastern-bloc countries. Schayes remembered that Larry Costello made one Romanian boy very happy when Costello gave him a pair of basketball shoes. Nine years had passed since Schayes made his first trip to Europe on a similar basketball excursion. In Sofia, Bulgaria, he remembered seeing anti-American slogans as the United States began to escalate its war in Vietnam.[42]

After Schayes returned to Syracuse and signed his contract, Wilt Chamberlain ended any rumors of retirement on August 17, when he signed a three-year contract worth $110,000 per year. If Chamberlain was not the best-paid athlete in American sport, he was near the top.

The 1965–66 Season

Before the 1965–66 season the 76ers traded Johnny Kerr and lost Larry Costello to retirement. Although not as flashy as Bob Cousy or Dick McGuire, individuals who played with and against him placed Costello in the group of elite guards of the late 1950s and early 1960s. Because Wilt Chamberlain did not like coming out of games, there was not much playing time for the backup center. Johnny Kerr, who had been a mainstay for the Nats and 76ers, was now expendable and was traded to the Baltimore Bullets for Wally Jones. Jones had been a high school star in Philadelphia who excelled at Villanova. Schayes remembered Jones as an explosive player, excellent on defense, and good in the locker room. Jones moved into the starting lineup, replacing Larry Costello. The 76ers also drafted Billy Cunningham, a six-foot-six forward, from the University of North

Carolina, who would have a Hall of Fame career. Blessed with springs in his legs, Cunningham became the 76ers' sixth man. He gave the 76ers instant offense and finished the season as the team's fourth-highest scorer, with 14.3 points per game.

In the fall of 1965 the 76ers got off to a fast start. On November 13 they beat the Knicks, as Hal Greer scored 38 points, keeping Philadelphia in first place with a 9-3 record. In this game Greer, in his eighth season, passed the 10,000-point career mark.[43] Four days later Chamberlain scored 46 points, which gave him 19,263 in his seventh season. This figure made Chamberlain the NBA's second-leading scorer, just ahead of Dolph Schayes. Bob Pettit's record of 20,880 was Chamberlain's next target.[44]

On December 3, 1965, tragedy struck the 76ers. In the first quarter of a game in Boston, Ike Richman, the co-owner, suffered a massive heart attack while watching the game on the 76ers' bench. He was just fifty-two.[45] Richman's death coincided with a 76er slump, as Philadelphia's record sank to 17-17. But then the 76ers won twenty-four of their next thirty-two games and were just two games back of Boston by mid-February. On February 14 Chamberlain scored 41 points, which raised his career totals to 20,884, 4 ahead of Pettit. Chamberlain also captured his 12,852th rebound, just ahead of Pettit, with only Russell ahead of him.[46] With seven games left in the season, the 76ers grabbed first place by percentage points over Boston. On March 20 the 76ers edged the Baltimore Bullets, 108–104, and finished one game ahead of Boston, ending Boston's nine-year streak as champions of the Eastern Division. The 76ers had won their last eleven games to dislodge the Celtics.[47] Schayes called winning the Eastern Division title "the biggest thrill of my life." He added, "We won this championship because we are a team." Boston and Cincinnati had to meet in a five-game playoff for the right to play the 76ers. Schayes was confident that "this team can beat anybody now."[48]

There was an amusing aspect to the final victory. Near the end of the game, Schayes was surprised that the Bullets did not foul Chamberlain when the 76ers led by just a 2-point margin. After the game Schayes approached Paul Seymour, Baltimore's coach, to ask about it. Seymour replied that he had instructed Jim Barnes to foul Chamberlain to get him on the free-throw line. When Barnes approached Wilt, the big center warned Barnes that if he fouled him, the 76er center would break both of his arms.[49]

Oddly, the day before Schayes celebrated the Eastern Division title, he had a rather embarrassing but, in retrospect, humorous experience. On March 19 Texas Western and the University of Kentucky met in Cole Fieldhouse on the campus of the University of Maryland to determine the NCAA basketball champion. The buildup to the game would make it one of college basketball's more memorable games. Sportswriters like a story line, and this contest had one. In the mid-1960s the civil rights movement provided the backdrop to this contest. Texas Western, coached by the relatively unknown Don Haskins, started an all-black team. Adolph Rupp, the legendary coach of Kentucky, had never recruited a black player. Moreover, the Southeastern Conference was just taking its first tentative steps to integrate athletics.

By 1966 Dolph had established a friendship with Eddie Gottlieb, whom he much admired. Because Gottlieb was still scouting for the San Francisco Warriors, he asked Dolph if he would drive him down to the game in his Cadillac. Ben Kerner, the owner of the St. Louis Hawks, would accompany them. When they reached Cole Fieldhouse, Dolph dropped Gottlieb and Kerner at one of the entrances and parked the car. The game proved to be a disappointment as a contest, since Texas Western controlled the game from the opening tip-off and won easily.

With about three minutes left in the game, Schayes left the arena so that he, Gottlieb, and Kerner could beat the crowd out of the parking lot. There was one problem. As Dolph stared at the mass of cars in the parking lot, he realized that he was unsure of the location of Gottlieb's Cadillac. As Dolph wandered around the parking lot, the crowd began to pour out of the arena. As cars whizzed by, the bewildered Gottlieb and Kerner trailed Schayes around the parking lot. As they searched for the car, an increasingly frustrated Kerner turned to Gottlieb and said, "Gotty—are you sure this guy is Jewish?" Schayes remembered that as they drove back to Philadelphia, you could have heard a pin drop in the car.[50]

In the immediate aftermath of the regular season, Chamberlain and Schayes won coveted league honors. For the second time in his career the players named Chamberlain the NBA's most valuable player. He got

181 points, comfortably ahead of Los Angeles's Jerry West, who drew 101 points. After the players honored Wilt, a committee of twenty-seven writers who covered the NBA named Dolph Schayes the NBA's coach of the year. Schayes garnered thirteen votes, and Red Auerbach followed with nine. In accepting the award, Schayes singled out Wilt Chamberlain for his "leadership and great desire to win which penetrated through the ranks."[51] While Chamberlain led the NBA in scoring for the seventh consecutive year, his 33.5 average was the lowest in his career. Because he also led the league in rebounding and his team in assists (fifth in the league), some believed, including Lloyd Milligan of the *New York Times*, that Schayes had succeeded in persuading Wilt to fit his game into a team concept.[52]

If Schayes was using the media to change the image of Chamberlain, Wilt remained a Jekyll-and-Hyde character. During the season he lived in Manhattan and commuted to practices in Philadelphia, which had to be held in the afternoon for his convenience. When the team traveled, Chamberlain was the only player to have a private suite. Practices continued to bore him. During pregame talks and time-outs, Chamberlain could be frustratingly disengaged. Whatever the gap between image and reality, nobody could doubt Chamberlain's sincerity when he said, after the regular season, "I want the big title. This is just the down payment on the big one."[53] Schayes and Chamberlain had the same goal; they just could not agree on all the steps to get there.

The Boston-Cincinnati series was as tough as expected. The Royals were led by Oscar Robertson and Jerry Lucas and won two of the first three games. With a chance to close out the series at the Cincinnati Gardens, the Royals fell, 120–103. Auerbach, who had announced that he was retiring as a coach, said, "I sure didn't want to end my career in Cincinnati."[54] After four games neither team had won on its home court, but in game five Boston broke that pattern with a 112–103 victory.

While the 76ers were the favorite going into the Eastern Division finals, they had not played a game for two weeks. In the interim Schayes remembered that the team had not practiced well. While the 76ers had the home-court advantage, the Ringling Brothers' circus occupied the Convention Hall, which meant that the series opener would be played at the smaller and rather dingy Philadelphia Arena. Before 6,563 fans packed into the arena, the Celtics forced nineteen turnovers and won easily, 115–96. Sam Jones with twenty-nine points and John Havlicek with twenty-two led the way for Boston. Chamberlain had twenty-five points and thirty-two rebounds, but no other 76ers had more than fifteen points.[55] The Celtics easily won the second game at the Boston Garden by a score of 114–93. Sam Jones led Boston with twenty-three, and six other Celtics were in double figures. Chamberlain led the 76ers with twenty-three, but the Celtics limited Hal Greer to seven points. The most exciting part of the game was a fight between Billy Cunningham and Larry Siegfried in the fourth quarter.[56]

When the series returned to Philadelphia, the circus had departed, and a standing-room-only crowd of 10,454 watched the 76ers top the Celtics, 111–105. Chamberlain had thirty-two points, and Greer bounced back with nineteen points. Havlicek with twenty-seven points and Sam Jones with twenty-five continued to lead the Celtics. In winning, the 76ers almost blew a twenty-four-point lead. With twenty-four seconds left in the game, Chamberlain grabbed a Havlicek miss to seal the victory for the 76ers.

There was one amusing aspect to the game that Dolph and Naomi still laugh about. As late as 1966 coaches did not have assistant coaches to track fouls, time-outs, and substitutions. Schayes relied on Harvey Pollack, Philadelphia's statistician, to help him with details. During the game, Dolph recalled that he was forgetting something as he got involved in the flow of the game. He failed to put Bill Cunningham in the game, and Naomi, who was watching the game with daughter Debbie, spotted this oversight. Naomi sent Debbie down to the bench with a note to remind Dolph to put Cunningham in the game. Dolph pocketed the note, thinking it had something to do with postgame activities. When Naomi sent Debbie with a second note, Dolph again failed to read it. Finally, Naomi sent Debbie down a third time, and with hands on her hips, she told her father, "Put Billy Cunningham in."[57]

The fourth game in Boston proved to be the crucial game of the series. Early in the third period the 76ers had a thirteen-point lead, but the Celtics kept their poise and took a 99–98 lead with a minute left to play. Greer's layup gave the 76ers a one-point lead, but K. C. Jones hit a free throw to tie the game at 100 at the end of regulation play. The Celtics outscored the 76ers 14–8 in the overtime and took a commanding lead in the series, 3–1. Chamberlain had thirty-three rebounds but just fifteen points. Hal Greer had twenty-five, and Al Bianchi had twenty to lead the 76ers. Havlicek and Sam Jones collected twenty-seven and twenty-two points, respectively.[58]

The Celtics had not won at Convention Hall since January 1964, but on April 12 they finished the series by a 120–112 margin to make the NBA finals for the tenth straight year. In an impressive performance Chamberlain had forty-six points and thirty-four rebounds, while Russell had eighteen points and thirty-one rebounds. Havlicek with thirty-two points and Sam Jones with thirty points continued to pace Boston. Despite Chamberlain's effort, he missed seventeen of twenty-five free-throw attempts, which proved costly. Wilt made nineteen of thirty-four field-goal attempts, more than 50 percent; the rest of the team made twenty-four of seventy-nine shots, not quite a third of their attempts. Yet the story line was not how well Chamberlain played or the poor shooting night of his teammates, but that once again Chamberlain had failed to nail down a championship. For playing in the Eastern Division finals the 76ers split $29,000. Nine players and Dolph Schayes were $2,550 richer.[59]

Within weeks of the season's end, newspapers began to speculate on the fate of Dolph Schayes's coaching career. On April 28 Bill Reddy reported that Irv Kosloff had flown to Los Angeles to determine whether Alex Hannum was interested in coaching the 76ers.[60] Just a month earlier Franklin Mieuli, the owner of the San Francisco Warriors, had replaced Hannum with Bill Sharman. The reason given was that Hannum would not devote twelve months to the job, preferring to spend the off-season in Los Angeles managing his construction business.[61] On May 2 the drama ended when Irv Kosloff announced that Hannum would replace Schayes as the coach of the 76ers. Kosloff stated that he was "very unhappy" that the Celtics had eliminated the 76ers in the playoffs. Because his goal was to win a championship, Kosloff said, "it seemed to me there was only one man for the job. That was Alex Hannum." Unlike San Francisco's Mieuli, Kosloff did not care what Hannum did in the summer as long as he won in Philadelphia. Kosloff did not say much about Schayes, except that he was a gentleman who did not push his players.[62]

There were two theories about Schayes's firing. The first was simply to take at face value that the 76ers failed to beat the Celtics and that the easiest move was to fire the coach. The second, proposed by Larry Merchant of the *New York Post*, was that in the contest of wills between Chamberlain and Schayes, Wilt won. In an interview Schayes said, "Wilt's a prima donna. He knows it, I know it, everyone knows it." Wilt demanded special privileges, and Schayes knew that "it did affect others, [but] I felt it wasn't costing us ball games which was the important thing, the main thing. Basically, I know that he had winning on his mind, period. So did I." In assessing himself, Schayes said, "I'm not dynamic, aggressive, outspoken like Auerbach. I think all you have to know is the game, treat players fairly and firmly. Shouting isn't important. That's how I am. If you're not the right kind of guy, you go into something else."[63]

Throughout Dolph Schayes's career, Naomi Schayes had stayed out of the papers. This time Leonard Lewin of the *New York Post* got her to talk. Along with sharing her frustrations, Naomi related an interesting story. During one of the 76er practices, Ike Richman approached her and said, "I'm going to make an S.O.B. out of your husband. One of my greatest joys is to have people call me that because then it means I'm a success." Well, Dolph Schayes did not become an SOB, and Naomi admitted that she was glad for it.[64]

The Aftermath

Alex Hannum was not particularly pleased that it was a friend that he replaced as the coach of the 76ers. Schayes and Hannum had been teammates, and Alex had coached Dolph for three years. Loyalty was a value that Hannum did not take lightly, but he knew that the 76ers were positioned to make another run at an NBA championship. The opportunity was too tantalizing to pass up. Besides, Hannum and Schayes understood the perils of the basketball business. In early May 1966, Bill Reddy reported that Hannum visited with Dolph Schayes and Danny Biasone at the Eastwood Sports Center, where they discussed the 76ers' personnel.[65] Between August 28 and September 4, Schayes conducted his annual basketball camp near Lake George, and Hannum, Luke Jackson, and Billy Cunningham participated.

Hannum's hunch about the 76ers proved prophetic. The 76ers ran away with the Eastern Division by setting a new record for a season by compiling a 68-13 record. Boston was eight games behind. Chamberlain averaged 24.1 points a game, the first time he averaged fewer than 33 points for a season. The trade-off was that Chamberlain finished third in assists, led the league in rebounding, and made his teammates more productive. Because Wilt still made fewer than half of his free throws, teams fouled him even when he did not have the ball. At the halfway point of the season, the NBA made a rule change that such a foul would be treated as a technical foul so that the fouled team would maintain possession of the ball after the free throw.[66]

In the playoffs Boston beat New York and Philadelphia eliminated Cincinnati to set up the third straight 76er-Celtic clash for the right to play in the NBA finals. With Red Auerbach moving up to the general manager's office, Bill Russell led Boston as its player-coach. In five games the 76ers eliminated the Celtics, ending their run of eight consecutive championships and nine in ten years. In game five in Philadelphia the 76ers clobbered the Celtics, 140–116. In the NBA finals the 76ers met the San Francisco Warriors, led by Rick Barry, the NBA's leading scorer, and Nat Thurmond, their leading rebounder. It took the 76ers six games to win the championship, but Philadelphia celebrated its first NBA title since 1956.[67]

For one season Philadelphia may have been the best team in the NBA's twenty-one-year history, but it produced no dynasty. While the 76ers won the division for a third straight time in 1968, Boston beat them in the 1968 Eastern Division finals.

In a normal year the Russell-Chamberlain rivalry could have been enjoyed without a second thought, but 1968 was not a normal year. The diversions caused by the Vietnam War and the long, hot summers as urban violence spread in urban ghettoes came to a head in 1968. The political implications of sport had a long history, but nowhere more so than in the Olympics. In October 1967 Harry Edwards, a black sociologist at San Jose University, organized the Olympic Project for Human Rights, which urged black athletes to boycott the Olympics unless certain demands were met to end the exploitation of black athletes and to increase opportunities for black coaches. On April 4, the day before the first scheduled game in the Eastern Division final, Martin Luther King Jr. was assassinated. Some players wanted to postpone the opener, but the game was played and won by the Celtics. The second game was delayed a day, and Philadelphia won it and the next two to take a commanding 3–1 lead in the series. Nonetheless, the Celtics rebounded to take the next three games in one of the NBA's most remarkable comebacks. Boston captured its tenth crown by beating Los Angeles 4–2 in the NBA finals.[68]

The 1967–68 season was also notable because it was the first year of the American Basketball Association. The eleven-team league was testimony to the growing popularity of professional basketball and the wealth of available talent. The NBA had not been standing still, as it added Chicago, Seattle, San Diego, Milwaukee, and Phoenix between 1966 and 1968. Pat Boone owned the Oakland Oaks in the ABA and signed Alex Hannum to coach his team. More eye catching was a trade that sent Wilt Chamberlain to the Los Angeles Lakers for Archie Clark, Darrall Imhoff, and Jerry Chambers. The result was that Philadelphia went from being a great to a good team, while the Lakers recaptured their dominant position in the Western Division.[69] In 1972 the Los Angeles Lakers captured their first NBA title. For Chamberlain it was his second and last championship ring. Whether it was with Elgin Baylor or Wilt Chamberlain, Jerry West had played in the finals eight times but had not played on a championship team until 1972.

Between 1966 and 1970, Dolph Schayes kept his fingers in the NBA game by serving as the supervisor of NBA officials. It was a job that Schayes did not particularly enjoy. He said he felt like a "fish out of water" and thought it was a position better suited for an experienced official. Schayes's major responsibilities were to schedule referees, identify new officials, and deal with complaints from owners. Schayes held a camp for officials, reviewed film, and mastered the rule book. If Schayes did not find his job very rewarding, he did enjoy the camaraderie with the officials. Norm Drucker, Earl Strom, Eddie Rush, Daryl Garretson, Jack Madden, Mendy Rudolph, Jake O'Donnell, Rich Powers, John Vanek, and Joe Gushue made up the core of officials at this time. All of the officials approached their job differently, which reflected their personalities. Schayes remembered that Earl Strom had a tendency to take over a game. He also knew how to disarm players who had a beef with one of his calls. One of Dolph's favorite examples of this involved a rookie who complained to Strom, "I notice that all the superstars get all the calls. When do I get a call?" Strom quickly replied, "When you become a superstar."[70]

One of the advantages of working for the NBA was that Schayes and his family could remain in Syracuse. The NBA office in New York City, still rather small in the late 1960s, was an easy commute from Syracuse. This convenience allowed Schayes to manage and expand a rental property business that had engaged him since the mid-1950s. When Dolph and Naomi bought their first home, it was a duplex, and Dolph rented out half of it. By 1966 Schayes had built twelve- and sixteen-unit complexes and was in the process of investing in a thirty-unit venture. Along with his NBA job and his business ventures, Schayes continued to operate an annual basketball camp near Lake George in the Adirondacks.[71]

On January 20, 1970, the NBA announced the addition of franchises in Cleveland, Portland, and Buffalo. The owners of the Buffalo franchise were Neuberger-Loeb, a New York investment firm. Philip Ryan and Peter Crotty headed the organizing group and made Carl Scheer president. A graduate of Colgate University and Marquette University Law School, Scheer resigned as the NBA's assistant commissioner to take the position. Scheer named Dolph Schayes the team's coach and Eddie Donovan its general manager. Donovan had played and coached at St. Bonaventure, so western New York was home for him. Before resigning as the general manager of the New York Knicks, Donovan had put together the roster that gave New York its first NBA championship in 1970.[72]

In stocking the new franchises, the NBA did not prove very generous. The expansion teams were given the seventh, eight, and ninth picks in the first round. Donovan chose to trade Buffalo's ninth pick to Baltimore for Mike Davis and Baltimore's first-round choice, the fifteenth overall. Davis had made the NBA all-rookie team in 1969. At this point Donovan chose to pass over Calvin Murphy, a five-foot-nine college scoring machine from Niagara University. Donovan also passed on Nate "Tiny" Archibald, who had starred at Texas El Paso and had graduated from DeWitt Clinton High School, Schayes's alma mater. Instead, Donovan selected John Hummer, a six-foot-nine forward from Princeton University. The only other draft choice to make the team was Cornell Warner, a six-foot-nine forward from Jackson State.[73]

The balance of the team came from an expansion draft held on May 11, 1970. Each NBA team could protect seven players, which meant the expansion teams were looking at players who came off the bench. One exception to that rule was Dick Garrett, who had started as a rookie for the Lakers and had made the NBA's all-rookie team. Another exception was Bailey Howell, who was nearing the end of his Hall of Fame career. Donovan traded Howell to Philadelphia for Bob Kauffman, a six-foot-eight forward who played center for the Braves. Rounding out the team were Emmett Bryant from the Celtics, George Wilson from Philadelphia, Herm Gilliam from Cincinnati, Freddie Crawford from Milwaukee, Paul Long from Detroit, Mike Lynn from Los Angeles, and Donnie May, Nate Bowman, Bill Hosket, and Mike Silliman from the Knicks.[74]

Lacking a real star and possessing a roster that would not strike fear into the hearts of any of the established NBA teams, the Braves had no chance to be very competitive. Schayes thought that one way to be more competitive was to stress defense, but developing defensive schemes was not one of his strengths. When he tried to hire Rollie Massimino, who would later coach Villanova to an NCAA title, Dolph was told that the team could not afford it. The team hired Johnny McCarthy, a former pro who starred at Canisius College, to scout. Later in the season, McCarthy would join Schayes on the bench.

As a business venture the Braves also faced another problem. In 1970 Seymour and Norty Knox purchased an expansion franchise in the National Hockey League. They had strong ties to the Buffalo community and had negotiated a lease with the Buffalo Memorial Auditorium that gave them Sundays and Thursdays for home hockey games. Canisius College had Saturdays, so the Braves were left Tuesdays and Fridays for their home games.

In gearing up for the season, Dolph Schayes and several players held basketball clinics throughout western New York. During the summer a slump in the stock market left the team's investors reeling, and they could not make the payments on their $3.7 million investment. In a state of panic, Paul Snyder, a Buffalo businessman, rescued the franchise. Snyder built Freezer Queen into a successful frozen-food business and sold it to Nabisco for a bundle of money. The ownership change would prove to be significant for Schayes. Most important, Carl Scheer was no longer the team's president. Because he and Schayes had worked together in the NBA office, they had a good relationship and recognized the difficult challenges faced by an expansion team. Snyder proved a less patient person.[75]

The season opened on a high note, as the Braves downed the Cleveland Cavaliers, 107–92, before 7,129 fans. Donnie May led all scorers with 24 points. The Braves lost their next nine games. While victories were infrequent, the Braves did surprise the NBA champion Knicks on December 4 by edging them 97–91. May, Garrett, and Kauffman scored 20 or more points to lead the Braves.[76]

On November 5 New York University inducted its first class of athletes into its new sports hall of fame. Schayes joined Howard Cann, his coach; Ken Strong, the only NYU football player in the Pro Football Hall of Fame; and Dr. Phil Edwards, a track star who represented Canada in the Olympics between 1928 and 1936, winning five medals. While Dolph's basketball schedule made it impossible for him to attend, Naomi; his father, Carl; and his brothers, Fred and Herman, were there to receive his award.[77]

When the season ended, Buffalo's record stood at 22-60. Bob Kauffman led the team in scoring with a 20.4 average, and Donnie May followed closely with a 20.2 average. May's season was rather remarkable because he had averaged a mere 2.6 points per game the previous season with the Knicks. During the season Dolph quickly recognized that May was the only player on the team who could consistently score from the outside, so he began to design plays for him. Probably few players, maybe none, saw such an increase in point production from one season to the next. At six foot eight, Kauffman had to play center and was too small for that position. One consolation for the Braves was that they won seven more games than the Cleveland Cavaliers. As an expansion team the Braves performed as expected. While the team struggled, Schayes remained upbeat and worked well with the press, which was becoming an important part of a coach's job. Jim Baker of the *Buffalo Courier-Press* wrote, "Dolph's strong point, I think, was being able to communicate with the fans of the area. He was tremendous on radio and television."[78] Dolph and Naomi had moved the family to Buffalo and enjoyed the city and made a number of friends. Their son Danny was the team's ball boy. During the season, however, Paul Snyder made it a habit of visiting the locker room after games and dressing down the players. Snyder got into everything, which complicated basketball operations.[79]

On March 29 the NBA held its draft, and the Braves selected Elmore Smith, a seven-foot-one center from Kentucky State. Smith had just led Kentucky State to the National Association of Intercollegiate Athletics championship. In the seventh round the Braves took Randy Smith, a superquick guard from Buffalo State who would blossom into a star.[80]

On October 13 the Braves opened their second season at the Memorial Auditorium before a sellout crowd. With Spencer Haywood scoring forty-two points, the Seattle Supersonics blew out the Braves, 123–90. After the game an irate Snyder fired Schayes and replaced him with assistant coach Johnny McCarthy. Snyder said, "We weren't happy with the performance. We felt we can have a better team with the talent we have."[81] One of the spectators at the game and seated with Snyder was his friend and former vice president Hubert Humphrey. Schayes speculated that Snyder's emotional reaction to the loss may have been influenced by seeing his team thrashed before Humphrey.[82] Ironically, the Braves ended the season with another 22-60 record, and Snyder fired McCarthy at the end of the season.

When Dolph Schayes agreed to coach the Buffalo Braves, he knew that he was taking a high-risk job. The change in ownership clearly altered the dynamics of the basketball operation. At forty-three, Dolph Schayes was finished with professional basketball.

Buffalo's NBA history proved as erratic as its owner. After firing McCarthy, Snyder hired Jack Ramsay, who had collegiate and NBA coaching experience. Ramsay suffered through a 21-61 season, but Eddie Donovan began to get him some talent. Bob McAdoo, Garfield Heard, Jim McMillian, and Ernie DiGregorio would lead the Braves to the playoffs in 1974, 1975, and 1976. After 1976 Ramsay left for Portland, and Snyder decided to sell the team to John Y. Brown, who had owned the ABA's Kentucky Colonels before the NBA absorbed Denver, San Antonio, Indiana, and New York in 1976. To reduce the $6.2 million purchase price, Brown allowed Snyder to keep the money from the sale of McAdoo and Moses Malone. While Snyder was dismantling the Braves, a most unusual trade took place. Irv Levin, the owner of the Boston Celtics, wanted to move his team to San Diego. Given the Celtic tradition, this idea was anathema to the NBA. It solved the problem by persuading Levin and Brown to trade franchises. As a result, Levin took the Buffalo franchise to San Diego after the 1977–78 season, ending the eight-year history of the Braves. The implosion of the Buffalo Braves was not unprecedented in professional sports. As usual, the only casualties of the move were the fans who had supported the team.[83]

5

A Life Well Lived

At the age of forty-three, Dolph Schayes's connection to professional basketball was over, but basketball remained an important part of his life. Beginning in the mid-1950s, he ran a basketball camp until the mid-1980s on Lake George in upstate New York. In the 1950s basketball camps were a novelty. In Dolph's camp, which lasted a week, most of the kids were from small towns or farms in central New York. During the day the campers would work on their basketball skills, and in the evening Dolph would organize a fun event such as a Las Vegas night, an action movie, a basketball game between the camp counselors, or an evening in Lake George.

Dolph stole an idea from the Professional Golfers' Association in the 1950s to motivate the campers. In order to promote golf, the PGA asked President Dwight D. Eisenhower to play a round of golf and submit his score, which was in the mideighties. If a golfer beat Ike's score, they would get an "I beat Ike" button. Dolph offered his campers a similar challenge. If anybody could beat him in a best-of-fifteen free-throw shooting contest, they would get an "I beat Dolph" button. To give the kids a chance, after making seven or eight in a row, Dolph would say that he would only count those remaining shots that were perfect swishes so that he wound up making less than a perfect fifteen for fifteen. As a result the campers were practicing their free throws during all their spare time. Dolph remembered that one eight-year-old camper, who could barely reach the rim when shooting, came up to him and said, "I beat you, Dolph—just ask my buddy."

The camp also provided an opportunity for Dolph's extended family to share a week together. Herman Schayes brought his family and helped Dolph with administrative duties. Many of the Syracuse Nats and 76ers helped Dolph in the early years of the camp. Other NBA stars such as Jo Jo White, Willis Reed, and Pete Maravich and coaches such as Jim Boeheim, who attended the camp as a teenager, and Press Maravich were there to instruct and dazzle the campers.[1]

Finally, Dolph used the camp to improve his own game. To improve his set shot Dolph developed a basketball rim that was only fourteen inches in diameter, four inches shorter than the standard rim. By increasing the challenge to shoot accurately, Schayes was forced to shoot the basketball with a higher arc and greater extension with his arms and fingers. Also, by shooting outside Dolph increased the backspin on the ball so that its trajectory would not be altered by a summer breeze. After practicing this way, Dolph found that during the regular season, the basket seemed twice as wide. One of the payoffs was an improvement in Dolph's free-throw-shooting percentage.

By the 1980s all the colleges and high schools were getting into the basketball-camp business as a method of raising money for their programs. With so many conflicts, Schayes decided to get out of this business. None-theless, for three decades the camp was a week in Dolph's life that gener-ated a host of great memories.

In 1977 Dolph Schayes had an experience that would have a profound impact on his life. Jewish basketball fans followed Schayes's career, and historians include him in any discussion of Jews and sports. As one of the NBA's first superstars, Schayes never thought of himself as a Jewish bas-ketball player, just a basketball player. He was driven by the desire to be the best and did not see his career as having some larger social meaning. For all his life, however, Dolph Schayes had an interest in history and was eager to visit Israel and learn more about its history and culture. For many years Haskell Cohen had worked in the NBA as the league's publicity director, but he was also deeply involved in Israeli sports and headed the United States Committee Sports for Israel. When Schayes expressed an interest in coaching the US team in the 1977 Maccabiah Games, or Jew-ish Olympics, Cohen readily agreed to make him the coach. Schayes con-ducted tryouts at New York Tech on Long Island. Three hundred players showed up, and with the help of Red Holzman, Fuzzy Levane, and Lou Carnaseca, Schayes selected his team. One of his players was a six-foot-ten center who had just graduated from high school—Danny Schayes. In July the team practiced at Kutsher's Country Club in the Catskill Mountains before flying to Tel Aviv.[2]

The Maccabiah Games were a cultural experience as well as an athletic competition. Jews from the Diaspora visited holy sites and immersed themselves in Israeli culture. In 2009 Dolph Schayes spoke at the International Jewish Hall of Fame at Wingate Institute for Physical Education and Sport at Netanya, Israel, and told the audience, "In life I was tall— 6'8". In Jewish life, I wasn't very tall—I was stunted. Beginning in 1977 I grew up as a Jew. Every time I come I grow up even more."[3] In 1977, when Schayes marched into the stadium with thousands of Jewish athletes from around the world before a crowd of tens of thousands, it was an emotional experience he would never forget.[4]

There were sixteen countries in the basketball competition. Israel had just won the European basketball tournament, and it was expected to win the Maccabiah Games. Other than the United States, no other nation posed a serious threat to the Israelis. Both teams breezed through the early rounds of the competition until they met in the championship game. Before a packed house in an exciting contest, the US team hit two free throws at the end of the game to take the championship.[5]

Dolph Schayes came of age during World War II. In the wake of the war and the Holocaust, Israel emerged as a nation-state in 1948. For Schayes to see what Israel had accomplished in politics, economics, science, technology, and the arts was breathtaking. In 1993 Dolph coached an American Masters basketball team in the Maccabiah Games. By then there were Jewish teams from Russia and Germany. During the opening ceremonies, Dolph traded his new warm-up with a Russian player for his rather tattered outfit. To this day Dolph says, "I still have it. I treasure it."[6]

The connection to the Maccabiah Games has become a Schayes family affair. Danny Schayes also played on the 1981 US team. Danny's son will soon participate in junior competitions in basketball.[7] Three of Dolph's granddaughters won silver medals in the 2001 volleyball competitions, and a grandson won a gold medal in the 400-meter relay in 2005.[8]

After starring at Jamesville-DeWitt High School, Danny chose to play his college basketball at Syracuse University. As a senior in high school,

19. Carl Schayes and his three sons enjoy a moment together. *From left:* Herman, Dolph, Carl, and Fred. Family photograph.

Danny attributed some of his success to the "skills I had acquired at my dad's summer basketball camp." He said, "My dad never really pushed me that much or gave me a lot of extra attention. A lot of what I learned came from the counselors." Danny also thought that playing one-on-one against his brother, David, who was two years older, helped to toughen him up. If Dolph was low-key as a father, he was not as a fan. Some of his most embarrassing moments as an adult occurred while watching Danny play basketball. Because Danny was six foot ten, Dolph was convinced that the referees were calling fouls against Danny because of his size. Unfortunately, Dolph could not contain his frustration and would leave his seat to give the officials a piece of his mind. Occasionally, to Dolph's chagrin, these outbursts would find their way into the local newspaper.[9]

While Danny improved as a player at Syracuse, Dolph's behavior as a fan remained unchanged. In a game against Villanova in Danny's senior year, Villanova's center created contact with Danny and then fell back as if he had been fouled by Danny. One of the officials bought this maneuver and called three or four fouls on Danny. As Dolph recalled, "I was in the stands going crazy." What was worse is that the television cameras periodically kept their sights on Dolph. After the game Dolph went down to the court and accidentally bumped into the official who had annoyed him, which was interpreted as a threatening action. Some game-management people saw it and took Dolph to a locker room, supposedly to cool off. The upshot of this incident was that Dolph received a letter from Syracuse's athletic director, informing him that if he could not behave, he would not be welcome at Syracuse basketball games.[10] Clearly, watching Danny play basketball was Dolph's Achilles' heel.

Danny's first three years at Syracuse were frustrating for Danny (and Dolph) because he was not a starter. This situation changed when as a senior Danny averaged 14.6 points per game, made the All–Big East first team, and won All-America and Academic All-America honors. In 1981 the Utah Jazz made Danny the thirteenth pick in the first round of the NBA draft. Dolph and Danny Schayes are one of the few father-son combinations to play in the NBA.

During Danny's pro career, Dolph seemed to mellow. Perhaps the officiating improved. Nonetheless, Dolph managed to get his name in the papers one more time. In 1996–97 Danny played for the Orlando Magic. In the playoffs the underdog Magic took the Miami Heat to the fifth and deciding game, played in Miami. Dolph was sitting in a section of the arena with other Magic fans and behaving himself. At one point in the game, the Miami mascot, dressed as a giant rabbit, decided to spray the Orlando section with his squirt gun. Outraged by the mascot's behavior, Dolph jumped up and started wrestling with the mascot. The police separated Dolph and the mascot, but the incident was widely reported in America's sport pages. Dolph was very embarrassed, but took some solace when the *San Jose Mercury* applauded him for standing up for fans who were victimized by team mascots across the country. Today Dolph can laugh about these antics and wonder who that crazy guy was.[11]

In his NBA career Danny played just over a season and a half before the Jazz traded him to the Denver Nuggets. Danny had his most productive years with the Nuggets, where he played for just over seven years. His best year was in 1987–88, when he averaged 13.9 points per game. After being traded to Milwaukee in 1990, Danny made stops as a backup center in Los Angeles, Phoenix, Miami, and Orlando. In 1999, at the age of thirty-eight, Danny Schayes played the last game of his eighteen years in the NBA. He played 1,138 regular-season games and scored 8,780 points for a 7.7 average.[12] During Danny's career Dolph managed to travel to about a dozen of Danny's games a year and watched most of the rest on his satellite dish. The NBA had changed drastically from 1948 when the Nats issued Dolph two pairs of shoes and two uniforms, one home and away, and when away games were broadcast via ticker tape.

Over the years Dolph Schayes's contribution to basketball was recognized in many ways. In 1971 a selection panel placed Schayes on the NBA's 25th Anniversary Team.[13] The following year Schayes received his greatest honor when he was inducted into the Basketball Hall of Fame in Springfield, Massachusetts. In 1979 he was inducted into the International Jewish Sports Hall of Fame, located on the campus of the Wingate Institute in Israel.

On October 29, 1996, NBA commissioner David Stern announced the NBA's 50th Anniversary All-Time Team. A panel of fifty drawn from the media, former players, coaches, and current and former general managers voted for the top-fifty players in the NBA's fifty-year history. One of those honored was Dolph Schayes.[14] In February 1997 forty-seven of the players traveled to Cleveland, where they were honored at the annual NBA All-Star Game. Dolph relished every minute of the festivities. He recalled that the gathering was "like a family."[15] At one point Naomi Schayes decided to summon up her courage and approach Wilt Chamberlain in an effort to mend the strained relationship between Wilt and Dolph. She told Wilt that it "pained her" that the legacy of the tension between Wilt and Dolph still lingered after thirty years. Naomi proposed that Wilt meet with Dolph, which he readily agreed to do. Dolph remembered the meeting as rather brief, but it was the beginning of a new relationship between the two men.[16] Sadly, in October 1999 Wilt Chamberlain passed away. Wilt's death shocked Dolph. He admitted, "Early on I wasn't a real Wilt fan, but now I realize that I underestimated him as a person. As the years

20. Dolph and Naomi Schayes at their home in Syracuse. Family photograph.

went by, we bonded a little but I found him to be a gregarious guy, a nice guy. And very sharp." Schayes said, "As you get older, you want to do things you didn't do when you were younger, and I wanted to get to know Wilt better. And because we were getting together a couple of times a year lately, I was starting to. But now, I'll never have the opportunity."[17] Six years later, when George Mikan died, the *Syracuse Post-Standard* asked Schayes to name the top-ten centers in NBA history. At the top of the list was Wilt Chamberlain because he was "simply unstoppable. Unstoppable. I picked him No. 1 because later in his career he decided to change his game, become an all-around player and win the championship. He became unselfish."

Any evaluation of Chamberlain immediately brings up comparisons to Bill Russell. The Chamberlain-Russell rivalry, Schayes stressed, was the first of its kind in NBA history and captured the attention of writers and fans. In their duel the press portrayed Chamberlain as Goliath and Russell as David. Statistically, Chamberlain consistently bested Russell, but the Celtic center won the championship rings. In watching Chamberlain and

Russell compete, Schayes noticed something remarkable. Chamberlain was capable of throwing down dunks with savage force. Schayes believed that with Russell's hands above the rim and vulnerable, Chamberlain purposely adjusted his shot to avoid injuring his nemesis. In assessing their duel, Schayes fell into the camp that argued that when Chamberlain entered the NBA, Russell had the advantage of being surrounded by a better mix of players. In 1967 that situation changed, as Chamberlain and the 76ers ended Boston's string of eight championships. Simply said, for Schayes, "Wilt Chamberlain was larger than life."[18]

As time passed, Dolph Schayes became Syracuse's link to its professional basketball past. This connection was strengthened by periodic reunions. In April 1985 the Nats celebrated the thirtieth anniversary of their championship season. All of the players from that team were still alive except Dick Farley, who had died of cancer at the age of thirty-six.[19] In 1990 the Nats met again and gave Al Bianchi, general manager of the New York Knicks at that time, an opportunity to reflect on the game. He remembered the Syracuse team as a family. There were parties at Biasone's home or at Schayes's home. "You don't see the fun anymore," Bianchi observed. Bianchi thought that the players of 1990 were more physically gifted than players of the 1950s, but he was not convinced that they "really know how to play the game." He was sure that Dolph Schayes would have excelled in any era.[20]

On Memorial Day 1992 Danny Biasone passed away at the age of eighty-three. At the funeral mass Schayes said, "He was like a father to us."[21] In November 1999 Danny Biasone's Eastwood Sports Center succumbed to the wrecking ball. Dolph Schayes remembered that the Sports Center's hamburgers were "the best in Syracuse." Before practice and road trips the team met at the Sports Center. After home games the team would go to Biasone's Sports Center and often hang around until tw in the morning. Naomi remembered that Danny would hold court a argue basketball or the meaning of life, often pounding his fist on bar to make his point. Dolph called Danny's place "our home away home."[22] Forever linked to the twenty-four-second clock, Biasone's tributions to basketball were recognized in 2000 when he was in posthumously into the Basketball Hall of Fame.

In May 1998 Paul Seymour died after a long battle with heart disease. Schayes was shocked because, "to me, he was indestructible." When Schayes was honored with a lifetime achievement award at the age of seventy, he said of Seymour, "I considered Paul my very best friend. He had no airs. He was just Paul and was like a brother to me. We sort of fit together like a couple of puzzle pieces."[23]

As the twenty-first century opened, diehard Nats fans of the mid-twentieth century read of the loss of a number of their old heroes—Larry Costello, George King, George Yardley, Johnny Kerr, and Al Cervi. Others had left Syracuse for a variety of reasons. Billy Gabor had stayed in Syracuse, but Dolph Schayes's story was the most compelling.

From growing up in the Bronx until he played his last game with the Philadelphia 76ers, Dolph Schayes pursued basketball excellence with an extraordinary single-mindedness. He was always trying to figure out a way to improve. When he broke his right wrist, he became a better shooter with his left hand. He took care of himself physically and was always prepared to give his best effort. As a rookie in 1960, Joe Roberts remembered rooming with Schayes on a road trip. When they returned to their room after a game, Dolph said to Joe, "Rook, at 10:00 p.m. we are going to shut the lights and television off." Sure enough, at 10:00 p.m., the lights and television were off. Roberts thought of Schayes as the "consummate pro," did all his teammates.[24]

There was one slight contradiction that emerged in Dolph's game. As a teenager and collegian, Schayes was the first pro to show emotion after making a basket. After scoring, Schayes would raise his fist in to the consternation of his opponents. Although Schayes was and tough, he was not otherwise a gifted athlete. He was not he led the team in rebounding, he could not dunk the basket. was always moving and had a great feel for the game that cessful. In the era in which he played, Dolph Schayes St. Louis Hawks were the two best forwards. Leonard basketball writers in the 1950s and 1960s, thought hooter, best passer, and the best all-around money best, Pettit or Schayes, they set the standard for

Why had the team's star stayed in town? It was simple. As Schayes repeatedly said, "I was a withdrawn loner type who just took out my frustrations and energies in the game."[25] The city embraced him, and in different ways Danny Biasone, Paul Seymour, and others helped him come out of his shell. Syracuse was also where he met and married Naomi Gross, whom he thought "the most beautiful girl in the world and maybe on Mars, too."[26] Syracuse became his town.

In his mideighties there is a certain rhythm to Dolph Schayes's life. He is still involved in his rental business, now assisted by his son David. After sixty years he still goes to the office and meets clients. There is plenty of time to engage in his other activities: raising money for the Maccabiah Games, attending Hall of Fame enshrinement ceremonies, and keeping an eye on his grandchildren. For the local sportswriters, Schayes is a treasure trove of stories and commentary on how professional basketball has changed in its sixty-five-year history. Today, professional basketball, according to Schayes, is a "fairyland. . . . It's show business. Everybody's prominence is magnified by marketing."[27] Dolph Schayes came to Syracuse uncertain of his future in basketball, became a star, and remains the Salt City's major connection to its professional basketball past. He has enjoyed a life well lived.

Notes

Works Cited

Index

Notes

1. New York's Golden Age of Basketball

1. Dolph Schayes, phone interviews, Sept. 3, 2010, Oct. 27, 30, 2011.

2. Gerard J. Pelisson and James A. Garvey III, *Castle on the Parkway*, http://www.castleontheparkway.com/alumni.php.

3. Schayes, phone interview, Sept. 3, 2010.

4. Len Heideman, "Tall Adolf Schayes of Clinton Scouted by Two *Heights News* Reporters," *New York University Heights Daily News*, Jan. 12, 1945, 2.

5. Schayes, phone interview, Sept. 3, 2010.

6. Joe Gergen, *The Final Four*, 36–39.

7. "Howard Cann," in *Basketball Hall of Fame: Class of 1994 Yearbook*, 24.

8. Schayes, phone interview, Oct. 30, 2011.

9. Schayes interview, Oct. 30, 2011; Norm Drucker, phone interview, Oct. 31, 2011.

10. Gary Bodingfield, "Baseball in Wartime," http://www.baseballinwartime.com.

11. Steven A. Riess, ed., *Sports and the American Jew*, 24–25; Peter Levine, *Ellis Island to Ebbets Field: Sport and the American Jewish Experience*, 26–51.

12. Al Figone, "Gambling and College Basketball: The Scandal of 1951," 45–49.

13. "Nat Holman: The Man, His Legacy, and CCNY," http://www.ccny.cuny.edu/library.

14. Norm Drucker, phone interview, Oct. 31, 2011; Charles Rosen, *Scandals of '51: How the Gamblers Almost Killed College Basketball*, 52.

15. Rosen, *Scandals of 1951*, 90–97, 210–17.

16. Nat Holman, "The Man, His Legacy, and CCNY."

17. Gus Alfieri, *Lapchick: The Life of a Legendary Player and Coach in the Glory Days of Basketball*, 14, 52, 74, 104–75, 180, 296.

18. "Clair Bee," in *Basketball Hall of Fame: Class of 1994 Yearbook*, 21.

19. Larry Dubrow, "NYU Seeks Eleventh Victory," *New York Heights Daily News*, Feb. 9, 1945, 2.

20. Schayes, phone interview, Sept. 3, 2010.

21. Adolph Schayes file, New York University.

22. Louis Effrat, "Notre Dame Stops N.Y.U. by 66 to 60 on Garden Court," *New York Times*, Feb. 11, 1945, S1.

23. Schayes, phone interview, Oct. 30, 2011.

24. Louis Effrat, "N.Y.U. Rally Beats Ohio State Quintet in Overtime, 70–65," *New York Times*, Mar. 25, 1945, 57.

25. Louis Effrat, "Oklahoma Aggies Down N.Y.U., 49–45," *New York Times*, Mar. 28, 1945, 26.

26. Louis Effrat, "N.Y.U. Five Upsets Notre Dame, 62–58, before 18,095 Fans," *New York Times*, Feb. 10, 1946, 75.

27. Louis Effrat, "N.Y.U. Rally Trips St. John's, 58–54," *New York Times*, Feb. 21, 1946, 24.

28. Howard Rosenblum and Leonard Heideman, "Violets Halt Desperate Owls in Last Minutes: To Win," *New York University Heights Daily News*, Feb. 25, 1946, 1.

29. Daniel J. Robins, "Round Ohio Field," *New York University Heights Daily News*, Mar. 11, 1946, 4.

30. Larry Dubrow, "Betting on Basketball?," *New York University Heights Daily News*, Mar. 11, 1945, 4.

31. Louis Effrat, "N.Y.U. Loses, 57–49, to North Carolina," *New York Times*, Mar. 22, 1946, 30.

32. *New York University Heights Daily News*, Mar. 8, 1946, 4.

33. Figone, "Gambling and College Basketball," 46–47; Schayes, phone interview, Oct. 27, 2011.

34. Louis Effrat, "N.Y.U. Five Downs Connecticut, 67–41, before 18,309 Fans," *New York Times*, Dec. 8, 1946, 27.

35. Louis Effrat, "Redmen Withstand Rally to Win, 57–56," *New York Times*, Mar. 5, 1947, 32.

36. *New York University Heights Daily News*, Mar. 13, 1947, 2.

37. Jonas Kiken, "The Sports Desk," *New York University Heights Daily News*, Mar. 13, 1947, 2.

38. "Basketball," in *New York University Yearbook, 1946–47*, 147.

39. Dave Glinert, "Story of Dolf [sic] Schayes," *New York University Heights Daily News*, Mar. 10, 1947, 2.

40. Editorial, "Beat Notre Dame," *New York University Heights Daily News*, Mar. 1, 1948, 2.

41. Editorial, "Sportsmanship," *New York University Heights Daily News*, Mar. 3, 1948, 2.

42. Norman Jackman, "More Jack: A Tribute to Donnie," *New York University Heights Daily News*, Mar. 3, 1948, 4.

43. Norman Jackman, "CCNY Downs Five in Thriller, 60–57; Schayes NYU Scoring Record," *New York University Heights Daily News*, Mar. 10, 1948, 1.

44. *New York Times*, Mar. 14, 1948, S5.

45. Joe Hirsch, "The Sports Desk," *New York University Heights Daily News*, Mar. 9, 1948, 1.

46. Stan Hochman, "Violets Nip Texas in Final Seconds, 45–43; Face DePaul Five in Tourney Semi-finals Tonight," *New York University Heights Daily News*, Mar. 15, 1948, 1.

47. Louis Effrat, "St. Louis Conquers N.Y.U. in National Invitational Basketball Final at Garden," *New York Times*, Mar. 18, 1948, 38.

48. Louis Effrat, "Baylor Tops N.Y.U. in Olympic Trials at Garden, 59–57," *New York Times*, Mar. 28, 1948, 20.

49. Adolph H. Grundman, *The Golden Age of Amateur Basketball: The AAU Tournament, 1921–1968*, 115.

50. *New York University Heights Daily News*, Mar. 1, 1948, 4.

51. Schayes file, New York University.

52. Schayes, phone interview, Oct. 27, 2011.

53. Ibid.

54. Grundman, *Golden Age of Amateur Basketball*, 76–77; Schayes, phone interview, Oct. 30, 2011.

2. The Syracuse Nationals: The Al Cervi Years

1. Robert Peterson, *Cages to Jump Shots: Pro Basketball's Early Years*, 95–100.

2. Ibid., 110–12.

3. Ibid., 109.

4. Murry R. Nelson, *The National Basketball League: A History, 1935–1949*, 11–51, 142–59.

5. Leonard Koppett, *24 Seconds to Shoot: The Birth and Improbable Rise of the NBA*, 13–19; Charles Rosen, *The First Tip-Off: The Incredible Story of the NBA*, 11–20.

6. Neil D. Isaacs, *Vintage NBA: The Pioneer Era, 1946–1956*, 229–35; Rosen, *First Tip-Off*, 21–24.

7. Koppett, *24 Seconds to Shoot*, 34–38.

8. Dolph Grundman, *Jim Pollard: The Kangaroo Kid*, 42.

9. Schayes, phone interview, Oct. 30, 2011.

10. Koppett, *24 Seconds to Shoot*, 39.

11. Neils Florio, "Only in America: Immigrant Plays Key Role in Early Years of Pro Basketball," *Red, White, and Green Sports*, Jan. 1984, Danny Biasone file, Basketball Hall of Fame; Nelson, *National Basketball League*, 159.

12. Bill Reddy, "Keeping Posted," *Syracuse Post-Standard*, Mar. 19, 1949, 10; *Syracuse Post-Standard*, Mar. 27, 1949, sec. 4, 37.

13. Al Bianchi, phone interview, Sept. 19, 2011; Richard Goldstein, "Larry Costello, 70, Player and Coach in the NBA, Is Dead," *New York Times*, Dec. 14, 2001, D13.

14. Lawrence J. Skiddy, "Skidding the Sports Field," *Syracuse Herald-Journal*, Dec. 14, 1949, D4; Schayes, phone interview, Nov. 12, 2010.

15. David Ramsey, *The Nats*, 98; Schayes, phone interview, Sept. 10, 2000.

16. Koppett, *24 Seconds to Shoot*, 35–37.

17. Schayes, phone interview, Nov. 2, 2010; Harold Rosenthal, "Schayes Is a Hustler"; Alex Hannum with Frank Deford, "Old Days and Changed Ways."

18. Johnny Macknowsky, phone interview, Sept. 28, 2010.

19. Ramsey, *The Nats*, 125–27.

20. Nelson, *National Basketball League*, 291, 241, 243.

21. Ibid., 220–21.

22. Bill Reddy, "Keeping Posted," *Syracuse Post-Standard*, Mar. 6, 1949, 35.

23. Koppett, *24 Seconds to Shoot*, 43.

24. Ibid., 42–45.

25. Schayes, phone interview, Nov. 2, 2010.

26. Alex Hannum, interview, Apr. 1, 1999.

27. Al Cervi to Dick Triptow, n.d., in possession of Dick Triptow.

28. Ibid.

29. Al Cervi scrapbook, Basketball Hall of Fame.

30. *Syracuse Herald-Journal*, Mar. 13, 1950, 19.

31. Vince Boryla, interview, Sept. 18, 2010.

32. Al Cervi, "Cervi Happy over Series Sweep," *Syracuse Herald-Journal*, Mar. 24, 1950, 50.

33. Lawrence J. Skiddy, "Skidding the Sports Field," *Syracuse Herald-Journal*, Mar. 26, 1950, 45.

34. Bud Vander Veer, "Merriwell Finish Wins for Syracuse," *Syracuse Herald-Journal*, Mar. 27, 1950, 50.

35. Bill Reddy, "Keeping Posted," *Syracuse Post-Standard*, Apr. 12, 1950, sec. 4, 1.

36. "Knicks, Syracuse in Garden Tonight," *New York Times*, Mar. 30, 1950, 41.

37. Louis Effrat, "Knicks Conquer Syracuse, Even Play-Off Series," *New York Times*, Mar. 31, 1950, 46.

38. Louis Effrat, "Syracuse Topples Knicks for Title," *New York Times*, Apr. 3, 1950, 33.

39. Johnny Macknowsky, phone interview, Sept. 28, 2010; Bill Reddy, *Syracuse Post-Standard*, Apr. 9, 1950, 1.

40. Bill Reddy, "Keeping Posted," *Syracuse Post-Standard*, Apr. 10, 1950, 1.

41. Al Cervi, *Syracuse Herald-Journal*, Apr. 10, 1958, 12.

42. Jack Andrews, *Syracuse Post-Standard*, Apr. 15, 1950, 1.

43. Jack Andrews, *Syracuse Post-Standard*, Apr. 17, 1950, 1.

44. Jack Andrews, *Syracuse Post-Standard*, Apr. 21, 1950, 1.

45. Lawrence J. Skiddy, "Minneapolis Lakers Rule Basketball," *Syracuse Herald-Journal*, Apr. 24, 1950, 21.

46. Bud Poliquin, *Syracuse Post-Standard*, Jan. 2010, found on Jay LaFountaine's website.

47. Charles Freedman, "Schayes Is Still Haunting the Knicks," *New York Times*, Nov. 22, 1958, 17.

48. Bob Houbregs, phone interview, Oct. 28, 2010.

49. Koppett, *24 Seconds to Shoot*, 48–49.

50. Ron Thomas, *They Cleared the Lane: The NBA's Black Pioneers*, 26–44.

51. Koppett, *24 Seconds to Shoot*, 60–61.

52. Schayes, phone interview, Nov. 2, 2010.

53. http://www.NBAUniverse.com.

54. Jack Andrews, "Scolari Sinks Vital Baskets at Philadelphia," *Syracuse Post-Standard*, Mar. 21, 1951, 19.

55. Jack Andrews, "Nationals Top Warriors in Series Final, 90–78," *Syracuse Post-Standard*, Mar. 23, 1951, 1.

56. Koppett, *24 Seconds to Shoot*, 53–55.

57. Louis Effrat, "Knicks Defeat Syracuse Quintet in Opener of Semi-final Series," *New York Times*, Mar. 29, 1951, 43.

58. Louis Effrat, "New Yorkers Lose in Play-Off, 102–80," *New York Times*, Mar. 30, 1951, 38.

59. Louis Effrat, "Knicks Rally Halts Syracuse by 77–75 in Overtime Game," *New York Times*, Apr. 1, 1951, 155.

60. Louis Effrat, "Nationals Defeat New York by 90–83," *New York Times*, Apr. 2, 1951, 33.

61. Louis Effrat, "Knicks Win, 83–81, Gain Final Series," *New York Times*, Apr. 5, 1951, 36.

62. Vince Boryla, interview, Sept. 18, 2010; Alex Peterson, "Up Close and Personal: Remembering the 'Thrill Kids,'" edited by George Edmonston Jr., http://www.osualum.com.

63. Schayes, phone interview, Nov. 12, 2010; Earl Lloyd, phone interview, Nov. 16, 2010.

64. Koppett, *24 Seconds to Shoot*, 12–63.

65. *Syracuse Herald-Journal*, Mar. 24, 1952. 18.

66. Bill Reddy, "Keeping Posted," *Syracuse Post-Standard*, Apr. 2, 1952, 18.

67. Louis Effrat, "New York Quintet Triumphs by 87–85," *New York Times*, Apr. 3, 1952, 50.

68. Louis Effrat, "Nats Down Knicks, Tie Series at 1-All," *New York Times*, Apr. 4, 1952, 29.

69. Louis Effrat, "Knicks Check Nats for 2–1 Lead, 99–92," *New York Times*, Apr. 6, 1952, 51.

70. Louis Effrat, "New York Quintet Triumphs, 100–93," *New York Times*, Apr. 9, 1952, 37.

71. Bud Vander Veer, "Syracuse Eliminated in New York," *Syracuse Herald-Journal*, Apr. 9, 1952, 23.

72. Naomi Schayes, phone interviews, Oct. 27, 29, 2011.

73. Earl Lloyd, phone interview, Nov. 16, 2010.

74. Ibid.

75. Ibid.

76. Ibid.

77. Ibid.

78. Bill Reddy, "Syracuse Nationals May Be Sold to Interests in Larger City," *Syracuse Post-Standard*, Mar. 7, 1953, 10; Jack Andrews, "Duffy Renews Offer for Nats' Franchise," *Syracuse Post-Standard*, Mar. 16, 1953, 10.

79. Nats Invade Boston Today in Quest of Playoff Series Ties," *Syracuse Post-Standard*, Mar. 21, 1953, 10.

80. Bill Reddy, "Nationals Beaten by Celtics in Fourth Overtime," *Syracuse Post-Standard*, Mar. 22, 1953, sec. 4, 31.

81. "Biasone Gives Assurance Nationals to Remain in Syracuse," *Syracuse Post-Standard*, Mar. 23, 1953, 10.

82. Bill Reddy, "Keeping Posted," *Syracuse Post-Standard*, Mar. 21, 1953, 10; Frank Woolever, "Scanning the Sports Field," *Syracuse Herald-Journal*, Nov. 28, 1951, 37.

83. Bill Reddy, "Keeping Posted," *Syracuse Post-Standard*, Mar. 17, 1954, 19.

84. "Syracuse Downs Boston, 96–95," *New York Times*, Mar. 18, 1954, 36.

85. "Syracuse Downs New York, 75–68," *New York Times*, Mar. 19, 1954, 27.

86. Jack Andrews, "Nats Nips Knicks, 103–99," *Syracuse Post-Standard*, Mar. 22, 1954, 12.

87. *Syracuse Post-Standard*, Mar. 23, 1954, 12.

88. Bud Vander Veer, "Nats Move to Boston for Second Game," *Syracuse Herald-Journal*, Mar. 26, 1954, 39.

89. Jack Andrews, "Riot in Boston as Nats Beat Celtics, 83–76," *Syracuse Post-Standard*, Mar. 28, 1954, 27.

90. *Syracuse Post-Standard*, Apr. 1, 1954, 16.

91. "Nationals Top Lakers by 62–60, Even Series at One Game Apiece," *New York Times*, Apr. 4, 1954, 81; *Syracuse Post-Standard*, Apr. 4, 1954, sec. 4, 31.

92. *Syracuse Post-Standard*, Apr. 5, 1954, 12.

93. *Syracuse Post-Standard*, Apr. 9, 1954, 38.

94. *New York Times*, Apr. 11, 1954, 51.

95. *Syracuse Post-Standard*, Apr. 12, 1954, 10.

96. *Minneapolis Morning Tribune*, Apr. 13, 1954, 10; Jack Andrews, "Nats Bow 87–80," *Syracuse Post-Standard*, Apr. 13, 1954, 14.

97. Cervi to Triptow, n.d., in possession of Triptow.

98. *Syracuse Post-Standard*, Apr. 18, 1954, 34; *Syracuse Post-Standard*, Mar. 29, 1954; *Syracuse Post-Standard*, Apr. 11, 1954, sec. 4, 31.

99. Dick Clarke, "For a Youngster, Nats Made Magic," *Syracuse Herald-Journal*, June 9, 1992, D3; Betsy Burton to Dolph Grundman, e-mail, July 14, 2011.

100. Koppett, *24 Seconds to Shoot*, 89–93.

101. Sam Smith, "Johnny Kerr the Original Iron Man," asksam@bulls.com, Feb. 2, 2009.

102. Leonard Koppett, "Strictly for Laughs," *New York Times*, Nov. 9, 1965, 56.

103. Bob Greene, "Commentary: Boss Ends Amazing Streak," CNN.US, June 14, 2009.

104. *Cincinnati Enquirer*, Mar. 19, 1964, 24.

105. Bianchi, phone interview, Jan. 31, 2011.

106. Greene, "Commentary."

107. Jim Tucker, phone interview, Jan. 4, 2011.

108. *Syracuse Herald-Journal*, Oct. 5, 1954, 20.

109. *New York Times*, Oct. 9, 1954, 13.

110. *Syracuse Post-Standard*, Mar. 5, 1955, 8.

111. Jack Andrews, "Nats Triumph over Celts in Opening Playoff Games," *Syracuse Post-Standard*, Mar. 23, 1955, 19.

112. Jack Andrews, "8,186 See Nats Repeat 116–110 over Celtics," *Syracuse Post-Standard*, Mar. 26, 1955, 28.

113. Jack Andrews, "13,091 Watch as Cousy Finds Scoring Touch," *Syracuse Post-Standard*, Mar. 27, 1955, 35; *Boston Globe*, Mar. 28, 1955, 30.

114. Jack Andrews, "Nats Trounce Boston to Enter NBA Finals," *Syracuse Post-Standard*, Mar. 28, 1955, 1.

115. Koppett, *24 Seconds to Shoot*, 21, 97–98.

116. Grundman, *Golden Age of Amateur Basketball*, 131, 137–39, 142, 147, 152.

117. Charley Rosen, *The Wizard of Odds: How Jack Molinas Almost Destroyed the Game of Basketball*, 127–41.

118. Koppett, *24 Seconds to Shoot*, 98.

119. Ben Tenny, *Fort Wayne (IN) News-Sentinel*, Mar. 28, 1955, 10.

120. Jack Andrews, "Nats Nip Pistons, 86–82, in First Tilt," *Syracuse Post-Standard*, Apr. 1, 1955, 31–33.

121. Ben Tenny, *Fort Wayne (IN) News-Sentinel*, Apr. 1, 1955, 13.

122. Jack Andrews, "Nats Nip Pistons in NBA Playoff, 87–84," *Syracuse Post-Standard*, Apr, 3, 1955, IV:37.

123. Ben Tenny, "Zs Win at Coliseum in Indy," *Fort Wayne (IN) News-Sentinel*, Apr. 4, 1955, 8.

124. Ben Tenny, "Pistons Shoot for Series Lead Thursday," *Fort Wayne (IN) News-Sentinel*, Apr. 6, 1955, 10.

125. Jack Andrews, "Cervi after Torrid Clash," *Syracuse Post-Standard*, Apr. 8, 1955, 30; Ben Tenny, "Zs Have Two Chances to Gain Championship," *Fort Wayne (IN) News-Sentinel*, Apr. 8, 1955, 12.

126. Ben Tenny, "Pistons Can Win World Crown Today," *Fort Wayne (IN) News-Sentinel*, Apr. 9, 1955, 20.

127. Bud Vander Veer, "Kerr and Farley Spark Contest," *Syracuse Herald-Journal*, Apr. 10, 1955, 49.

128. Jack Andrews, "Beat Pistons in Thrilling Finals, 92–91," *Syracuse Post-Standard*, Apr. 11, 1955, 16.

129. Jack Andrews, "Cervi Lauds His Athletes in Greatest Moment of Glory," *Syracuse Post-Standard*, Apr. 11, 1955.

130. Jack Andrews, *Syracuse Post-Standard*, Apr. 12, 1955, 1.

131. Vince Boryla, interview, Sept. 18, 2010.

132. Koppett, *24 Seconds to Shoot*, 100–101.

133. Bill Reddy, "Celtics Trounce Nats in Opening Playoff," *Syracuse Post-Standard*, Mar. 18, 1956, sec. 4, 31.

134. Bill Reddy, "Nats Beat Celtics to Square Series," *Syracuse Post-Standard*, Mar. 20, 1956, 14.

135. Bill Reddy, "Nats Triumph, 102–97 to Eliminate Celts," *Syracuse Post-Standard*, Mar. 22, 1956, 25.

136. Rich Westcott, *Eddie Gottlieb, Philadelphia Legend and Pro Basketball Pioneer*.

137. *Dunkirk (NY) Evening Observer*, Mar. 21, 1956, 9.

138. Bill Reddy, "Nats Whip Warriors, 122–118, to Tie Series," *Syracuse Post-Standard*, Mar. 26, 1956, 12.

139. *New York Times*, Mar. 28, 1956, 36.

140. Bud Vander Veer, "George King Sparkles as Nats Win 4th Game," *Syracuse Herald-Journal*, Mar. 29, 1956, 49.

141. Jack Andrews, "Nats Eliminated by Warriors, 109 to 104," *Syracuse Post-Standard*, Mar. 30, 1956, 16.

142. Bud Vander Veer, "Nats Eliminated," *Syracuse Herald-Journal*, Mar. 20, 1956, 22.

143. Earl Lloyd, phone interview, Nov. 16, 2010.

144. *Syracuse Herald-Journal*, Apr. 26, 1956, 62.

145. Schayes, phone interview, Nov. 12, 2010.

146. Earl Lloyd, phone interview, Nov. 16, 2010.

3. Dolph Schayes Rewrites the Record Book

1. Bob Hopkins, phone interview, Jan. 4, 2011.

2. Jack Andrews, "Nats Face Pistons," *Syracuse Post-Standard*, Nov. 29, 1956, 27.

3. Arnie Burdick, "Cage Fan Sees Thriller," *Syracuse Herald-Journal*, Dec. 11, 1957, 28.

4. *Boston Daily Globe*, Mar. 10, 1957, 20.

5. *Boston Daily Globe*, Mar. 11, 1957, 18.

6. *Boston Daily Globe*, Mar. 17, 1957, 18.

7. *Boston Daily Globe*, Mar. 19, 1957, 18.

8. Koppett, *24 Seconds to Shoot*, 107–11.

9. Clif Keane, *Boston Daily Globe*, Mar. 20, 1957, 30.

10. Clif Keane, *Boston Daily Globe*, Mar. 22, 1957, 1, 23.

11. Clif Keane, *Boston Daily Globe*, Mar. 24, 1957, 45, 50.

12. *New York Times*, Mar. 25, 1957, 31.

13. Bianchi, phone interview, Jan. 31, 2011.

14. Kevin Cook, "Rochester Royals: The Story of Professional Basketball"; Donald M. Fisher, "Lester Harrison and the Rochester Royals, 1945–1957: A Jewish Entrepreneur in the NBA."

15. Koppett, *24 Seconds to Shoot*, 116–17.

16. Richard Goldstein, "Larry Costello, 70, Player and Coach in the NBA, Is Dead," *New York Times*, Dec. 14, 2001, D13.

17. Wayne Embry with Mary Schmitt Boyer, *The Inside Game: Race, Power, and Politics in the NBA*, 256.

18. Dave Gambee, phone interview, Aug. 9, 2011.

19. Goldstein, "Larry Costello, 70, Player and Coach in the NBA, Is Dead."

20. Koppett, "Schayes 'Best' Gives Nats Easy Win in New York," *Syracuse Herald-Journal*, Dec. 4, 1957, 39.

21. Clif Keane, "Nats Topple Knicks, 105 to 102, Battle Storm to Get Here for Game," *Syracuse Herald-Journal*, Feb. 8, 1958, 9.

22. *Syracuse Herald-American*, Feb. 9, 1958, 50.

23. Ibid.

24. Togo Palazzi, phone interview, Jan. 24, 2011.

25. *Syracuse Herald-Journal*, Feb. 13, 1958, 43.

26. *Syracuse Post-Standard*, Feb. 21, 1958, 5.

27. *New York Times*, Mar. 16, 1958, S3.

28. Bud Vander Veer, "Seymour Blasts Officials," *Syracuse Herald-Journal*, Mar. 17, 1958, 21.

29. Bill Reddy, "Warriors Ousts Nats from Playoffs, 101–88," *Syracuse Post-Standard*, Mar. 19, 1958, 14.

30. Bill Reddy, "Schayes Smashes All-Time Pro Scoring Record," *Syracuse Post-Standard*, Jan. 13, 1958, 10.

31. *New York Times*, Mar. 2, 1958, S9.

32. *Hoopedia*, s.v. "Hal Greer."

33. George Yardley, "Basketball's Original 'Bird,'" http://www.JockBio.com.

34. Schayes, phone interview, Dec. 15, 2010.

35. Bill Reddy, "Keeping Posted," *Syracuse Post-Standard*, Mar. 2, 1959, 12.

36. Arthur Daley, "Sports of the Times," *New York Times*, Oct. 22, 1958, 47.

37. Michael Strauss, "Nationals Defeat Knicks in Play-Off Opener," *New York Times*, Mar. 14, 1959, 28.

38. Bill Reddy, "Keeping Posted," *Syracuse Post-Standard*, Mar. 15, 1959, 12.

39. Joseph Sheehan, "Nationals Eliminate Knick Five," *New York Times*, Mar. 16, 1959, 34.

40. "Brawls Spice Nats Victory," *Syracuse Post-Standard*, Feb. 20, 1959, 1; "Brawling Marks Syracuse Victory," *New York Times*, Feb. 20, 1959, 29.

41. *Boston Evening Globe*, Mar. 16, 1959, 30.

42. Clif Keane, *Boston Evening Globe*, Mar. 16, 1959, 32.

43. Jack Barry, *Boston Evening Globe*, Mar. 22, 1959, 27.

44. *Boston Evening Globe*, Mar. 26, 1959, 25.

45. Clif Keane, *Boston Evening Globe*, Mar. 26, 1959, 30.

46. Jack Andrews, *Syracuse Post-Standard*, Mar. 27, 1959, 12.

47. Clif Keane, "Celtics Favorite in Climax Battle," *Boston Evening Globe*, Apr. 1, 1959, 28.

48. Francis Rosa, "Crowd Carries Ace Off Floor," *Boston Daily Globe*, Apr. 2, 1959, 29.

49. "'Greatest Game I've Seen,' Says Sharman after Win," *Boston Daily Globe*, Apr. 2, 1959, 32.

50. "Referee, Fan Tangle," *Boston Daily Globe*, Apr. 2, 1959, 30.

51. Louis Effrat, "Basketball Man Always in Motion," *New York Times*, Feb. 19, 1959, 32.

52. Schayes, phone interview, Dec. 17, 2010; Milton S. Katz, *Breaking Through: John B. McLendon, Basketball Legend and Civil Rights Pioneer*, 84–92; Bud Poliquin, "One Old Syracuse National, Dick Barnett, Recalls 'the Boss' . . . and, Yes, He Does So Fairly Fondly," *Syracuse Post-Standard*, July 20, 2010, 20; William Leggett, "A New Knick with a Knack."

53. "Nats Beat Celtics as Yardley, Schayes Star," *Syracuse Post-Standard*, Jan. 13, 1960, 15.

54. "Dolph Runs up 15,000."

55. Deane McGowen, "Rookie Dominates 125–115 Contest," *New York Times*, Jan. 23, 1960, 17.

56. Bill Reddy, "Nats Beat Warriors to Tie Playoff Series," *Syracuse Post-Standard*, Mar. 14, 1960, 12; "Syracuse Scores 125–119 Decision," *New York Times*, Mar. 14, 1960, 33; "First-Half Drive Decisive, 132–112," *New York Times*, Mar. 15, 1960, 49.

57. Grundman, *Golden Age of Amateur Basketball*, 191, 193, 212.

58. Charles Salzberg, *From Set Shot to Slam Dunk: The Glory Days of Basketball in the Words of Those Who Played It*, 174.

59. Koppett, *24 Seconds to Shoot*, 57.

60. Halbrook scrapbook, in possession of Mary Kay Halbrook.

61. Ibid.

62. Gerald Astor, "A Matter of Size"; Beaver Eclips, Oregon State University Alumni Association.

63. Grundman, *Golden Age of Amateur Basketball*, 165–66.

64. "Swede Halbrook Dies in Portland at Age 55," *Portland Oregonian*, Apr. 5, 1988, 20.

65. Gambee, phone interviews, Aug. 9, Sept. 22, 2011.

66. "Schayes of Nats Is Hailed," *New York Times*, Nov. 22, 1960, 45; "Robertson Is Selected," *New York Times*, Jan. 1, 1961, 52; "Schayes Hits 17,000," *New York Times*, Jan. 28, 1961, 15.

67. Bill Reddy, "Nats Upset Warriors in Opener, 115–107," *Syracuse Post-Standard*, Mar. 15, 1961, 16; Jack Andrews, "Nats Halt Warriors' Rally in Dramatic Win," *Syracuse Post-Standard*, Mar. 17, 1961, 20; "Nats Sweep Series against Warriors, 106–103," *Syracuse Post-Standard*, sec. 4, 31.

68. "Boston Registers 128–115 Triumph," *New York Times*, Mar. 20, 1961, 31.

69. Bill Reddy, "Nats Battle to 115–98 Triumph over Celts," *Syracuse Post-Standard*, Mar. 22, 1961, 18.

70. "Celtics Top Nats in 133–110 Game," *New York Times*, Mar. 24, 1961, 38; "Russell Sparks 123–101 Victory," *New York Times*, Mar. 27, 1961, 35.

71. Koppett, *24 Seconds to Shoot*, 143–48.

72. Ben Green, *Spinning the Globe: The Rise, Fall, and Return to Greatness of the Harlem Globetrotters*, 308–9.

73. Bianchi, phone interview, Dec. 18, 2011.

74. Lee Shaffer, phone interview, Dec. 17, 2011.

75. Ibid.

76. Arthur Daley, "Sports of the Times," *New York Times*, Nov. 15, 1961, 54.

77. "N.Y.U. Varsity Club to Honor Mele and Schayes on November 13," *New York Times*, Nov. 1, 1961, 47.

78. "Baylor Selected on All-Star Team," *New York Times*, Dec. 23, 1961, 19.

79. "Schayes Streak Ends at Record 764 Games," *New York Times*, Dec. 28, 1961, 33.

80. "Warriors Down Nats 110 to 103," *New York Times*, Mar. 17, 1962, 19; "Warriors Beaten by Nats," *New York Times*, Mar. 20, 1962, 46; Bill Reddy, "Nats Win, 106–99, Tie Series with Warriors," *Syracuse Post-Standard*, Mar. 21, 1962, 14; "Warriors Reach Play-Off Finals," *New York Times*, Mar. 23, 1962, 39.

81. Chet Walker with Chris Messenger, *Long Time Coming: A Black Athlete's Coming of Age in America*, 12–13, 60–61, 127–28, 183–89, 214–32.

82. *Syracuse Post-Standard*, May 13, 1962, 35.

83. Koppett, *24 Seconds to Shoot*, 155.

84. Ted Meier, "First 1,000 Games Hardest, 15-Year Vet Schayes," *Baltimore Sun*, Jan. 23, 1963, 20.

85. *Syracuse Post-Standard*, Mar. 3, 1963, 32.

86. Bill Reddy, "Celtics Win Cousy's Finale Here, 125–121," *Syracuse Post-Standard*, Mar. 17, 1963, sec. 4, 29.

87. Schayes, phone interview, Jan. 8, 2013.

88. Bill Reddy, "Keeping Posted," *Syracuse Post-Standard*, Feb. 6, 1963, 18.

89. Bill Reddy, "Nats Edge Royals in Rugged Opener, 123–120," *Syracuse Post-Standard*, Mar. 20, 1963, 16.

90. Jim Schottelkotte, "Nats Bashed, 133–115," *Cincinnati Enquirer*, Mar. 22, 1963, 41.

91. Jim Schottelkotte, "Nats One-Up," *Cincinnati Enquirer*, Mar. 24, 1963, D1.

92. "Royals Win, Tie Series," *Cincinnati Enquirer*, Mar. 25, 1963, 35.

93. Jack Andrews, "Cincinnati Downs Nats in Overtime, 131–127," *Syracuse Post-Standard*, Mar. 27, 1963, 15.

94. "Nats Five Is Sold for $500,000 and Will Move to Philadelphia," *New York Times*, May 16, 1963, 44.

95. Naomi Schayes, phone interview, Oct. 27, 2011.

96. Jack Andrews, "Departing Nats Left Exciting Memories," *Syracuse Post-Standard*, May 19, 1963.

97. *Hoopedia*, s.v. "Walter Kennedy."

4. The Transition Game: From Player to Coach

1. Schayes, phone interview, Feb. 2, 2011; Naomi Schayes, phone interview, Oct. 27, 2011.

2. Bill Reddy, "Keeping Posted," *Syracuse Post-Standard*, July 17, 1963, 15.

3. Frank Fitzpatrick, "Les Keiter, 89; Famed Big Five Broadcaster," *Philadelphia Inquirer*, Apr. 16, 2009, http://alt.obituaries.com; Schayes, phone interview, Oct. 27, 2011.

4. Leonard Koppett, "Knicks Sell Guerin to St. Louis Five and Buy Chappell from Philadelphia," *New York Times*, Oct. 21, 1963, 43.

5. Leonard Koppett, "76ers Crush Knicks, 118–101, but Triumph Proves Costly," *New York Times*, Nov. 21, 1963, 64; Leonard Koppett, "Pistons Lose to 76ers," *New York Times*, Dec. 2, 1963, 67.

6. "Greer's 50 Points Help Rout Boston," *New York Times*, Feb. 22, 1964, 27.

7. *New York Times*, Dec. 29, 1963, 114.

8. *New York Times*, Feb. 9, 1964, S5.

9. Jim Schottekottle, "Cincinnati Tops 76ers by 130–124," *Cincinnati Enquirer*, Mar. 30, 1964, 41.

10. Phil Elderkin, "Schayes Erects Invisible Line," *Christian Science Monitor*, Jan. 1, 1964, Schayes file, New York University.

11. Leonard Koppett, *24 Seconds to Shoot*, 167.

12. Ibid., 163–65.

13. Arthur Daley, "Mutiny on the Bounty," *New York Times*, Jan. 23, 1964, 40.

14. Bill Reddy, "Keeping Posted," *Syracuse Post-Standard*, Jan. 13, 1964, 14.

15. Jack Andrews, "Dan Biasone Honored at NBA All-Star Game," *Syracuse Post-Standard*, Jan. 14, 1965, 24.

16. Koppett, *24 Seconds to Shoot*, 169.

17. Shaffer, phone interview, Dec. 16, 2011.

18. Schayes, interview, Aug. 20, 2010.

19. "Philly Fans Storming the Gates to See Wilt Play for 76ers."

20. Koppett, *24 Seconds to Shoot*, 150.

21. Leonard Koppett, "Wither Wilt," *New York Times*, Jan. 15, 1965, 27.

22. Jim Schottelkotte, "Schayes Boosts His Sport," *Cincinnati Enquirer*, Mar. 22, 1963, 41.

23. Dolph Schayes, "Wilt Chamberlain as We Knew Him."

24. *Philadelphia Daily News*, Jan. 16, 1962, 30.

25. Schottelkotte, "Schayes Boosts His Sport," 41.

26. Wilt Chamberlain, *View from Above*, 75.

27. Schayes, phone interview, Feb. 2, 2011.

28. "76ers Top Royals and Bullets Set Back Hawks in Opening N.B.A. Playoffs," *New York Times*, Mar. 25, 1965, 46.

29. "Royals, Hawks Gain in Playoffs," *New York Times*, Mar. 27, 1965, 19.

30. "Winner Leads 2–1, in East Playoffs," *New York Times*, Mar. 29, 1965, 50.

31. "76ers Down Royals, 119–112, and Enter N.B.A. Eastern Finals against Celtics," *New York Times*, Apr. 1, 1965, 46.

32. Gordon S. White Jr., "Russell Victor in Rebound Duel," *New York Times*, Apr. 5, 1965, 40.

33. Gordon S. White Jr., "Playoff Series Is Evened at 1-1," *New York Times*, Apr. 7, 1965, 50.

34. "Celtics Set Back 76ers by 112–94," *New York Times*, Apr. 9, 1965, 23.

35. "76ers Defeat Celtics in Overtime by 134–131," *New York Times*, Apr. 10, 1965, 24.

36. Wilt Chamberlain with Bob Ottum, "I'm Punchy from Basketball, Baby, and Tired of Being a Villain."

37. "Wilt Protests His Magazine Article," *Syracuse Post-Standard*, Apr. 10, 1965, 9.

38. Gordon S. White Jr., "Celtics Top 76ers, 114–108, and Take 3–2 Lead in Series," *New York Times*, Apr. 12, 1965, 45.

39. Gordon S. White Jr., "Victors Thwart Late Boston Bid," *New York Times*, Apr. 14, 1965, 49.

40. Ibid.

41. Gordon S. White Jr., "Havlicek Stars in 110–109 Game," *New York Times*, Apr. 16, 1965, 19; Schayes, phone interviews, Feb. 2, Dec. 23, 2011; Salzberg, *From Set Shot to Slam Dunk*, 213; Terry Pluto, *Tall Tales: The Glory Years of the NBA in the Words of the Men Who Built Pro Basketball*, 262.

42. Schayes, phone interview, Mar. 7, 2011.

43. "Greer's 38 Points Set Scoring Pace," *New York Times*, Nov. 14, 1965, S2.

44. "Wilt Climbs Past Dolph's Point Total," *Syracuse Herald-Journal*, Nov. 18, 1965, 50.

45. "Richman, Owner of the 76ers, Dies after Coronary at Game," *New York Times*, Dec. 9, 1965, 25.

46. "Chamberlain Gets 20,884th Point for a Record," *New York Times*, Feb. 15, 1966, 45.

47. "76ers Top Bullets and End Celtics' 9-Year Hold on Eastern Title," *New York Times*, Mar. 21, 1966, 40.

48. "Still Want the Big One—Wilt," *Syracuse Herald-Journal*, Mar. 21, 1966, 21.

49. Schayes, phone interview, Feb. 2, 2011.

50. Ibid.

51. "Schayes Is NBA Coach of the Year," *New York Post*, Mar. 31, 1966, 40.

52. Lloyd R. Milligan, "Chamberlain Rises to Challenge of Team Play with Philadelphia," *New York Times*, Mar. 21, 1966, 40.

53. Schayes, phone interview, Feb. 2, 2011; *Syracuse Herald-Journal*, Mar. 21, 1966, 21.

54. Gordon S. White Jr., "Sam Jones Paces Boston's Attack," *New York Times*, Mar. 31, 1966, 51.

55. Gordon S. White Jr., "Boston Defense Shackles Rivals," *New York Times*, Apr. 4, 1966, 38.

56. Gordon S. White Jr., "Runaway Causes Last-Period Fight," *New York Times*, Apr. 7, 1966, 67.

57. Gordon S. White Jr., "76ers Turn Back Celtics, 111 to 105," *New York Times*, Apr. 8, 1966, 15; Schayes, phone interview, Feb. 2, 2011.

58. Gordon S. White Jr., "Champions Take 3–1 Series Lead," *New York Times*, Apr. 11, 1966, 50.

59. Gordon S. White Jr., "Boston Captures East Series, 4–1," *New York Times*, Apr. 13, 1966, 48; "76ers Divide $29,000," *New York Times*, Apr. 14, 1966, 50.

60. Bill Reddy, "Keeping Posted," *Syracuse Post-Standard*, Apr. 28, 1966, 34.

61. "Warriors Dismiss Hannum and Name Sharman as Coach," *New York Times,* Mar. 23, 1966, 51.

62. "Schayes Replaced by Hannum," *New York Times,* May 3, 1966, 58.

63. Larry Merchant, "Wilt and the Firing," *New York Post,* May 3, 1966, Schayes file, New York University.

64. Leonard Lewin, "Dolph's Wife Looks . . . and Calls a 'Foul,'" *New York Post,* May 3, 1966, Schayes file, New York University.

65. Bill Reddy, "Keeping Posted," *Syracuse Post-Standard,* May 10, 1966, 21; Joe Beamish, "City and Country Life," *Syracuse Herald-Journal,* June 10, 1966, 11.

66. Koppett, *24 Seconds to Shoot,* 183–84.

67. Ibid., 188–92.

68. Ibid., 205.

69. Ibid., 197–207.

70. Schayes, phone interview, Mar. 7, 2011.

71. Ibid.

72. "Schayes Will Coach N.B.A. Team," *New York Times,* Apr. 1, 1970, 71.

73. "Buffalo Braves History," http://www.buffalobraves.blogspot.com.

74. Ibid.

75. "Buffalo Rising: Remember the Buffalo Braves?," http://www.buffalorising.com; Schayes, phone interview, Mar. 7, 2011.

76. "Braves Down Cavaliers," *New York Times,* Oct. 15, 1970, 68; "Braves Top Knicks, 97–91, as May Paces Last-Period Rally against Ex-Team," *New York Times,* Dec. 5, 1970, 46.

77. "Dolph Misses His NYU Night," *New York Post,* Nov. 5, 1970, 68.

78. "Buffalo Braves History."

79. Schayes, phone interview, May 7, 2011.

80. *New York Times,* Mar. 30, 1971, 29.

81. *New York Times,* Oct. 14, 1971, 59.

82. Schayes, phone interview, Mar. 7, 2011.

83. Buffalo Braves, "Historical Moments," http://www.chriscreamer.com.

5. A Life Well Lived

1. Danny Schayes, phone interview, May 1, 2011; Schayes phone interview, Dec. 5, 2011.

2. Schayes, phone interview, Apr. 30, 2011.

3. Steve Klein, "NBA Hall-of-Famer Says Games in Israel Forged His Jewish Identity," http://www.Haaretz.com.

4. Schayes, phone interview, Apr. 30, 2011.

5. Danny Schayes, phone interview, May 1, 2011.

6. Schayes, phone interview, Apr. 30, 2011.

7. Danny Schayes, phone interview, May 1, 2011.

8. Klein, "NBA Hall of Famer Says Games in Israel Forged His Jewish Identity."

9. Danny Schayes, http://www.BasketballReference.com; Dick Clarke, "Sharp Schayes a Success Story," *Syracuse Herald-American*, Jan. 30, 1977, 30; Schayes, phone interview, Dec. 5, 2011.

10. Schayes, phone interview, Dec. 5, 2011.

11. Ibid.

12. Danny Schayes, http://www.BasketballRefeerence.com.

13. *Wikipedia*, s.v. "NBA 25th Anniversary Team."

14. "The NBA at 50," http://NBA.com.

15. Bud Poliquin, "Schayes Takes Trip Back to Glory Days," *Syracuse Herald-Journal*, Feb. 12, 1997.

16. Naomi Schayes, phone interview, Apr. 16, 2011.

17. Bud Poliquin, "Dolph Was Just Getting to Know Wilt Better," *Syracuse Post-Standard*, Oct. 16, 1999, C1.

18. Bud Poliquin, "Wrath of Mikan Recalled," *Syracuse Post-Standard*, June 14, 2005, D1.

19. Bud Vander Veer, "Nats Recall Thrill of Being NBA Kings," *Syracuse Herald-Journal*, Apr. 8, 1985, C4.

20. Bud Vander Veer, "Nats Reunite Remember Their Old Days," *Syracuse Herald American*, July 22, 1990, E9.

21. Bud Poliquin, "Biasone Ascends to Basketball Heaven," *Syracuse Herald-Journal*, May 29, 1992, D1.

22. Sean Kirst, "Basketball League Was Born at Syracuse's Old Sports Center," *Syracuse Post-Standard*, Nov. 22, 1999, B1.

23. David Ramsey, "Seymour's Spirit Defined the Nats," *Syracuse Herald-Journal*, May 7, 1998, D1.

24. Joe Roberts, phone interview, Dec. 20, 2011.

25. David Ramsey, "He Was Timid, Shy and One of the NBA Greats," *Syracuse Herald-Journal*, June 4, 1992, C1.

26. Bud Poliquin, *Central New York Magazine*, Jan.–Feb. 2007.

27. Bud Poliquin, "NBA of Today Is Nothing Like the World of the Nats, Schayes Says," *Syracuse Herald-Journal*, Jan. 30, 1997, D6.

Works Cited

Archives

Biasone, Danny. File. Basketball Hall of Fame, Springfield, MA.
Schayes, Adolph. File. New York University.

Newspapers

Baltimore Sun
Boston Daily Globe
Boston Evening Globe
Christian Science Monitor
Cincinnati Enquirer
Dunkirk (NY) Evening Observer
Fort Wayne (IN) News-Sentinel
Minneapolis Morning Tribune
New York Post
New York Times
New York University Heights Daily News
Philadelphia Daily News
Philadelphia Inquirer
Portland Oregonian
Syracuse Herald-American
Syracuse Herald-Journal
Syracuse Post-Standard

Other Sources

Alfieri, Gus. *Lapchick: The Life of a Legendary Player and Coach in the Glory Days of Basketball*. Guilford, CT: Lyons Press, 2006.

Astor, Gerald. "A Matter of Size." *Sports Illustrated*, Feb. 15, 1955, 54–55.

Basketball Hall of Fame: Class of 1994 Yearbook. West Springfield, MA: Bordeaux, 1994.

Chamberlain, Wilt. *View from Above*. New York: Villard Books, 1991.

Chamberlain, Wilt, with Bob Ottum. "I'm Punchy from Basketball, Baby, and Tired of Being a Villain." *Sports Illustrated*, Apr. 12, 1965, 32–43.

Cook, Kevin. "Rochester Royals: The Story of Professional Basketball." *Rochester History* 58 (Winter 1966): 10–18.

"Dolph Runs Up 15,000." *Sports Illustrated*, Jan. 25, 1960, 25–26.

Embry, Wayne, and Mary Schmitt Boyer. *The Inside Game: Race, Power, and Politics in the NBA*. Akron, OH: Akron University Press, 2004.

Figone, Al. "Gambling and College Basketball: The Scandal of 1951." *Journal of Sport History* 16, no. 1 (1989): 45–49.

Fisher, Donald M. "Lester Harrison and the Rochester Royals, 1945–1957: A Jewish Entrepreneur in the NBA." In *Sports and the American Jew*, edited by Steven A. Riess, 232–40. Syracuse, NY: Syracuse University Press, 1988.

Gergen, Joe. *The Final Four*. St. Louis: Sporting News, 1987.

Green, Ben. *Spinning the Globe: The Rise, Fall, and Return to Greatness of the Harlem Globetrotters*. New York: HarperCollins, 2005.

Grundman, Adolph H. *The Golden Age of Amateur Basketball: The AAU Tournament, 1921–1968*. Lincoln: University of Nebraska Press, 2004.

———. *Jim Pollard: The Kangaroo Kid*. Minneapolis: Nodin Press, 2009.

Hannum, Alex, with Frank Deford. "Old Days and Changed Ways." *Sports Illustrated*, Nov. 25, 1968, 36–44.

Isaacs, Neil D. *Vintage NBA: The Pioneer Era, 1946–1956*. Indianapolis: Masters Press, 1996.

Katz, Milton S. *Breaking Through: John B. McLendon, Basketball Legend and Civil Rights Pioneer*. Fayetteville: University of Arkansas Press, 2007.

Koppett, Leonard. *24 Seconds to Shoot: The Birth and Improbable Rise of the NBA*. 1968. Reprint, Kingston, NY: Total Sports Illustrated Classics, 1999.

Leggett, William. "A New Knick with a Knack." *Sports Illustrated*, Jan. 17, 1966, 18–26.

Levine, Peter. *Ellis Island to Ebbets Field: Sport and the American Jewish Experience*. New York: Oxford University Press, 1992.

Nelson, Murry R. *The National Basketball League: A History, 1935–1949*. Jefferson, NC: McFarland, 2009.

Peterson, Robert. *Cages to Jump Shots: Pro Basketball's Early Years*. New York: Oxford University Press, 1990.

"Philly Fans Storming the Gates to See Wilt Play for 76ers." *Sporting News*, Feb. 27, 1965, 37.

Pluto, Terry. *Tall Tales: The Glory Years of the NBA in the Words of the Men Who Built Pro Basketball*. New York: Simon and Schuster, 1992.

Ramsey, David. *The Nats*. Utica, NY: North Country Books, 1995.

Riess, Steven A., ed. *Sports and the American Jew*. Syracuse, NY: Syracuse University Press, 1998.

Rosen, Charles. *The First Tip-Off: The Incredible Story of the NBA*. New York: McGraw-Hill, 2009.

———. *Scandals of '51: How the Gamblers Almost Killed College Basketball*. New York: Holt, Rinehart, and Winston, 1978.

———. *The Wizard of Odds: How Jack Molinas Almost Destroyed the Game of Basketball*. New York: Seven Stories Press, 2001.

Rosenthal, Harold. "Schayes Is a Hustler." *Sport*, Feb. 1958, 40–41, 72–73.

Salzberg, Charles. *From Set Shot to Slam Dunk: The Glory Days of Basketball in the Words of Those Who Played It*. New York: Dell, 1987.

Schayes, Dolph. "Wilt Chamberlain as We Knew Him." *Sport*, Aug. 1960, 23–24.

Thomas, Ron. *They Cleared the Lane: The NBA's Black Pioneers*. Lincoln: University of Nebraska Press, 2002.

Walker, Chet, and Chris Messinger. *Long Time Coming: A Black Athlete's Coming of Age in America*. New York: Grove Press, 1995.

Westcott, Rich. *Eddie Gottlieb, Philadelphia Legend and Basketball Pioneer*. Philadelphia: Temple University Press, 2008.

Index